HERACLITUS: *HOMERIC PROBLEMS*

Society of Biblical Literature

Writings from the Greco-Roman World

John T. Fitzgerald, General Editor

Editorial Board

Number 14

HERACLITUS: *HOMERIC PROBLEMS*

Volume Editor
David Konstan

HERACLITUS: *HOMERIC PROBLEMS*

Edited and Translated by

Donald A. Russell

and

David Konstan

Society of Biblical Literature
Atlanta

HERACLITUS: *HOMERIC PROBLEMS*

Copyright © 2005 by the Society of Biblical Literature

Library of Congress Cataloging-in-Publication Data

Heraclitus, 1st cent.
   [Allegoriae Homericae. English & Greek]
   Heraclitus : Homeric problems / edited and translated by Donald A. Russell and David Konstan.
          p. cm. — (Writings from the Greco-Roman world ; v. 14)
   Includes bibliographical references and indexes.
   Commentaries in English; texts in Greek with parallel English translation.
   ISBN-13: 978-1-58983-122-3 (alk. paper)
   ISBN-10: 1-58983-122-5 (alk. paper)
   1. Homer—Religion. 2. Gods, Greek, in literature. 3. Heraclitus, 1st cent. Allegoriae Homericae. I. Title: Homeric problems. II. Russell, D. A. (Donald Andrew) III. Konstan, David. IV. Title. V. Series.
   PA4035.H4 2005
   883'.01—dc22   2005013284

13 12 11 10 09 08 07 06 05   5 4 3 2 1

Printed in the United States of America on acid-free, recycled paper
conforming to ANSI/NISO Z39.48-1992 (R1997) and ISO 9706:1994
standards for paper permanence.

CONTENTS

PREFACE

The idea of preparing a translation of Heraclitus, along with Cornutus and the allegorical scholia to Hesiod, was first proposed in the Society of Biblical Literature by members of the Section on Hellenistic Moral Philosophy and Early Christianity, an interdisciplinary program unit that already had produced a translation of Philodemus's treatise on frankness of speech. At an early stage in the Heraclitus project, it became known that a full translation, along with selected notes, already had been prepared by the eminent scholar of ancient literary criticism, Donald A. Russell. Dr. Russell kindly made his translation available to the SBL group, and he agreed to its publication in the series, Writings from the Greco-Roman World. David Konstan, in accord with the practice of the series, was asked to serve as volume editor, and he worked closely with Dr. Russell on the final version. He also drafted the introduction, which was in turn edited by Dr. Russell. Because of their close collaboration in the preparation of this volume, Dr. Russell asked that Prof. Konstan's name be paired with his as the joint authors of this work. As a result of this happy circumstance, Prof. Konstan's name appears as both volume editor and co-author. As General Editor of the series, I am pleased to join Dr. Russell and Prof. Konstan in expressing our thanks to Ilaria Ramelli, who made available to us the manuscript of her book (Ramelli 2004) prior to its publication and who read the whole text through with her unfailing critical eye.

John T. Fitzgerald

ABBREVIATIONS

The abbreviations used for the citation of ancient texts and modern scholarly literature follow, in general, the guidelines of the Society of Biblical Literature as published in *The SBL Handbook of Style* (1999). Those used in this volume include the following:

ANRW	*Aufstieg und Niedergang der römischen Welt: Geschichte und Kultur Roms im Spiegel der neueren Forschung.* Edited by Hildegard Temporini and Wolfgang Haase. Berlin: de Gruyter, 1972–.
CP	*Classical Philology*
CQ	*Classical Quarterly*
FGH	*Die Fragmente der griechischen Historiker.* Edited by Felix Jacoby. Leiden: Brill, 1954–1964.
JHS	*Journal of Hellenic Studies*
JRS	*Journal of Roman Studies*
LCL	Loeb Classical Library
PGL	*Patristic Greek Lexicon.* Edited by G. W. H. Lampe. Oxford: Oxford University Press, 1968.
SH	Hugh Lloyd-Jones and P. J. Parsons, eds. *Supplementum Hellenisticum.* Texte und Kommentare 11. Berlin: de Gruyter, 1983.
SVF	*Stoicorum veterum fragmenta.* Hans von Arnim. 4 vols. Leipzig: Teubner, 1903–1924.
TAPA	*Transactions of the American Philological Association*
Theol.	Cornutus, *Epidromê tôn kata tên Hellênikên theologian paradedomenôn* (*Summary of the Traditions concerning Greek Theology*)
Vit. poes. Hom.	Pseudo-Plutarch, *De vita et poesi Homeri* (*On the Life and Poetry of Homer*)
ZPE	*Zeitschrift für Papyrologie und Epigraphik*

INTRODUCTION

The book by Heraclitus—sometimes called "the Grammarian" or "the Allegorist" to distinguish him from his more famous namesake, the presocratic philosopher (called "the Obscure")—begins with the dramatic pronouncement: "It is a weighty and damaging charge that heaven brings against Homer for his disrespect for the divine. If he meant nothing allegorically, he was impious through and through, and sacrilegious fables, loaded with blasphemous folly, run riot through both epics." The text that follows is intended to rescue Homer from that charge by demonstrating that what Homer says about the gods is in fact meant allegorically, and, so understood, conforms to the high-minded view of divinity entertained by the most sober thinkers, such as the Stoics, in Heraclitus's own time.

NAME AND DATE

Heraclitus's own time was perhaps toward the end of the first or the beginning of the second century A.D. He refers explicitly to earlier writers, such as Apollodorus of Athens (7) and Crates of Mallus (27), who can be dated to the second century B.C., and also to Crates' disciple, Herodicus of Babylon (11). He must, then, belong to the first century B.C. or later. How much later? Perhaps the chief argument for a relatively early date is the absence of the kind of mystical allegory one finds in the neo-Platonic and Pythagorean writers, such as Porphyry, though this in itself is an insecure basis for dating (see Buffière 1962, ix–x). In any case, there does seem to be a mystical streak, or at least a disposition to employ the rhetoric of the mysteries, in Heraclitus. He writes, for example (53): "anyone who is prepared to delve deeper into Homer's rites and be initiated in his mystical wisdom will recognize that what is believed to be impiety is in fact charged with deep philosophy." And he concludes (76): "After all this, can Homer, the great hierophant of heaven and of the gods, who opened up for human souls the untrodden and closed paths to heaven, deserve to be condemned as impious?" This may be conventional solemnity, but it is possible that Heraclitus was familiar with more mystical currents of allegorical interpretation, and borrowed something of their tone.

There is perhaps another bit of evidence, until now overlooked, that suggests a date around A.D. 100 for the composition of this text. Concerning the open battle among the gods that Homer describes in book 20 of the *Iliad*, one of the episodes that most offended staid readers of the epic, Heraclitus writes (53): "Some think that Homer in this episode has revealed the conjunction of the seven planets in a single zodiacal sign. Now whenever this happens, total disaster ensues. He is therefore hinting at the destruction of the universe, bringing together Apollo (the sun), Artemis (the moon), and the stars of Aphrodite, Ares, Hermes, and Zeus. I have included this allegory, which is plausible rather than true, just so far as not to be thought ignorant of it." Heraclitus goes on to offer instead an ethical interpretation of the conflict (54): "What he has done in fact is to oppose virtues to vices and conflicting elements to their opposites." Heraclitus's way of introducing the astrological interpretation suggests that it was something of a novelty in his day, and this may well have been the case. Astrology in general was a relatively recent import into the Greek world, arriving from the east some time after 300 B.C. (Pingree 1997). A couple of centuries may have elapsed before it was applied to the allegorical reading of Homer. Now, Plutarch (ca. A.D. 46–ca. 120), in his early essay, *How a Youth Should Listen to Poems*, in which he too seeks to extract a more noble meaning from Homer and other poets than a superficial reading would indicate, criticizes certain writers who force the text "with what used to be called undersenses [*huponoiai*] but are now called allegories. These people say that Helios reveals the adultery of Aphrodite with Ares [in the *Odyssey*, book 8], because when Ares' star joins that of Aphrodite it predicts adulterous births, but they do not remain concealed when the Sun is ascendant and descendant. In turn, Hera's beautification for Zeus and her trick with [Aphrodite's] girdle [*Il.* 14] signify, they say, the purification of the air as it nears the fiery element—as though the poet himself did not provide the solutions." Plutarch explains that, in the latter episode, "Homer excellently demonstrated that sex and gratification deriving from potions and magic and accompanied by deception are not only transient, quick to surfeit, and precarious, but also mutate into enmity and anger when the pleasurable part abates. For Zeus himself threatens this and says to Hera, 'so you may see whether sex and the bed help you, which you enjoyed when you came to me apart from the gods and deceived me' [*Il.* 14.32–33]" (19E–20B). Plutarch's interpretation, while ethical in character, is not allegorical, but depends rather on showing that Homer's own words provide reason to suppose that he disapproved of Hera's conduct. But he too seems to be attacking a relatively recent development in Homeric criticism, in which the gods are not just equated with planets—this was nothing new, since the planets bore the names of gods—nor with physical elements as such, but with complex astronomical conjunctions that are predictive of events in the world. Since Heraclitus and Plutarch refer to different episodes, they are not dependent on a single excerpt, and they may well have been familiar with the same text, conceivably one that was popular shortly before they wrote. If so, then Heraclitus may have been composing his work as early as the end of the first century A.D. But it must be acknowledged that all this is highly speculative. Nothing more is known about Heraclitus, apart from his name, which is reasonably securely transmitted by the oldest, though fragmentary, manuscript of the work (M). From this same manuscript is derived the title, *Homeric Problems*, or, more fully, *Homeric Problems concerning What Homer Has Expressed Allegorically in Respect to the Gods.*

The Beginnings of Allegory

Heraclitus himself explains (5) that allegory is, as the word implies (*alla* = "other," *agoreuein* = "say"), "the trope which says one thing but signifies something other [*alla*] than what it says." This definition accords with that of the ancient grammarians, such as Trypho (first century B.C.), in his work, *On Tropes.* Trypho notes (3.191 Spengel) that a trope "is a word [or phrase: *logos*] that is uttered by way of an alteration of the proper sense," and among the fourteen tropes he identifies, which include metaphor, catachresis, metonymy, and synecdoche, he defines allegory (3.193 Spengel) as "a word or phrase that signifies one thing in the proper sense, but provides a notion [*ennoia*] of something else most often by way of similarity" (cf. 3.215–216 Spengel, from a treatise that West [1965] has shown to derive also from Trypho; Cocondrius 3.324 Spengel; Ps.-Choeroboscus 3.244 Spengel). Heraclitus's definition, then, belongs to the sphere of rhetorical theory, and, like metonymy and the other figures, allegory could be and was employed for any number of purposes, such as literary elegance or persuasiveness in oratory. Heraclitus is making a particular use of it to salvage Homer's reputation in respect to religious piety.

Not that this function of allegory was unprecedented. In fact, it may well have been the earliest purpose to which allegorical criticism, and more particularly criticism of the Homeric epics, was put. We are told by later writers that as early as the sixth century B.C., Greek thinkers were already applying allegorical methods to Homer. Thus, Theagenes of

Rhegium, according to a note by Porphyry on *Il.* 20.67 (1.240.14 Schrad. =
Diels-Kranz 8A2), affirmed that Homer spoke not literally but allegorically, and identified deities with elements such as hot and cold, dry and
moist, and also with psychological dispositions such as foolishness,
amorousness, and so forth. There are similar reports concerning Pherecydes, who lived in the early sixth century, and Metrodorus, coeval with
Theagenes (Diels-Kranz 7B5, 61A4; cf. also Diogenes Laertius 8.21 on
Pythagoras). It is not clear from these accounts just what the purpose of
these intepretations might have been, and more particularly whether they
were intended to explain Homer's view of the gods. There is perhaps
some likelihood that they were, in light of the attacks on Homer—more
or less contemporary with the above writers—precisely for his primitive,
if not impious, representation of divinity. The most famous of these writers is Xenophanes of Colophon, a philosophical poet of the sixth century
B.C. Xenophanes alleged that "Homer and Hesiod have ascribed to the
gods all those things that among human beings are shameful and blame-
worthy: thieving, adultery, and mutual deception" (Sextus, *Math.* 9.193;
cf. 1.289, Diogenes Laertius 9.18, Aulus Gellius, *Noct. att.* 3.11, Clement of
Alexandria, *Strom.* 5.109–110, 7.22). Xenophanes did not write with the
intention of absolving Homer, and so he had no need to develop or apply
an interpretative method such as allegory in order to do so. But it is plausible that Theagenes and others—including Metrodorus of Lampsacus
and Diogenes of Apollonia, who may have been inspired in turn by
Anaxagoras (Diogenes Laertius 2.11, following Favorinus; cf. Tatian, *Or.*
21, other testimonia in Diels-Kranz 61, 64)—developed their analyses in
response to such charges.

Among the presocratic philosophers, we may observe that Heraclitus too attacked Homer and wanted him expelled from poetic contests
(frg. 42 Diels-Kranz); he refers to him ironically as "wisest of the Greeks"
(frg. 56 Diels-Kranz), a sign that Homer already had a reputation for
being the fount of all knowledge. Heraclitus introduced the term
sêmainein (frg. 93 Diels-Kranz) in reference to the interpretation of ora-
cles, which, he asserted, neither speak openly nor conceal their meaning,
but rather "indicate" it; it is possible that such a style of explication was
already being applied to the Homeric texts. Indeed, I would venture, very
tentatively, the possibility that criticism such as Xenophanes', and
responses to it like that of Theagenes (if indeed this was his purpose),
may have arisen still earlier, and in tandem with Homeric epic. For it may
not always be the fancy of later critics that finds in Homer himself allegorical significance, and we need not imagine that these sophisticated
poems evolved in isolation from the intellectual currents of their time.
Our own Heraclitus (5) points to the self-conscious use of allegory by
poets as early as Archilochus and Alcaeus (seventh century B.C.) as evi-

dence that the technique was not foreign to Homer. But this kind of speculation takes us away from the work under consideration.

THE AUTHORITY OF HOMER

Whatever the focus and intention of Theagenes' interpretations, or those
of his successors, it was of course possible to exploit the allegorical style
of reading for other ends than that of defending Homer's piety, whether
in respect to epic poetry or myth in general, just as one might explain
away ostensibly licentious stories about the gods by other means than
allegory, as Plutarch does, for example, in the passage cited above. I
have mentioned that Homer was often regarded as an authority on all
the arts and sciences, and a source of every kind of wisdom: this view
lies at the heart of Plato's little dialogue, *Ion*, in which Socrates seeks to
explain how it is that Homer, and via Homer the rhapsode Ion, can talk
knowledgeably about all the crafts, though they are trained in none of
them (Socrates decides that it must be a consequence of divine inspira-
tion). The geographer Strabo (first century B.C.) held that Homer was the
"founder of the science of geography" (*Geogr.* 1.1.2), but he named certain locations in a "riddling way" (*hupainittetai*) by means of certain
signs (*tekmêria*, 1.1.3; compare also Pseudo-Plutarch, *Life and Poetry of
Homer* 200–211, on Homer's knowledge of medicine); failure to understand his technique, according to Strabo, explains why some have cast
doubt on his learning in this domain.

One might also resort to allegory in order to enlist Homer as a witness or source for a philosophical doctrine. An example is the idea that
Homer anticipated the teaching of Thales, that the source of all things is
water, in the passage in which he describes Ocean as the source (*genesis*)
of all the gods (*Il.* 14.201 = 14.302) and "of all [sc. things]" (*Il.* 14.246; cf.
Plato, *Theaet.* 152E, 180C; Aristotle, *Metaph.* 983b27–984b5; Cornutus,
Theol. ch. 8 = 8.10–11 Lang; Heraclitus, *All.* ch. 22; for the view that Homer
means rather "of all rivers," see Panchenko 1994). The Stoics in particular
seem to have been fond of appealing to Homer in this way, and held the
view, which seemed paradoxical in antiquity, that only a sage could be a
poet (*SVF* 3.654 = Stobaeus 2.61.13 W.; cf. Strabo, *Geogr.* 1.2.3). Thus they
affirmed, for example, that the seat of intelligence was in the heart
(*SVF* 2.884–890 = Galen, *On the Doctrines of Plato and Hippocrates* 3.5; cf. *SVF*
2.911), and invoked passages from Homer in support of the notion (considered bizarre by other schools, apart from the Epicureans). This kind of
appeal, however, did not involve the decipherment of Homer's words
according to a symbolic code; Homer was presumed to speak plainly,
and as such to confirm, as a wise bard, the Stoic thesis. But the Stoics

might also appeal to passages that were, as they supposed, mysteriously meant. For example, the Stoics held that Zeus permeates the entire universe, and that the other gods are specific manifestations of his powers (cf. *SVF* 2.1021 = Diogenes Laertius 7.147–148), and for this view too they found support in the Homeric texts (*SVF* 2.622 = Dio Chrysostom, *Or.* 36.55; *SVF* 2.1009 = Aetius 1.6, etc.). Both Zeno and Chrysippus wrote works on Homer (*SVF* 1.274 = Dio Chrysostom, *Or.* 63.41), in which they offered numerous specific exegeses. It does not necessarily follow, however, that they employed the allegorical method systematically, or that they held that there was a profound and hidden sense to every passage in Homer that relates to the characterization of the gods. The fragments do not permit a firm conclusion concerning their approach in this regard (see esp. Boys-Stones 2003a; Ramelli 2004, 79–145).

THE NATURE OF ALLEGORY

Again, some passages in Homer were obscure even to critics in antiquity: the diction of the poems was archaic, and invited speculation about the meaning of various words. This very circumstance may have inspired an interest in language among the presocratics and sophists of the fifth century B.C. Sometimes they resorted to metonymical interpretations in order to make sense of a phrase, or else proposed exotic etymologies to account for the evolution or original sense of a term (Plato's *Cratylus* provides a rich sample). Trypho (both versions) illustrates metonymy by using the name Hephaestus to indicate fire, since he is the god who discovered fire, and Demeter to mean wheat. Such metonymies were commonplace; only a simpleton, like Polyphemus in Euripides' *Cyclops* (521–527), would imagine that the god Dionysus actually inhabited a wine flask. On a more sophisticated level, one might explain the transferred sense of terms in Homer, and more specifically his use of divine names, as a consequence of the lack of an abstract vocabulary in earlier times. Thus, Plutarch, in the essay cited above, observes that the name Zeus in Homer may represent the deity, but may also stand for fate or chance. The ancient poets resorted to such imagery, Plutarch explains, because they did not yet have a specific term for the concept of accident or *tukhê* (24A), though they knew, of course, that events occur randomly. Whenever malice, or some other quality incompatible with his rational nature, is ascribed to Zeus, Plutarch adds, one may be certain that the poet is speaking metaphorically (cf. 24B).

Today, critics frequently treat allegory, as opposed to metonymy, as the systematic application of transferred or hidden senses of terms in an extended passage or argument. Perhaps one might specify that allegory should involve, at a minimum, two such terms, and in addition some relation (it may be an activity) that obtains between them, and which is also understood symbolically. Thus, the mere use of the name Hephaestus for fire is an image, not yet an allegory. The metonymy becomes allegory proper when two such labels are related by some bond or action, e.g., when Zeus and Mnemosyne, that is, "Memory," are said to be the parents of the Muses. Cornutus, for example (*Theol.* ch. 14 = p. 14.3–5 Lang), interprets this relationship as indicating that "it was Zeus who introduced the forms of knowledge relevant to culture [*paideia*]." Again, to say that Zeus is *pneuma*, or is the divine principle that permeates the universe, does not, on the definition I have offered, quite constitute an allegory. It begins to approach one, however, when the family relationship between Zeus and other gods is interpreted metaphorically to indicate how Zeus's divinity is variously manifested in the world (cf. *SVF* 2.1070, where the elements of ether and air, equated with Zeus and Hera, are virtually described as marrying).

Approaches to Myth

Recourse to the authority of Homer did not necessarily require allegorizing, of course. I have mentioned that the early Stoics, like the Epicureans, held, contrary to the prevailing opinion, that the intellectual faculty was located in the chest rather than in the head, and cited passages in Homer to prove the point. One might also appeal to Homer for models or paradigms of virtuous behavior. The Stoics and Cynics, in particular, invoked Odysseus, along with Heracles, as exemplars of wisdom and endurance in service of the good (cf. *SVF* 3.467 = Galen, *On the Doctrines of Plato and Hippocrates* 4.7, from Chrysippus's *On the Passions*). This same approach might be put to use in defense of Homer's morality: heroes of such exceptional integrity as Achilles or Odysseus are a sign of the poet's rectitude. Thus, Heraclitus observes (78): "In Homer, everything is full of noble virtue: Odysseus is wise, Ajax brave, Penelope chaste, Nestor invariably just, Telemachus dutiful to his father, Achilles totally loyal to his friendships." Odysseus was also notoriously given to lying, and Achilles to rage, and here was an opportunity to explain their actions allegorically, but it was not obligatory to do so, even for admirers of Homer.

Not all rationalizing interpretations of myth involve allegory. They are sometimes employed to explain how a myth arose, and in this case they point not to a hidden meaning of the myth, but to its origin. Examples are the historicizing approach to myth adopted by Palaephatus (fourth century B.C.) and Euhemerus (third century B.C.). Thus Palaephatus, who devoted his exegeses to lesser myths rather than to the nature of the Olympian gods, offers the following explanation (7) for the story that Actaeon, because he chanced to see Artemis naked at her bath, was transformed by the goddess into a stag and then devoured by his own hunting dogs. Actaeon, he suggests, was a powerful ruler back at the time when agriculture was the principal occupation of men, but he was so attached to hunting that he wholly neglected his property. And so his life, or livelihood (*bios*), was consumed in hunting, and the saying went round that he was "eaten up by his own dogs." Poets composed the mythicized version, Palaephatus says, so that "their hearers might not offend against the divine." Euhemerus purported to have discovered evidence on the imaginary island of Panchaea that the gods of Greek myth were originally great kings and human benefactors. The difference between such an analysis and allegory proper is not always evident, since one may say that the original historical event constitutes the implicit content or meaning of the surface story, but the intentions behind the two procedures are clearly distinct. Heraclitus offers a Palaephatean interpretation of the story that the goddess Dawn fell in love with the hero Orion (68), and again of the tale, recounted by Homer, that the mortal king Lycurgus pursued Dionysus violently (35): "Lycurgus, who was the owner of an estate good for winegrowing, had gone out in the autumn, when Dionysus's crops are harvested, to the very fertile region of Nysa." But the brunt of Heraclitus's treatment of this latter episode is not so much historical as symbolic, as he explains that "Dionysus was 'in terror,' because fear turns the mind, just as the fruit of the grape is 'turned' as it is crushed to make wine," and so forth.

Greek religion was not a uniform system, nor was it based on an exclusive set of sacred texts. Alongside the stories of the Olympian gods, as constituted chiefly by the poems of Homer and Hesiod (cf. Herodotus, *Hist.* 2.53), there were alternative mythical narratives associated with such mysterious figures as Orpheus and Musaeus. Thanks to a recently discovered papyrus (the Derveni papyrus), we now have documentary evidence of allegorical interpretation in a cultic context as early as the fourth century B.C. (see Henry 1986; Laks and Most 1997; Janko 2001, 2002; Obbink 2003). This extraordinary text takes the form of a commentary on an Orphic poem. As the author (anonymous, though various guesses have been made) writes, Orpheus "speaks in sacred language [*hierologeitai*] from the first word to the last" (column 7, lines 7–8). The connection between religious cult and allegory is noteworthy, and shows that the interpretative strategy was put to wider use than that of redeeming Homer and the traditional poets. Indeed, it is possible that some of the impetus to the allegorization of the Homeric gods was derived from just such cultic contexts, which lent an immediate religious urgency to the enterprise. There can be little doubt that the method was already practiced well before the author of the Derveni papyrus penned his commentary.

Plato famously made use of myths, or at all events stories concerning the afterlife, to communicate truths that were not expressible in ordinary language, for example at the end of the *Gorgias*, the *Phaedo*, and the *Republic* (the dream of Er). He was also familiar with allegorical modes of interpretation of traditional myths: Protagoras's handling of the story of Prometheus, in Plato's *Protagoras*, shows how philosophers were already adept at constructing allegorical narratives in the service of their moral or anthropological theories (cf. also Prodicus's fable of Heracles at the crossroad between Virtue and Vice, reported by Xenophon *Memorabilia* 2.1.20–33 and popular among moralists ever afterwards). In the *Phaedrus* (229 C–E), Socrates pokes fun at the rationalization of the rape of Oreithyia by Boreas, the north wind, according to which the girl was simply blown off a cliff by a strong gust. The more metaphysical flights of Plato's fancy were to have a great influence on neo-Platonic interpretations of myth, to which we shall return below. But it was Plato's denunciation of Homer, precisely for the impiety entailed in his treatment of the gods, that had the greatest immediate impact on philosophical approaches to myth.

PLATO'S ATTACK ON HOMER AND ITS AFTERMATH

In the second book of Plato's *Republic*, Socrates explains that "there are two kinds of speech [*logoi*], one true, the other false," and then observes: "We must instruct by means of both, but first by means of falsehoods." His meaning is that "we first tell children stories [*muthoi*], and this is a falsehood, speaking generally, but there are also true things in them" (376E11–377A6). There are, nevertheless, some myths that should not be recited at all, such as Hesiod's narrative about Cronus's castration of his father, Uranus (377E6–378A1)—even if, Socrates says, they are true (378A2–3, 378B2–3), though he is sure that they are not (378C1). For, Socrates observes, the young cannot appreciate the tacit meaning (*huponoia*) in such stories (378D7–9), if indeed there is one. Thus, Socrates comes to the reluctant conclusion that Homer and the other poets must either cease to sing such lies, or else be banished from the ideal city that he envisions (379C, 398A; cf. 595B).

It may have been in part because of the authority of Plato and the severity of his critique that subsequent interpreters of myth and poetry, above all in and around the camp of the Stoics, were moved to come to Homer's defense. Zeno, the founder of the Stoic school, in addition to writing a treatise called *Homeric Questions* (*Problêmata Homêrika*, the same title as that of Heraclitus's essay) in five books (Diogenes Laertius 7.4), and very possibly other works on Hesiod and on Homer, wrote a *Republic* of his own that was renowned, not to say notorious, in antiquity, and that certainly was conceived in answer to Plato's great work. Chrysippus, the so-called Second Founder of Stoicism, also wrote a treatise *On the Republic* (Diogenes Laertius 7.34, 186), along with a book *On the Gods.* The Epicurean philosopher Philodemus (first century B.C.), many of whose writings have been recovered, in mutilated condition, from the lava that poured from Mount Vesuvius in A.D. 79, claims in his treatise, *On Piety* (13) that Chrysippus sought to base Stoic theology specifically in the poets, and Fritz Wehrli (1928) and Glenn Most (1989) have argued that the emphasis on theology in the interpretation of Homer is a Stoic innovation. Of later critics associated more or less closely with the Stoics, we may mention Chrysippus's disciple, Diogenes of Babylon, who wrote a book *On Athena.* In his edition of *On Piety* (1996), Dirk Obbink observes (19) that "Diogenes' treatise *On Athena* is treated at some length (*P.Herc.* 1428 cols. 8,14–10,8 = *SVF* iii, Diogenes 33)," and from Philodemus's summary (translated by Obbink on p. 20), it is clear that Diogenes, in good Stoic style, rejected anthropomorphic gods and equated Apollo with the sun, Artemis with the moon, "and that the part of Zeus which extends into the sea is Poseidon, that which extends into the earth Demeter, that which extends into the air Hera." Diogenes was in turn the teacher of Apollodorus of Athens, also the author of an *On the Gods,* whom Heraclitus cites, as we have seen, along with Crates of Mallos (identified in the *Suda* κ 2342 as a Stoic) and Crates' disciple, Herodicus of Babylon. These latter scholars, more grammarians and literary critics than philosophers in the narrow sense of the term, may or may not have been responding specifically to Plato. But Heraclitus himself, centuries later, still feels the sting of Plato's attack (4): "Away too with Plato, the flatterer, Homer's dishonest accuser, who banishes him from his private Republic as an honored exile, garlanded with white wool and with his head drenched with costly perfumes! Nor need we trouble ourselves with Epicurus," Heraclitus adds, "who cultivates his low pleasure in *his* private garden, and abominates all poetry indiscriminately as a lethal allurement of fable" (the Epicureans did employ allegory, as when Lucretius interprets the torments of hell as signifying the insatiable desires of ignorant human beings [3.978–1023], but they used it principally to account for the false beliefs of the ignorant; cf. Gale 1994, 26–38; Obbink 1995a; for Epicurus's early interest in Hesiod's creation story, Diogenes Laertius 10.2). Heraclitus goes on to note that "the irony is that both these philosophers found the basis of their doctrines in Homer, and are ungrateful as well as impious towards the person from whom they gained most of their knowledge" (cf. 17, 76–79).

Even if the Stoics, then, adduced Homer to support their own doctrines, and took an interest in etymologies in the first instance for the sake of their linguistic theory rather than as a means of interpreting Homer (they, like the Epicureans, held that the original meanings of words were truest or most natural), they may very well have been broadly concerned to defend an icon of Greek culture against Plato's attack. Their theological interests may thus have squared nicely with an allegorical approach to Homer, though of course they were free to use other methods as well to explicate his meaning, including philological criticism (see Ramelli 2004). On the other side, writers influenced by Platonism were perhaps more reluctant to adopt the allegorical method. Cicero, in *On the Nature of the Gods*, expresses Academic doubts about the use of allegory (1.41; cf. the Stoic reply, 2.63–71), and Plutarch, also an adherent of the Academy, generally avoids applying it to Homer, whom he sought to rescue from Plato's censure by other means, although he occasionally exploits the method in other contexts, as in his observation, in the treatise *On Isis and Osiris* (372E5), that "Isis is the feminine principle of nature," or his equation, in the tract *On the Face in the Moon* (942D–943D), of Demeter and Core with the earth and the moon (cf. Dawson 1992, 52; Boys-Stones 2001, 99–122).

THE VARIETIES OF ALLEGORY

It is important, as has been indicated, to distinguish allegory proper from other critical approaches to myth and the Homeric poems, such as the recognition of metonymy, an interest in etymology, the search for the origins of myths in historical events, the appeal to epic heroes as paradigms of virtue, or citation of Homer in support of a given ethical or philosophical doctrine, even if these approaches were often amalgamated by the ancient critics themselves. In turn, it is desirable to be clear about the different purposes to which these several methods, including allegory, might be put. It is one thing to defend Homer against a charge of impiety, another to demonstrate his omniscience in all fields of knowledge or simply to explicate a puzzling passage that resists a surface reading, as the grammarians and textual critics did. In addition, allegory itself, even when used to prove Homer's religious propriety, assumed different forms, in accord with the model or master narrative that subtended it.

We have already noted several such master narratives that provide the reference for the surface allegory. One is cosmological or physical, according to which deities and other figures are identified with elements such as ether, air, fire, or water, or sometimes cosmic forces such as attraction and repulsion. This approach seems to be particularly identified with the Stoics, but it goes back, it would appear, to the very earliest allegorizers, for example Theagenes. Heraclitus makes regular use of it, as in his affirmation that "Apollo is identical with the Sun" (6), which forms the basis of his lengthy analysis of the plague that Apollo visits upon the Greeks at the beginning of the *Iliad*, or in his interpretation of the two cities on the shield of Achilles (49) as emblematic of Empedocles' Strife and Love. Related to this are the scientific interpretations, such as the inference from a single epithet applied to night that Homer knew the relative sizes of the sun and earth (46), or the proof that Homer's earth is spherical. A second reference paradigm is ethical or psychological, as when Athena is equated with wisdom and Aphrodite with foolishness (30); this style too is doubtless ancient. Related to this model is the identification of Ares, for example, with war (31), which comes complete with an etymological explanation (*arê* = "harm"). For while, on one level, this substitution may be treated simply as metonymy, Ares is simultaneously taken to represent the traits associated with a violent temperament in human beings: like Ares, "all men who fight are full of madness, boiling with zeal for mutual murder" (cf. 54; also 37 on the Prayers). Sometimes, a description in Homer informs us of the structure of the soul: thus, Plato is said to have derived his theory of the psyche entirely from Homer (17), though he ungratefully expelled him from his Republic. Myths may also refer to philosophy itself, as when the three heads of Cerberus are equated with the three branches of philosophical investigation (33). We have also had occasion to remark on the astrological version of allegory, which Heraclitus mentions only to dismiss. The fourth-century thinker Sallustius duly classifies several types of myth, such as theological, natural, spiritual, and material (*On Gods and the Cosmos* 4).

All the above modes of allegory presuppose that once the code of interpretation is provided, the hitherto hidden meaning of the text is entirely clear, whether it refers to scientific, psychological, or other areas of knowledge. What seems like a battle between gods is just the conflict between wisdom and folly, and so forth. The key to unlocking a given association between a symbol and its referent might vary—it could be based on etymology, or homophony, or a similarity of attributes, or mere contiguity—but once the connection is made, the deeper sense displaces the surface meaning. But there was also a style of allegorical reading that saw more complex, and even ineffable, meanings dwelling behind the surface of the text. Proclus (fifth century A.D.) writes that the inventors of myth "fashion likenesses of the indivisible by way of division, of the eternal by what moves in time, of the noetic by the perceptible; they represent the immaterial by the material, what is without extension by way of discontinuity, and that which is steadfastly established through change" (*On the Republic* 1.77 Kroll). Even the most indecent of myths, including Cronus's castration of his father, can be assigned transcendent meanings in this scheme of things. To understand such stories, moreover, it is not enough to have a key by which to decipher the individual symbols; rather, their effect is psychagogic, leading the mind on to intuitions of a higher reality.

Wolfgang Bernard has recently (1990) distinguished between what he calls "substitutive" and "diaeretic" allegory. Substitutive allegory, according to Bernard, posits a one-to-one correspondence between characters in a narrative and elements or other abstract concepts, e.g., Hera = air, Aphrodite = sexual desire (1); he takes this type, moreover, to be characteristic of the Stoics, and cites Heraclitus as his chief illustration of the approach (15–21). Diaeretic allegory, which Bernard attributes above all to the Platonists, differs from the substitutive in that it treats, not individual figures, but rather an episode as a whole, which it reads as referring to another realm of experience or ontological order (cf. 7–8). The difference between the two is not a matter of content, such as physical versus moral reference, but of method. Thus, whereas Heraclitus's analysis of the theomachy in the *Iliad* gives us precise substitutions, such as "Poseidon stands for moisture, Apollo for the sun," or "Hermes is reason, Leto forgetfulness" (74–75), Proclus, in his commentary on Plato's *Republic* (1.90.13–21), takes the scene as a whole to mean that "'the creative unity,' that is Zeus, remains above the multiplicity of gods"; this is why Zeus has no opponent (80).

Nevertheless, the ancient allegorists do not divide so neatly into distinct camps. Plutarch, a Platonist, would appear to offer an exemplary summary of the diaeretic method in his instructions on how to read the sacred stories concerning Isis and Osiris (*On Isis and Osiris* 358E11–359A2): "You know that they in no way resemble the dry fables [*mutheumata*] and empty fictions [*plasmata*] that poets and public speakers weave and spin out like spiders, generating from themselves unsubstantiated premises; rather, they contain as it were puzzles [*aporiai*] and narrative accounts [*diêgêseis*] of phenomenal properties [*pathê*; cf. Plato, *Phaedr.* 96C]. And just as scientists say that the rainbow is an indirect expression [*emphasis*] of the sun that is variegated by the rebound of the image against a cloud, so too myth here is an indirect expression of reason that deflects the mind to other things." Yet, as we have seen, in this same treatise Plutarch identifies Isis as "the feminine principle of nature" (372E5; cf. Babut 1969, 379), and he in fact refers positively to Stoic interpretations, as Daniel Babut points out (378, citing *On Isis and Osiris* 367C).

The later neo-Platonic exegetes were perhaps more systematic in their approach to allegory than earlier writers, as Bernard maintains, but they too posited elementary symbolic equivalences. Robin Jackson (1995, 293) notes that for the sixth-century neo-Platonist Olympiodorus, the Minotaur slain by Theseus "represents our bestial passions, Ariadne's thread is the divine power that we depend on, and the Labyrinth is the complex nature of life" (Olympiodorus, *Commentary on Plato's Gorgias* 44.5), and he affirms that the source of this approach is precisely the Stoics. It might seem that, by assigning an emblematic significance not only to the Minotaur, who is a character in the story, but also to the thread and the labyrinth, which pertain to the narrative context, Olympiodorus's interpretation goes beyond the substitutive method as defined by Bernard, but this is not exclusive to the neoplatonists. Heraclitus reads the legend that Heracles pierced the right breast of Hera with a three-pronged arrow (*Il.* 5.392–394) as symbolizing the philosopher who casts his mind up toward the heavens like a dart, adding for good measure that the three points of the arrow denote the three parts of philosophy, that is, logic, ethics, and physics (34). Heraclitus indeed had praise for the Stoics (33.1), as opposed to Plato, but this does not make of him a faithful practitioner of a Stoic style of exegesis. We have seen that he too regards the surface meanings of Homer as pointing to teachings accessible only to initiates, as in the mystery cults, even if he does not develop so elaborate an allegorical structure in this respect as, say, Porphyry does in his interpretation of the cave of the Nymphs in the *Odyssey*. The question of Heraclitus's philosophical allegiances, at all events, remains open (cf. Alesso 2002; Ramelli 2003, 49–50).

ALLEGORY AND LITERARY CRITICISM

Today, allegorical criticism of literature is unfashionable and is applied only to works that self-consciously declare themselves to be allegories, such as Spenser's *Faerie Queene*. Compositions of this sort emerged as a genre relatively late in antiquity; examples are Prudentius's *Psychomachia* and Martianus Capella's *On the Marriage of Mercury and Philology* (fifth century A.D.). In turn, they fell out of favor after the Renaissance. As W.H. Auden has observed (1951, 15): "Revolutionary changes in sensibility or style are rare. The most famous is, perhaps, the conception of *amor* that appeared in Europe in the twelfth century. The disappearance, during the sixteenth, of allegory as a common literary genre is another." The eclipse of allegorical criticism duly followed. The effect of this sea change upon classical criticism is strikingly evident in the scant space allotted to allegorical interpretation in recent histories and anthologies of literary criticism in antiquity (cf., e.g., Grube 1965, 55–56; Russell and Winterbottom 1972; Kennedy 1989, 85–86, 209–10, 320–22; see Struck 2004, 7–8). The interest in allegory lay elsewhere. As Donald Russell has put it (1981, 95–96): "The long and complex history of ancient allegorical interpretation ... has to do with the history of religion and ethics more than with that of literary criticism." Under these circumstances, it is perhaps not entirely surprising that the version presented here is the first translation into English of the most extended example of pagan allegorical criticism to survive from classical antiquity.

We are inclined to think of allegorical criticism as forcing arbitrary meanings upon an innocently transparent text, finding abstruse significance where none was intended. The approach smacks of astrology or dream manuals, like that of Artemidorus in antiquity or Freud's own *Interpretation of Dreams,* with their lists of symbolic equivalences. It is not difficult to poke fun at some of the more extravagant products of ancient allegorical criticism, but a remark by John Frow (1995, 58) may serve as a warning against too facile a dismissal of the method: "There are no codes of reading to which there will not correspond (at least potentially) a set of codes of writing." The tradition of allegorical interpretation developed out of, and in turn inspired and influenced, practices of allegorical composition, and this not only in the form of large-scale, systematically symbolic narratives. Poets like Virgil and, I have suggested, even Homer changed registers from naturalistic description to symbolic figuration as freely as modern writers exploit resonances of imagery and metaphor. But the importance of allegory in the history of criticism goes beyond its application to individual texts. For allegorical interpretation may also have been the chief ancient forerunner of what counts today as literary criticism per se.

In an article entitled "The Reader in History," Jane P. Tompkins, taking as her point of departure Longinus's analysis in *On the Sublime* of a vivid description by Herodotus of travel up the Nile, concluded that Longinus "has no interest in the meaning of the passage.... Once the desired *effect* has been achieved, there is no need, or room, for interpretation" (Tompkins 1980, 203). She goes on to affirm:

> Behind Longinus's handling of the passage from Herodotus lies an attitude toward literature and language that is characteristic of classical antiquity and fundamentally alien to twentieth-century modes of understanding literature and art. For Longinus, language is a form of power and the purpose of studying texts from the past is to acquire the skills that enable one to wield that power.... All modern criticism—whether response-oriented, psychological, structuralist, mythopoeic, thematic, or formalist—takes *meaning* to be the object of critical investigation, for

unlike the ancients we equate language not with action but with signification. (ibid., emphasis added)

Tompkins notes further that "The equation of language with power ...
explains the two most prominent characteristics of literary criticism in
antiquity: its preoccupation with matters of technique and its debates
over the morality of literary production" (203–4). Moreover, the ancient
critic "faces toward the future and writes in order to help poets produce
new work.... The text as an object of study or contemplation has no
importance in this critical perspective" (204). Tompkins would not, perhaps, have drawn so sharp a contrast between ancient and modern
attitudes toward the text had she taken account of the allegorical tradition of interpretation. As Peter Struck observes (2004, 13): "Without
reckoning the ancient developments of allegory within the context of literary criticism more generally, it becomes impossible to discern the
history that runs from ancient to modern symbol theories." I have cited
Tompkins's discussion, however, not in order to disparage it, since she
captures quite elegantly the different purposes of ancient rhetorical
theory, as represented by Aristotle, Horace, and Longinus, and modern
criticism (cf. Struck 2004, 39–76), but rather to call attention to two of its
implications. First, it points up the distinct character of allegorical and
related styles of criticism in relation to the better-known rhetorical
mode of classical literary analysis. And second, it indicates once again
the neglect of ancient allegorical interpretation, if it escaped the notice
of so fine and learned a critic as Jane Tompkins.

Today the situation has changed, thanks to the publication of several excellent studies, along with editions and translations of many of
the major texts, and the study of ancient allegory, in its literary as well
as in its philosophical and religious applications, is coming into its own
(see, e.g., Buffière 1956; Buffière 1962; Coulter 1976; Pépin 1981; Lamberton 1986; Whitman 1987; Most 1989; Lamberton and Keaney 1992;
Blönnigen 1992; Dawson 1992; Hillgruber 1994–1999; Boys-Stones 2001;
Ford 2002; Boys-Stones 2003b; Ramelli 2003; Ramelli 2004; Struck 2004).
There is thus no need here for a detailed survey of the ancient allegorical tradition (for recent overviews, the reader is referred to Ramelli
2003, especially the "Saggio Integrativo"; Ramelli 2004; Struck 2004).
The interconnection between pagan, Jewish and Christian allegory is
also being actively investigated. While that subject is beyond the scope
of this introduction, it may be noted that Philo of Alexandria, who
offers rich allegorical interpretations of stories in the Old Testament
(cf., e.g., *Allegories of the Laws*), visited Rome, perhaps in the company
of the Stoic Chaeremon, also favorably disposed to allegory (if not to
Judaism), at the time when Cornutus was active there (A.D. 39–40; cf.

Philo, *On the Embassy to Gaius;* Eusebius, *Hist. eccl.* 6.19.8); nor should
one forget that Paul several times resorts to allegorical interpretations
(1 Cor 5:6–8; 9:8–10; 10:1–11), in one instance (Gal 4:24) using the term
itself.

Heraclitus's Treatise

Heraclitus's treatise follows the order of the Homeric poems, beginning with the first book of the *Iliad* and concluding with the slaying of
the suitors at the end of the *Odyssey* (a large lacuna has swallowed up
Heraclitus's interpretations of the episodes between books 11 and 20 of
the *Odyssey*). A brief methodological introduction and defense of allegorical interpretation (1–5), and a few polemical paragraphs addressed
principally to Plato at the end (76–79), round off the essay (on these, see
Russell 2003). A substantial portion of the treatise (6–16) is devoted to
the plague sent by Apollo in book 1 of the *Iliad*. This was evidently a
much debated question among critics of Homer, and it gives Heraclitus
the opportunity to display his erudition in a number of areas, including
medical theory and meteorology, by which he determines that the
season during which the *Iliad* takes place must have been summer.
There follows an analysis of Athena's intervention in the quarrel
between Achilles and Agamemnon (17–20), which includes a general
discussion of Homeric psychology and Plato's debt to it, and of the
ancient battle among the Olympian gods and the attempted binding of
Zeus (21–25), which provides the occasion for a cosmological interpretation. Heraclitus concludes his treatment of *Iliad* 1 with an allegorical
account of the tossing out of Hephaestus from Olympus (26–27), which,
like all episodes of strife among the immortals, piqued Homer's moral-
izing critics.

After brief comments on Paris's seduction of Helen, at Aphrodite's
instigation, in book 3 of the *Iliad* (28), and on Homer's account of Hebe
and Eris in book 4 (29), Heraclitus turns to the wounding of Aphrodite
and Ares by Diomedes (30–31), for which he offers a psychologizing allegory, and other attacks upon gods by mortals, including Heracles'
wounding of Hera, mentioned in the fifth book (33–34). These episodes
were clearly a sore point, as was Dionysus's terrified flight before the
tyrant Lycurgus in book 6 (35). Heraclitus deals briefly with the golden
chain that Zeus let down from Olympus (36), the manifestly symbolic
description of the Prayers in book 9 (37), and the destruction of the
Achaean wall in book 12 (38), before turning to the more notorious
topics of Hera's seduction of Zeus in book 14 (39), which Heraclitus
treats as an allegory of spring, the binding of Hera in book 15 (40–41), in

which he sees an allegory of the creation of the universe, and Zeus's tears for Sarpedon in book 16 (42). After this, he devotes several chapters to the Shield of Achilles (43–51), which is the occasion for a scientific digression on the spherical shape of the earth, among other things, and to the battle of the gods in book 21 (52–58), concluding his treatment of the *Iliad* with a brief discussion of Hermes' role in leading Priam to Achilles in book 24, whereupon he signals the transition to the discussion of the *Odyssey* (60).

Heraclitus explains Athena's appearance, in disguise, to Telemachus in the opening book of the *Odyssey* as a sign of Telemachus's newly achieved wisdom (61–63), and the story of Proteus in book 4 (64–67) as another allegorized cosmogony. He briefly considers the mention of Orion as the lover of the Dawn (68), along with other such couplings, and the infamous story of Aphrodite's adultery with Ares (69), narrated by Demodocus in book 8, before embarking on the series of adventures recounted by Odysseus in books 9–12 (70–74), where, however, the account breaks off in the middle of Odysseus's journey to the underworld in book 11. The text resumes (75) with a comment on Homer's knowledge of eclipses, and the discussion of the *Odyssey* concludes with a reference to Athena's role, again in her metaphorical capacity as wisdom, in assisting Odysseus in his vengeance against the suitors.

Heraclitus's style has been described as "pretentious, highly metaphorical, and distinctly non-Atticizing" (Russell 2003, 217), although it is not without a certain charm; the failure to conform to the canons of classical Attic prose is a further argument, though scarcely a secure one, for a relatively early date, since close adherence to classical models became the norm only in the period of the Second Sophistic, in the second and early third centuries. Defending Homer systematically against the charge of maligning the gods was a challenge to the skills of a professional public speaker or rhetor, and Heraclitus rises to it enthusiastically, in the manner of those orators who enjoyed taking the part of legendary reprobates (e.g., Gorgias's and Isocrates' apologies for Helen of Troy). A forensic tone and a certain delight in paradox do not mean, of course, that Heraclitus believed his case to be weak. It is central to his argument that Homer intentionally invited allegorical exegesis (apparently the view of the later Stoics: cf. Boys-Stones 2003a), but the proof of necessity is mainly indirect, showing at best that his text is susceptible to such interpretation (cf. Russell 2003, 228–29). Heraclitus portrays Homer as a consummate artist who embellished whatever historical core there may have been to the Trojan War with imaginative mythological fictions that demanded to be read allegorically. These are the passages that were controversial in antiquity, and they are the focus of Heraclitus's analysis.

For whom did Heraclitus write his essay? Given its sophistication, it was probably not addressed primarily to schoolboys or youths, like Cornutus's treatise. It may have been a showpiece, or, given its length, an earnest defense of Homer's piety. Anything more precise is guesswork.

TEXT AND TRANSLATION

The present translation and brief commentary are intended to make the text of Heraclitus available to a wider public than that which has hitherto enjoyed access to it. The notes, like the introduction, are designed to facilitate the understanding of Heraclitus's meaning; no attempt has been made to provide an exhaustive collection of parallel passages (a full commentary remains a desideratum). The facing Greek text has been constructed chiefly on the basis of the Teubner (Te) and Budé (Bu) editions, with the help of the apparatus criticus appended to each, and corresponds to what is translated in the English version. A brief discussion of some passages and conjectures will be found in Russell's contribution to a volume of essays in honor of J. F. Kindstrand (Uppsala, forthcoming). On the whole, the text is closer to the Teubner (Oelmann 1910) than to the Budé (Buffière 1962), which, in the judgment of the translators and editors of this volume, is too ready to neglect conjectural improvements in the text made by its predecessors. The reader should be aware that the manuscripts have not been independently collated, and hence the present work is in no sense a new critical edition. The apparatus to the Greek text records some plausible alternatives to what is printed in the text, as well as some less than plausible readings of the Teubner or Budé editions that have been rejected, along with translations, where possible, of the alternative readings. In this way, the reader who does not know Greek, or know it well, can obtain a sense of what is at stake in the editorial choices adopted here.

Heraclitus's treatise is preserved principally in two manuscripts dating to the fifteenth century: the one, now in the Vatican Library (Vat. Gr. 871), is designated by the letter A, the other, in the British Royal Library, designated by G (cf. also B = Vat. Gr. 951). These two derive from a common archetype, related to the earliest (thirteenth century), but very fragmentary, manuscript M, in the Ambrosian Library in Milan. Two manuscripts, also fragmentary, represent a different tradition: these are D (Vat. Gr. 305), dated to 1314, and O, in New College in Oxford, from the fourteenth century. In addition to these witnesses, the Aldine edition (1505) seems to have used a manuscript that is now lost, and thus has some independent authority (it is indicated by the letter a). There are also extensive quotations from Heraclitus in various manuscripts containing scholia to the Homeric epics, which provide independent testimony: although readings are often altered or adapted to the new context, there is also a considerable coincidence with readings in D and O, and their evidence should not be neglected in establishing the text of Heraclitus (contrast the approach of the Budé edition, p. liii: "Il n'est à peu près aucune lecture [sc. in the scholia] qui soit plus satisfaisante que celles du groupe A B G a"; and cf. pp. lv–lvii, where Buffière [1962] dismisses D and O in comparable terms). The reader is referred to the relevant pages of the introductions to the Teubner and Budé editions for a more thorough description of the manuscript tradition.

David Konstan

HERACLITUS, *HOMERIC PROBLEMS:*

TEXT AND TRANSLATION

ΗΡΑΚΛΕΙΤΟΥ

ΟΜΗΡΙΚΑ ΠΡΟΒΛΗΜΑΤΑ
εἰς ἃ περὶ θεῶν Ὅμηρος ἠλληγόρησεν

1.1 Μέγας ἀπ' οὐρανοῦ καὶ χαλεπὸς ἀγὼν Ὁμήρῳ καταγγέλλεται περὶ τῆς εἰς τὸ θεῖον ὀλιγωρίας· πάντα γὰρ ἠσέβησεν, εἰ μηδὲν ἠλληγόρησεν,[1] **1.2** ἱερόσυλοι δὲ μῦθοι καὶ θεομάχου γέμοντες ἀπονοίας δι' ἀμφοτέρων τῶν σωματίων μεμήνασιν· **1.3** ὥστε εἴ τις ἄνευ φιλοσόφου θεωρίας μηδενὸς αὐτοῖς ὑφεδρεύοντος ἀλληγορικοῦ τρόπου νομίζοι κατὰ ποιητικὴν παράδοσιν εἰρῆσθαι, Σαλμωνεὺς ἂν Ὅμηρος εἴη καὶ Τάνταλος,

> "ἀκόλαστον γλῶσσαν" ἔχων, "αἰσχίστην νόσον."

1.4 Ὥστε ἔμοιγε καὶ σφόδρα συμβέβηκε θαυμάζειν, πῶς ὁ δεισιδαίμων βίος ὁ ναοῖς καὶ τεμένεσι καὶ ταῖς δι' ἔτους [ἐν ταῖς] περὶ[2] θεῶν προτρεπόμενος ἑορταῖς οὕτω τὴν Ὁμηρικὴν ἀσέβειαν ἐνηγκάλισται φιλοστόργως, τοὺς ἐναγεῖς λόγους διὰ στόματος ᾄδων. **1.5** Εὐθὺς γὰρ ἐκ πρώτης ἡλικίας τὰ νήπια τῶν ἀρτιμαθῶν παίδων διδασκαλίᾳ παρ' ἐκείνῳ τιτθεύεται, καὶ μονονοὺκ ἐνεσπαργανωμένοι τοῖς ἔπεσιν αὐτοῦ καθαπερεὶ ποτίμῳ γάλακτι τὰς ψυχὰς ἐπάρδομεν· **1.6** αὐξομένῳ[3] δ' ἑκάστῳ συμπαρέστηκε καὶ κατ' ὀλίγον ἀπανδρουμένῳ, τελείοις δ' ἐνακμάζει, καὶ κόρος οὐδὲ εἷς ἄχρι γήρως, ἀλλὰ παυσάμενοι διψῶμεν αὐτοῦ πάλιν· **1.7** καὶ σχεδὸν ἓν πέρας Ὁμήρῳ παρ' ἀνθρώποις, ὃ καὶ τοῦ βίου.

2.1 Δι' ὧν σαφὲς οἶμαι καὶ πᾶσιν εὔδηλον, ὡς[4] οὐδεμία κηλὶς ἐναγῶν μύθων τοῖς ἔπεσιν ἐνέσπαρται·[5] καθαρὰ δὲ καὶ παντὸς ἁγνεύουσα[6] μύσους Ἰλιὰς πρώτη καὶ μετὰ ταύτην Ὀδύσσεια σύμφωνον ἑκατέρα περὶ τῆς ἰδίας εὐσεβείας κέκραγε φωνήν·

---

1. Full stop in Te, Bu.
2. Perhaps delete also περί so as to let θεῶν depend on ἑορταῖς: "the religious life, which is stimulated by temples and precincts and annual festivals of the gods, should have...," etc.
3. αὐξομένῳ Wyttenbach, Te; mss., Bu read ἀρχομένῳ, "as we begin."
4. ὡς (= "that") O, Te; omitted in M, which indicates a lacuna, and by Bu without comment.
5. ἐνέσπαρται Mehler, literally "is implanted in"; Te, Bu retain the mss. ἐνεσπείρηται = "is coiled up in" (but Bu translates "parsemés," as though he read ἐνέσπαρται).
6. Bu with some mss. reads καθαρὰν ... ἁγνεύουσαν, modifying "voice."

HERACLITUS

HOMERIC PROBLEMS
On Homer's Allegories Relating to the Gods

1 It is a weighty and damaging charge that heaven brings against Homer for his disrespect for the divine. If he meant nothing allegorically, he was impious through and through, and sacrilegious fables, loaded with blasphemous[1] folly, run riot through both epics.[2] And so, if one were to believe that it was all said in obedience to poetical tradition without any philosophical theory or underlying allegorical trope, Homer would be a Salmoneus[3] or a Tantalus,[4]

"with tongue unchastened, a most disgraceful sickness."[5]

Hence I have come to feel amazed that the religious life, whose concern with the gods is stimulated by temples and precincts and annual festivals, should have embraced Homer's impiety so affectionately and learned to chant his abominable stories from memory. From the very first age of life, the foolishness of infants just beginning to learn is nurtured on the teaching given in his school. One might almost say that his poems are our baby clothes,[6] and we nourish our minds by draughts of his milk. He stands at our side as we each grow up and shares our youth as we gradually come to manhood; when we are mature, his presence within us is at its prime; and even in old age, we never weary of him. When we stop, we thirst to begin him again. In a word, the only end of Homer for human beings is the end of life.[7]

2 For these reasons, it is, I think, perfectly plain and evident to all that no stain of abominable myth disfigures his poems. They are pure and innocent of all pollution—first the *Iliad* and, second, the *Odyssey*, each raising its voice in unison to proclaim its own piety:

---

1. This sense of *theomakhos* is not recognized in LSJ, but see *PGL*, s.v., where *theomakhon gnômên* is cited from Macarius Magnes, *Apocriticus ad Graecos* 10 (p. 15,15 Blondel).

2. For *sômation* in this sense, see Longinus, *Subl.* 9.13.

3. The arrogant ruler of Elis who imitated Zeus's thunder and lightning and was struck down by a thunderbolt sent by Zeus; the story is told in Virgil, *Aen.* 6.585–594; for earlier references, cf. Hesiod, frg. 10.3 = Scholia to Pindar, *Pyth.* 4.143; Euripides, *Aeolus* frg. 14.4.

4. Punished in Hades for perjury, for stealing nectar and ambrosia, or for revealing the gods' secrets; another stock example of impiety.

5. Euripides, *Orest.* 10; quoted again in ch. 78.

6. For the metaphor of swaddling clothes (*enesparganômenoi*), cf. Longinus, *Subl.* 44.3.

7. Cf. Dio Chrysostom, *Or.* 18.8, on Homer as the poet for all ages of life.

Οὐκ ἂν ἔγωγε θεοῖσιν ἐπουρανίοισι μαχοίμην·

Νήπιοι, οἳ Ζηνὶ μενεαίνομεν ἰσοφαρίζειν.

2.2 Οἷος μὲν ἐν οὐρανῷ διὰ τῶν ἐπῶν καθιέρωται Ζεὺς ἀφανεῖ νεύματι σείων· ὡς δὲ Ποσειδῶνος ὁρμήσαντος αἰφνιδίως "τρέμεν οὔρεα μακρὰ καὶ ὕλη." **2.3** Τὰ αὐτὰ δ᾽ ὑπὲρ Ἥρας ἄν τις εἴποι·

Σείσατο δ᾽ εἰνὶ θρόνῳ, ἐλέλιξε δὲ μακρὸν Ὄλυμπον.

2.4 Ὁμοίως δὲ Ἀθηνᾶν παρεστάναι·

Θάμβησεν δ᾽ Ἀχιλεύς, μετὰ δ᾽ ἐτράπετ᾽, αὐτίκα δ᾽ ἔγνω
Παλλάδ᾽ Ἀθηναίην, δεινὼ δέ οἱ ὄσσε φάανθεν.

Οἴη δ᾽ Ἄρτεμις εἶσι κατ᾽ οὔρεος ἰοχέαιρα
ἢ κατὰ Τηΰγετον περιμήκετον ἢ Ἐρύμανθον
τερπομένη κάπροισι καὶ ὠκείαις ἐλάφοισιν.

2.5 Ἃ μὲν γὰρ ἐξ ἴσου καὶ κατὰ κοινὸν ὑπὲρ ἁπάντων ἱεροπρεπῶς τεθεολόγηται, τί δεῖ καὶ λέγειν; "μάκαρες θεοὶ αἰὲν ἐόντες" καὶ "ἄφθιτα μήδε᾽ ἔχοντες" ἢ νὴ Δία "δωτῆρες ἐάων" καὶ "ῥεῖα ζώοντες"·

Οὐ γὰρ σῖτον ἔδουσ᾽, οὐ πίνουσ᾽ αἴθοπα οἶνον,
τοὔνεκ᾽ ἀναίμονές εἰσι καὶ ἀθάνατοι καλέονται.

"I would not fight against the gods of heaven";[1]

"We are fools to want to match ourselves with Zeus."[2]

How magnificently is Zeus sanctified in heaven in the lines in which he makes it tremble with an imperceptible nod![3] How the "great mountains and the forest shake"[4] on a sudden when Poseidon starts on his way. And the same could be said of Hera:

"she trembled on her throne and made
all great Olympus quake";[5]

or of Athena's epiphany:

"Achilles was amazed, and turned, and knew
Pallas Athena: fearful flashed her eyes";[6]

or

"Like Artemis the archer on the mountain,
on great Taygetus or Erymanthus,
delighted with the boars and the swift deer."[7]

As for the sacred solemnity with which he speaks of all the gods equally and in general, there is surely no need to illustrate this at length: "blessed gods who live forever," "with thoughts immortal," "givers of blessings," "living in ease";

"they eat no food and drink no gleaming wine,
are bloodless and are called immortals."[8]

---

1. *Il.* 6.129 (Diomedes to Glaucus).

2. *Il.* 15.104 (Hera to the other gods), with "match ourselves" (*isopharizein*) substituted for *aphradeontes* or *aphroneontes* (= "to contend thoughtlessly with Zeus"). A passage or two from the *Odyssey* seems to be missing (unless Heraclitus has misremembered and attributed the second verse to the *Odyssey*); cf. 4.78 for the idea.

3. Cf. *Il.* 1.528.

4. *Il.* 13.18; cf. Longinus, *Subl.* 9.8.

5. *Il.* 8.199.

6. *Il.* 1.199–200.

7. *Od.* 6.102–104.

8. *Od.* 8.306, *Il.* 24.88, *Od.* 8.325, *Od.* 4.805, *Il.* 5.341–342; compare Ps.-Plutarch, *Vit. poes. Hom.* 2.112.

3.1 Τίς οὖν ἐπὶ τούτοις Ὅμηρον ἀσεβῆ λέγειν τολμᾷ;

Ζεῦ κύδιστε. μέγιστε, κελαινεφές, αἰθέρι ναίων.
Ἠέλιός θ', ὃς πάντ' ἐφορᾷς καὶ πάντ' ἐπακούεις,
καὶ ποταμοί, καὶ γαῖα, καὶ οἳ ὑπένερθε καμόντας[1]
ἀνθρώπους τίνυσθον, ὅ τις[2] κ' ἐπίορκον ὀμόσσῃ,
ὑμεῖς μάρτυροι ἔστε

τῆς Ὁμήρου θεοσεβοῦς προαιρέσεως, ὅτι πάθεσιν ἐξαιρέτοις ἅπαν νεωκορεῖ τὸ δαιμόνιον, ἐπεὶ καὐτός ἐστι θεῖος. **3.2** Εἰ δ' ἀμαθεῖς[3] τινες ἄνθρωποι τὴν Ὁμηρικὴν ἀλληγορίαν ἀγνοοῦσιν οὐδ' εἰς τὰ μύχια τῆς ἐκείνου σοφίας καταβεβήκασιν, ἀλλ' ἀβασάνιστος αὐτοῖς ἡ τῆς ἀληθείας κρίσις ἔρριπται, καὶ τὸ φιλοσόφως ῥηθὲν οὐκ εἰδότες, ὃ μυθικῶς δοκεῖ πλάσαι προαρπάζουσιν,[4] οὗτοι μὲν ἐρρέτωσαν. **3.3** ἡμεῖς δ' οἳ τῶν ἀβεβήλων ἐντὸς περιρραντηρίων ἡγνίσμεθα, σεμνὴν ὑπὸ νόμῳ[5] τῶν ποιημάτων τὴν ἀλήθειαν ἀνιχνεύωμεν.[6]

4.1 Ἐρρίφθω δὲ καὶ[7] Πλάτων ὁ κόλαξ καὶ Ὁμήρου συκοφάντης, ἔνδοξον ἀπὸ τῆς ἰδίας πολιτείας τὸν φυγάδα προπέμπων λευκοῖς ἐρίοις ἀνεστεμμένον καὶ πολυτελεῖ μύρῳ τὴν κεφαλὴν διάβροχον. **4.2** Οὐδ' Ἐπικούρου φροντὶς ἡμῖν, ὃς τῆς ἀσέμνου περὶ τοὺς ἰδίους κήπους ἡδονῆς γεωργός ἐστιν, ἅπασαν ὁμοῦ ποιητικὴν ὥσπερ ὀλέθριον μύθων δέλεαρ ἀφοσιούμενος. **4.3** Πρὸς οὓς μέγα δή τι στενάξας εἴποιμ' ἂν εὐλόγως·

Ὦ πόποι, οἷον δή νυ θεοὺς βροτοὶ αἰτιόωνται.

4.4 Καὶ τὸ πικρότατον, ἀρχὴν ἑκάτεροι τῶν παρ' ἑαυτοῖς δογμάτων ἔχοντες Ὅμηρον, ἀφ' οὗ τὰ πλεῖστα τῆς ἐπιστήμης ὠφέληνται, περὶ τοῦτον ἀχαρίστως εἰσὶν ἀσεβεῖς. **4.5** Ἀλλ' ὑπὲρ μὲν Ἐπικούρου καὶ Πλάτωνος αὖθις

---

1. καμόντας (= "the dead") with Te (and OCT *Iliad*), rather than καμόντες (modifying "those who dwell below") with Bu; see the edition of West (1998, 103).

2. Te, following the Aldine edition; mss., Bu read ὅστις. Cf. 23.4.

3. ἀμαθεῖς Heyne, Te; ἀμαθῶς mss., Bu = "ignorantly."

4. προαρπάζουσιν Wyttenbach (cf. Plato, *Gorg.* 454C); προσαρπάζουσιν M, Te; προσαρμόζουσιν O, Bu, translated as "s'attachent" (intransitive).

5. ὑπὸ νόμῳ is odd; perhaps read ὑπονόμῳ, "by a hidden tunnel": one must go deep to understand Homer. Alternatively, perhaps, ὑπονοίᾳ, "by way of allegory," but this term (on which, see the introduction, p. xix) does not occur elsewhere in the book.

6. ἀνιχνεύωμεν G, Te; ἰχνεύωμεν A, B, Aldine, Bu.

7. Omitted in M, Bu.

3 After this, who dares call Homer impious?

"Zeus, mighty god of storm clouds, heaven-dwelling....
O Sun, who seest and hearest everything;
O rivers, earth, and ye who dwell below
and punish the dead, if any man swear falsely,
be witnesses..."[1]

to Homer's pious plan, that he honors[2] all divine beings with exceptional expressions of feeling,[3] because he is divine himself. If some ignorant people fail to recognize Homeric allegory and have not descended into the secret caverns of his wisdom but instead have risked a hasty judgment of the truth without proper consideration, and if then they seize hastily on what they take to be his mythical invention, because they do not know what is said in a philosophical sense—well, off with them and good riddance! But let us, who have been hallowed within the sacred enclosure, methodically track down the grand truth of the poems.

4 Away too with Plato, the flatterer, Homer's dishonest accuser, who banishes him from his private Republic[4] as an honored exile, garlanded with white wool and with his head drenched with costly perfumes! Nor need we trouble ourselves with Epicurus, who cultivates his low pleasure in *his* private garden, and abominates all poetry indiscriminately as a lethal allurement of fable.[5] In the face of these two, I might very reasonably groan and cry

Ah me, how mortals put the blame on gods![6]

And the irony is that both these philosophers found the basis of their doctrines in Homer, and are ungrateful as well as impious toward the person from whom they gained most of their knowledge.[7] But we shall have

---

1. *Il.* 2.412 + 3.277–280, repeated (less the final half-verse) in ch. 24. Heraclitus incorporates the quotation into his own argument (cf. Longinus, *Subl.* 9.8).

2. For *neôkorei* = "honor" or "tend," cf. Cornutus, *Theol.* 28 = p. 52.17 Lang, where Hestia is honored (*neôkoreitai*) by virgins because she is a virgin herself. Homer is frequently called "divine," e.g., Aristophanes, *Ran.* 1034, Plato, *Phaed.* 95A.

3. Compare (perhaps) Longinus, *Subl.* 9.13 for *pathesin* in this sense.

4. *Resp.* 398A.

5. Frg. 229 Usener; see ch. 79, and, e.g., Asmis (1995, 16–22).

6. *Od.* 1.32 (Zeus speaking).

7. For Epicurus's plagiarism of Homer, see Sextus Empiricus *Against the Grammarians* (= *Math.* 1) 273 with David Blank (1997, 290). For Plato's "plagiarism," see Ps.-Plutarch, *Vit.*

ἐξέσται λέγειν.

5.1 Νυνὶ δ' ἀναγκαῖον ἴσως μικρὰ καὶ σύντομα περὶ τῆς ἀλληγορίας τεχνολογῆσαι· σχεδὸν γὰρ αὐτὸ τοὔνομα καὶ λίαν ἐτύμως εἰρημένον ἐλέγχει τὴν δύναμιν αὐτῆς. **5.2** Ὁ γὰρ ἄλλα μὲν ἀγορεύων τρόπος, ἕτερα δὲ ὧν λέγει σημαίνων, ἐπωνύμως ἀλληγορία καλεῖται. **5.3** Καθάπερ Ἀρχίλοχος μὲν ἐν τοῖς Θρακικοῖς ἀπειλημμένος δεινοῖς τὸν πόλεμον εἰκάζει θαλαττίῳ κλύδωνι λέγων ὡδέ πως· **5.4**

Γλαῦχ' ὅρα, βαθὺς γὰρ ἤδη κύμασιν ταράσσεται
πόντος, ἀμφὶ δ' ἄκρα Γυρέων ὀρθὸν ἵσταται νέφος,
σῆμα χειμῶνος· κιχάνει δ' ἐξ ἀέλπτίης φόβος.

5.5 Ἐν ἱκανοῖς[1] δὲ καὶ τὸν Μυτιληναῖον μελοποιὸν εὑρήσομεν ἀλληγοροῦντα· τὰς γὰρ τυραννικὰς ταραχὰς ἐξ ἴσου χειμερίῳ προσεικάζει καταστήματι θαλάττης· **5.6**

Ἀσυνέτημι τῶν ἀνέμων στάσιν·
τὸ μὲν γὰρ ἔνθεν κῦμα κυλίνδεται,
τὸ δ' ἔνθεν· ἄμμες δ' ἂν τὸ μέσσον
νᾶι φορήμεθα σὺν μελαίνᾳ,
χείμωνι μοχθεῦντες μεγάλῳ μάλα·
πὲρ μὲν γὰρ ἄντλος ἱστοπέδαν ἔχει,
λαῖφος δὲ πᾶν ζάδηλον ἤδη
καὶ λάκιδες μέγαλαι κὰτ' αὐτο·
χόλαισι δ' ἄγκυραι.

5.7 Τίς οὐκ ἂν εὐθὺς ἐκ τῆς προτρεχούσης περὶ τὸν πόντον εἰκασίας ἀνδρῶν πλωιζομένων θαλάττιον εἶναι νομίσειε φόβον; ἀλλ' οὐχ οὕτως ἔχει· Μύρσιλος γὰρ ὁ δηλούμενός ἐστι καὶ τυραννικὴ κατὰ Μυτιληναίων

---

1. ἐν ἱκανοῖς is odd; perhaps emend to εἰκασμοῖς (Russell), "by means of likenesses."

other opportunities to discuss Epicurus and Plato.[1]

5 For the moment, it is probably essential to give a little technical account of allegory, quite briefly.[2] The word itself, which is formed in a way expressive of truth, reveals its own significance. For the trope which says [*agoreuôn*] one thing but signifies something other [*alla*] than what it says receives the name "allegory" precisely from this. Thus Archilochus, for example, caught up in the perils of Thrace, compares the war to a surge of the sea as follows:

> Look, Glaucus, how the deep sea now is troubled by the waves,
> and over Gyrae's heights a cloud stands towering high,
> sign of a storm: the unexpected brings us face to face with fear.[3]

Again, we shall find the lyric poet of Mytilene[4] often enough using allegory. He likewise compares the disturbances of a tyranny to a stormy sea:

> How the winds set, I cannot tell:
> waves roll from this side
> and from that, and in between
> in our black ship we drift,
>
> and labor in the monstrous storm:
> the bilge is rising round the mast,
> you can see through
> the sail, it's all in tatters,
>
> and now the anchor too is loosed![5]

Who would not conclude, from the image of the sea preceding this passage,[6] that what was meant was the fear of the sea felt by a party of

---

poes. Hom. 122, with Hillgruber (1994–1999, 1:266–68), and below, ch. 17. Dionysius of Halicarnassus, *Pomp.* 1.13, accuses Plato of jealousy toward Homer.

1. See below, chs. 76–79.

2. By "technical" in this context Heraclitus means "grammatical"; he gives a standard definition (cf. Trypho 3.193 Spengel; Lausberg 1998, sec. 895), and points out that the word itself displays its meaning (*etumôs*).

3. Frg. 54 Bergk = 105 West.

4. I.e., Alcaeus.

5. Frg. Z2 Page = 326 Lobel and Page; see Page (1955, 185–89). The allegory was imitated by Horace, *Carm.* 1.14; see Nisbet and Hubbard (1970, 179–81).

6. *Protrekhousês* indicates that the image precedes the explanation rather than following it; cf. Quintilian, *Inst.* 8.3.77 for this way of classifying similes.

ἐγειρομένη σύστασις. **5.8** Ὁμοίως δὲ τὰ ὑπὸ τούτου <πραχθέντ'>[1]
αἰνιττόμενος ἑτέρωθί που λέγει·

> Τὸ δ' ηὖτε κῦμα τῶν προτέρων ὄνω
> στείχει, παρέξει δ' ἄμμι πόνον πόλυν
> ἄντλην, ἐπεί κε νᾶος ἐμβᾷ.

5.9 Κατακόρως ἐν ταῖς ἀλληγορίαις ὁ νησιώτης θαλαττεύει καὶ τὰ πλεῖστα
τῶν διὰ τοὺς τυράννους ἐπεχόντων κακῶν πελαγείοις χειμῶσιν εἰκάζει.

5.10 Καὶ μὴν ὁ Τήιος Ἀνακρέων ἑταιρικὸν φρόνημα καὶ σοβαρᾶς
γυναικὸς ὑπερηφανίαν ὀνειδίζων τὸν ἐν αὐτῇ σκιρτῶντα νοῦν ὡς ἵππον
ἠλληγόρησεν οὕτω λέγων· **5.11**

> Πῶλε Θρηκίη, τί δή με λοξὸν ὄμμασιν βλέπουσα
> νηλεῶς φεύγεις, δοκέεις δέ μ' οὐδὲν εἰδέναι σοφόν;
> ἴσθι τοι, καλῶς μὲν ἄν τοι τὸν χαλινὸν ἐμβάλοιμι,
> ἡνίας δ' ἔχων στρέφοιμ<ί σ'>[2] ἀμφὶ τέρματα δρόμου.
> Νῦν δὲ λειμῶνάς τε βόσκεαι κοῦφά τε σκιρτῶσα παίζεις·
> δεξιὸν γὰρ ἱπποπείρην[3] οὐχ ἔχεις ἐπεμβάτην.

5.12 Καθόλου μακρὸς ἂν εἴην ἐπεξιὼν ἕκαστα τῶν παρὰ ποιηταῖς καὶ συγ-
γραφεῦσιν ἠλληγορημένων· ἀπόχρη <δ'>[4] ὀλίγαις εἰκόσι τὴν ὅλην τοῦ
πράγματος τεκμηριώσασθαι φύσιν. **5.13** Ἀλλ' οὐδ' αὐτὸς Ὅμηρος ἀμφι-
βόλοις ἔσθ' ὅτε καὶ ζητουμέναις ἔτι ταῖς ἀλληγορίαις εὑρίσκεται χρώμενος·
5.14 ἐναργῆ τὸν τρόπον ἡμῖν τῆς ἑρμηνείας παραδέδωκε τοῦτον, ἐν οἷς
Ὀδυσσεὺς τὰ πολέμου καὶ μάχης κακὰ διεξιὼν φησίν· **5.15**

> Ἧς τε πλείστην μὲν καλάμην χθονὶ χαλκὸς ἔχευεν,
> ἀμητὸς δ' ὀλίγιστος, ἐπὴν κλίνῃσι τάλαντα
> Ζεύς.

5.16 Τὸ μὲν γὰρ λεγόμενόν ἐστι γεωργία, τὸ δὲ νοούμενον μάχη· πλὴν ὅμως
δι' ἐναντίων ἀλλήλοις πραγμάτων τὸ δηλούμενον ἐπιγιγνώκομεν.[5]

---

1. Te indicates a lacuna here; the supplement follows a hint in Te apparatus criticus. Bu
ignores the hiatus and follows the mss.

2. Bergk.

3. So Page; Bergk, followed by Te and Bu, emended to ἱπποσείρην, "lead you by the
reins."

4. Gale; Bu, following Te, reads γάρ.

5. Tentatively adopted on a suggestion in Te apparatus criticus; Bu, following Te, reads
ἐπείπομεν, and translates "on fait entendre," but the word must mean "added" or "uttered."
Heyne proposed ἐπεῖπεν, which makes Homer the subject (perhaps rightly).

sailors? But it is not so. What is meant is Myrsilus and the conspiracy[1] of tyranny being formed against the people of Mytilene. He gives a similar enigmatic hint of the actions of this man in another passage:

> Here comes a higher wave than these:
> when the ship takes it, bailing out
> will cost us dear.[2]

Indeed, our island poet loves being at sea in his allegories, and compares most of the troubles due to the tyrants to storms at sea.

Again, Anacreon of Teos, attacking a courtesan's airs and the pride of an arrogant woman, describes the frisky spirit in her allegorically as a horse:

> Why look at me, Thracian filly, from the corner of your eye,
> and mercilessly run away and think I'm just a fool?
> For, let me tell you, I could curb you nicely,
> and take the reins and steer you round the course.
> Just now, you graze the meadows, jump and play,
> because you've got no skillful rider who can break you in.[3]

It would be tedious of me to go through all the instances of allegory in the poets and prose-writers. It is enough to illustrate the general nature of the thing by a few examples. Homer himself is sometimes found using allegories which are neither ambiguous nor still in dispute: he has given us a very lucid account of this mode of expression in the passage where Odysseus, enumerating the evils of war and battle, says

> In this, the bronze spills most straw on the ground,
> but the harvest is least, when Zeus tips up the scales.[4]

The words here speak of farming, though what is intended is battle; and yet we understand[5] the true significance from the pair of contrasting opposites.

---

1. The idea of "conspiracy" is hinted at in Alcaeus's use of *stasis* in verse 1, for this word means "conflict" or "civil strife" as well as "setting" or "position."

2. Frg. A6 Page (1955, 182).

3. Frg. 417 (= Anacreon 72) Page, *Poetae Melici Graeci* (1962); the fragment is known only from this passage.

4. *Il.* 9.222–224.

5. The "true significance" is presumably the wastefulness of war, which the contrast of "most" and "least" emphasizes. Or perhaps Heraclitus means that we understand "the

6.1 Ὁπότ᾽ οὖν συνήθης μὲν ἅπασι τοῖς ἄλλοις ὁ τῆς ἀλληγορίας τρόπος, ἠγνόηται δὲ οὐδὲ παρ᾽ Ὁμήρῳ, τί παθόντες, ὅσα φαύλως ἔχειν δοκεῖ περὶ θεῶν, οὐ διὰ τοιαύτης ἀπολογίας θεραπεύσομεν; **6.2** Τάξις δέ μοι γενήσεται τῶν λόγων ἡ τῶν Ὁμηρικῶν ἐπῶν τάξις, ἐν ἑκάστῃ ῥαψῳδίᾳ διὰ λεπτῆς ἐπιστήμης ἐπιδεικνύντι τὰ περὶ θεῶν ἠλληγορημένα.

6.3 Ὁ τοίνυν μιαρὸς ἀεὶ καὶ βάσκανος φθόνος οὐδὲ τῆς πρώτης ἐν ἀρχῇ πέφεισται· πολὺς δ᾽ αὐτῷ θρυλεῖται περὶ τῆς Ἀπόλλωνος ὀργῆς λόγος, ὅτι τοὺς οὐδὲν αἰτίους Ἕλληνας οἱ μάτην ἀφεθέντες ὀϊστοὶ παρανάλωσαν, **6.4** καὶ οὕτως ἄδικός ἐστιν ἡ τούτου μῆνις, ὥσθ᾽ ὁ μὲν ὑβρίσας Χρύσην Ἀγαμέμνων οὐδὲν ἐξαίρετον ἔπαθεν, ὀφείλων εἴπερ ἠδίκει κολασθῆναι, οἱ δ᾽ ἐπιβοήσαντες

αἰδεῖσθαί θ᾽ ἱερῆα καὶ ἀγλαὰ δέχθαι ἄποινα

τῆς ἀγνωμοσύνης τοῦ μὴ πεπεισμένου γεγόνασι παρανάλωμα. **6.5** Πλὴν ἔγωγε τὴν ὑποκειμένην[1] ἐν τοῖς ἔπεσιν ἀλήθειαν ἀκριβῶς διαθρήσας οὐκ Ἀπόλλωνος ὀργὴν οἶμαι ταῦτα, λοιμικῆς δὲ νόσου κακόν, οὐ θεόπεμπτον, ἀλλ᾽ αὐτόματον φθοράν, συστᾶσαν[2] τότε καὶ πολλαχῇ, ὥστε καὶ μέχρι τῶν δεῦρο χρόνων ἐκνέμεσθαι τὸν ἀνθρώπινον βίον. **6.6** Ὅτι μὲν τοίνυν ὁ αὐτὸς Ἀπόλλων ἡλίῳ, καὶ θεὸς εἷς δυσὶν ὀνόμασι κοσμεῖται, σαφὲς ἡμῖν ἔκ τε τῶν μυστικῶν λόγων, οὓς αἱ ἀπόρρητοι τελεταὶ θεολογοῦσι, καὶ τοῦ δημώδους ἄνω καὶ κάτω θρυλουμένου·[3]

ἥλιος Ἀπόλλων, ὁ δέ γ᾽ Ἀπόλλων ἥλιος.

7.1 Ἠκρίβωται δ᾽ ἡ περὶ τούτων ἀπόδειξις καὶ Ἀπολλοδώρῳ, περὶ πᾶσαν ἱστορίαν ἀνδρὶ δεινῷ. **7.2** Τοῦτ᾽[4] ἔγωγε τὴν ἐπὶ πλέον ἐξεργασίαν καὶ

---

1. ὑποκειμένην Russell; ὑπολελημένην AB; Te emends to ὑπολελειμμένην, "remaining in," Bu to ὑπολελησμένην, "lying concealed beneath."
2. συστᾶσαν O, Te; συστάντος M, Bu.
3. τὸ δημῶδες ... θρυλούμενον M, Bu.
4. So mss. Schow reads διὰ τοῦτ᾽, while Te in apparatus criticus suggests τούτου τοίνυν. But perhaps τοῦτ᾽ can stand in the sense of "therefore"; see LSJ s.v. οὗτός VIII.1.

6 So, since the trope of allegory is familiar to all other writers and known even to Homer, what should prevent us mending his alleged wrong notions about the gods by this kind of justification? My discussion will follow the order of the Homeric poems, and I shall use subtle learning to expound the allegorical statements about the gods in each book [*rhapsôidia*].[1]

Envy, always vile and malicious, has not even spared the opening of the first book. It has had a good deal to say about the anger of Apollo, claiming that his randomly discharged arrows incidentally destroyed the innocent Greeks, and that his wrath is so unjust that Agamemnon, despite the offence he did to Chryses, suffered no extraordinary consequences (though he did wrong, and ought to have been punished), whereas the people who called upon him to

respect the priest, and take the splendid ransom[2]

became the incidental victims of the folly of the man they failed to persuade. However, looking carefully at the truth underlying these lines, I believe that they do not describe Apollo's anger, but the misfortune of a plague, which is a spontaneous rather than a divinely sent disaster. It is one that happened both then and on many occasions besides, and ravages humanity even in our own day. That Apollo is identical with the Sun, and that one god is honored under two names, is confirmed both by mystical doctrines taught by secret initiations and by the popular and widely quoted line,

the sun's Apollo, and Apollo the sun.[3]

7 A scholarly exposition of these things is to be found in Apollodorus,[4] who is an authority in every branch of learning. I shall therefore

---

true reference," that is, to war, from the opposition between bronze and straw and between the harvest and the image of Zeus's scales, which are normally mentioned in connection with battle.

1. In Heraclitus, *rhapsôidia* usually designates a book of the poem.

2. *Il.* 1.23.

3. The line in this form is not otherwise known, although the identification is found already in the classical period (Euripides, *Phaethon* 224–226 Diggle), and is common later (see Pease [1955–1958] on Cicero, *Nat. d.* 2.68 for a list of passages). It does not seem, despite Heraclitus's claim, to have been particularly a mystical doctrine.

4. Apollodorus (second century B.C.), born in Alexandria, later moved to Athens; he wrote on history, religion, geography, and mythology (the extant work attributed to him is later by several centuries), in particular a treatise *On the Gods*, which was also a source for

ἀκαίρου λόγου περιττὸν ὑπερθήσομαι μῆκος· **7.3** ἐκεῖνο δ᾽ ὃ ἐκ τῆς ἡμετέρας εἰκασίας ἀναγκαῖον εἰπεῖν, οὐ παρήσω, δεικνὺς ὅτι καὶ καθ᾽ Ὅμηρον αὐτός ἐστιν Ἀπόλλων καὶ ἥλιος. **7.4** Τοῦτο δ᾽ εἰ λεπτῶς ἐθέλει σκοπεῖν τις, ἐξ ἁπάντων εὑρήσει τῶν ἐπιθέτων γνώριμον. **7.5** Ἀμέλει Φοῖβον αὐτὸν εἴωθε συνεχῶς ὀνομάζειν, οὐ μὰ Δία οὐκ ἀπὸ Φοίβης, ἣν Λητοῦς φασὶν εἶναι μητέρα· **7.6** σύνηθες γὰρ Ὁμήρῳ τοῖς πατρόθεν ἐπιθέτοις χρῆσθαι, τὰ δ᾽ ἐκ μητέρων οὐκ ἂν εὕροι τις ὅλως παρ᾽ αὐτῷ· **7.7** Φοῖβον οὖν <ὡς>[1] ἀπὸ τῶν ἀκτίνων λαμπρὸν αὐτὸν ὀνομάζει, τὸ μόνον ἡλίῳ προσὸν ἐξ ἴσου κοινώσας Ἀπόλλωνι. **7.8** Καὶ μὴν οὐδ᾽ ἑκάεργον εἰκός ἐστιν Ἑκάεργης ὁμώνυμον εἶναι τῆς ἐξ Ὑπερβορέων <τὰς>[2] ἀπαρχὰς ἐπὶ Δῆλον ἐνεγκούσης, ἀλλ᾽ ἔστιν ἐτύμως ἑκάεργος, ὁ τὰ ἕκαθεν ἐργαζόμενος· **7.9** τουτέστιν ὁ ἥλιος, ὁ πόρρωθεν ἀφεστὼς τῆς ἡμετέρας γῆς, ὡρῶν ἐπετείων[3] γεωργοῖς[4] εὐκαίρως ἐφίσταται, πνίγη χειμῶσιν ἀντιμετρῶν καὶ ἀρότου τε καὶ σπορᾶς ἀμήτου τε καὶ τῶν κατὰ γεωμορίαν ἔργων αἴτιος ἀνθρώποις γενόμενος. **7.10** Λυκηγενή[5] δὲ προσηγόρευσεν αὐτὸν οὐχ ὡς ἐν Λυκίᾳ γεγενημένον — ἔξω γὰρ οὖν τῆς Ὁμηρικῆς ἀναγνώσεως οὗτος ὁ νεώτερος μῦθος —, ἀλλ᾽ ὥσπερ οἶμαι τὴν ἡμέραν ἠριγένειαν ὀνομάζει, τὴν τὸ ἦρ γεννῶσαν, ὅπερ ἐστὶν ὄρθρον, οὕτω λυκηγενή προσηγόρευσε τὸν ἥλιον, ἐπειδὴ τοῦ κατὰ τὴν αἴθριον[6] ὥραν λυκαυγοῦς αὐτός ἐστιν αἴτιος· **7.11** ἢ ὅτι τὸν λυκάβαντα γεννᾷ, τουτέστι τὸν ἐνιαυτόν, ὅρος γὰρ ἐτησίου χρόνου διαδραμὼν ἥλιος ἐν μέρει τὰ δώδεκα ζῴδια. **7.12** Καὶ μὴν χρυσάορον αὐτὸν ὠνόμασεν οὐχ ὡς ὑπεζωσμένον χρυσοῦν ξίφος — ἀνοίκειον γὰρ Ἀπόλλωνι τὸ ὅπλον, τοξότης γὰρ ὁ θεός —, **7.13** ἀλλ᾽ ἐπειδήπερ ἐξ ἀνατολῶν χρυσῷ μάλιστα τὸ φέγγος ὁραθὲν ἔοικεν, εὑρέθη πρέπον ἐπίθετον ἡλίῳ διὰ τὰς ἀκτῖνας τὸ χρυσάορον.[7] **7.14** Ὅθεν οἶμαι κἂν τῇ θεομαχίᾳ Ποσειδάωνι ἵσταται διαμιλλώμενος· ἀεὶ γὰρ ἄσπειστος[8] ἔχθρα πυρὶ καὶ ὕδατι, τῶν δύο στοιχείων ἐναντίαν πρὸς

---

1. Added by Russell.
2. Added by Te; A, B, Bu indicate a lacuna.
3. ἐπετείων, Mehler; ἐπιγείων = "earthly" seasons, G, Bu; O, Te, read ἐπιτηδείων, seasons "serviceable to" farmers.
4. γεωργοῖς Russell, following O[2]; Te, Bu retain γεωργός = "presides as a farmer."
5. Λυκηγενῆ Homeric scholia, Te, *Il.* 4.101, 119; Λυκηγενέτην M, O, Bu.
6. Mss., Bu; Te has ὄρθριον, "at the dawn hour."
7. O, Te; M, Bu, read ὁ χρυσάορ, "he of the golden sword."
8. ἄσπειστος Pierson, Te; ἄσπονδος Homeric scholia; ἄπιστος M, Bu, who translates "incroyable"; but the sense "incredible" is not appropriate in this context.

dispense with a more elaborate explanation and the unnecessary prolixity of irrelevant argument. But I shall not pass over the point which is essential for my interpretation, namely to show that in Homer too Apollo is identified with the Sun. Anyone who is prepared to consider this with some subtlety will find it made evident by all the epithets the poet uses. Of course, he regularly calls Apollo "Phoebus"; but this is not because of Phoebe, who is said to be Leto's mother, since it is normal for Homer to use epithets derived from the father and no instance of an epithet derived from the mother can be found anywhere in his works. No: he calls him Phoebus because of the brightness of his rays,[1] giving Apollo an equal share in a characteristic unique to the sun. Again, it is unlikely that *hekaergos* should come from Hekaerge, the woman who brought the firstfruits from the Hyperboreans to Delos:[2] no, he is literally *hekaergos*, he who "works from afar"—that is, the sun, though distant from our earth, presides punctually over the seasons of the year for the benefit of farmers, balancing summer heat against winter storms, and allowing men to plough and sow and harvest and do all the works of agriculture. Again, Homer called him *lykêgenês*, not as being born in Lycia[3]—this is a modern myth, not to be found in Homer—but (in my opinion) because he is the cause of the twilight glow [*lykauges*][4] seen in clear weather: compare the epithet *êrigeneia*—producing *êr*, i.e., the dawn—applied to the day. Alternatively, it is because he produces the *lykabas*, that is, the year, since the sun passes in turn through the twelve signs of the zodiac and thus sets the limit of the annual period. Again, Homer calls Apollo *chrysaoros*, not because he has a golden sword at his belt[5]—that would be an inappropriate weapon for an archer god—but because the light seen at sunrise is most like gold; *chrysaoros* was thought of as an appropriate epithet for the sun, because of his rays. And this, I suppose, is also why, in the Battle of the Gods, he stands over against Poseidon, for an irreconcilable enmity

---

Cornutus. The present passage = *FGH* 244F98; cf. the Geneva scholium to *Il.* 21.472 = *FGH* 244F97.

1. For *lampron*, "bright," as the explanation of the epithet Phoebus, cf. Cornutus, *Theol.* ch. 32 = 66.18 Lang. Whereas Cornutus offers various derivations of divine epithets, without necessarily choosing among them, Heraclitus typically approves those that support his interpretation of Homer and rejects alternatives.

2. According to Callimachus, *Hymn to Delos* 291–293, the daughters of Boreas, who were called Oupis, Loxo, and Hekaerge, brought the firstfruits to Delos from the Arimaspoi; the connection with the epithet *hekaergos* was made by Phanodicus, according to the scholium on *Il.* 21.472 = *FGH* 397F5

3. A connection between Apollo and Lycia was known to Homer; see *Il.* 16.514; the scholia to *Il.* 4.101 explain *Lykêgenês* as born in, or dwelling in, Lycia.

4. Cf. Macrobius, *Saturnalia* 1.17.36–40 (but *lukophôs*, not *lukaugês*).

5. *Chrysos* = "gold," *aor* = "sword."

ἄλληλα φύσιν ἀποκεκληρωμένων· **7.15** διὰ τοῦθ' ὁ Ποσειδῶν, ὑγρά τις ὕλη καὶ παρὰ τὴν πόσιν οὕτως ὠνομασμένος, ἐξ ἀντιπάλου μάχεται ταῖς διαπύροις ἀκτῖσι τοῦ ἡλίου. Πρὸς γὰρ Ἀπόλλωνα ποίαν ἔχει πρόφασιν ἐξαίρετον ἀπεχθείας;

8.1 Ταῦτα τοίνυν εἰρήσεται, ἀνθ' ὅτου ποτὲ τὸν αὐτὸν ἀπεφηνάμην ἥλιον Ἀπόλλωνι, καὶ τί πειρώμενος κατασκευάζειν. αἱ λοιμικαὶ νόσοι τὴν μεγίστην ἔχουσι τῆς φθορᾶς¹ πρόφασιν τὸν ἥλιον. **8.2** Ὅταν μὲν γὰρ ἡ θέρειος [αὐτοῦ]² μαλακὴ καὶ πραεῖα δι' εὐκράτου τῆς ἀλέας ἡσυχῇ διαθάλπηται, σωτήριον ἀνθρώποις ἐπιμειδιᾷ φέγγος· **8.3** αὐχμηρὰ δὲ καὶ διάπυρος ἐκκαείσα νοσηροὺς ἀπὸ γῆς ἀτμοὺς ἐφέλκεται,³ κάμνοντα δὲ τὰ σώματα καὶ διὰ τὴν ἀήθη τοῦ περιέχοντος τροπὴν νοσοῦντα λοιμικοῖς πάθεσιν ἀναλοῦται. **8.4** Τῶν δ' ὀξέων συμφορῶν αἴτιον Ὅμηρος ὑπεστήσατο τὸν Ἀπόλλωνα, διαρρήδην τοῖς αἰφνιδίοις θανάτοις ἐπιγράφων τὸν θεόν· φησὶ γάρ·

Ἐλθὼν ἀργυρότοξος Ἀπόλλων Ἀρτέμιδι ξὺν
οἷς ἀγανοῖσι βέλεσσιν⁴ ἐποιχόμενος κατέπεφνεν.

8.5 Ἐπειδήπερ οὖν ἕνα μὲν καὶ τὸν αὐτὸν ὑφίσταται τῷ Ἀπόλλωνι τὸν ἥλιον, ἐκ δὲ τοῦ ἡλίου τὰ τοιαῦτα τῶν παθημάτων συνίσταται, φυσικῶς ἐπέστησε τῷ λοιμῷ τὸν Ἀπόλλωνα.

8.6 Καὶ ὅτι, καθ' ὃν καιρὸν συνέβαινε τοὺς Ἕλληνας ἐν τῷ λοιμῷ νοσεῖν, θέρειος ἦν ὁ καιρός, ἤδη πειράσομαι διδάσκειν·⁵ ὥστε οὐκ ὀργὴν Ἀπόλλωνος, ἀλλ' αὐτόματον φθορὰν ἀέρος εἶναι τὸ συμβεβηκός. **8.7** Αὐτίκα τῶν ἡμερῶν τὸ μῆκος, εἰς πλείστην ἀμετρίαν ἐκτεινόμενον, ἐλέγχει τὴν ἀκμὴν τοῦ θέρους· "ὅτε τ' ἤματα μακρὰ πέλονται." **8.8** Μία γὰρ ἀπὸ τῆς Ἀγαμέμνονος ἀριστείας ἐπὶ τὴν Ἀχιλλέως ἄνοπλον ἔξοδον ἡμέρα παρατείνεται καί, τὸ μεῖζον, οὐδ' ὁλόκληρος·

"Ἥλιον" γὰρ "ἀκάμαντα βοῶπις πότνια Ἥρη
πέμψεν ἐπ' Ὠκεανοῖο ῥοὰς ἀέκοντα νέεσθαι,"

χρεοκοπήσασα τῶν ὑπολειπομένων ὡρῶν οὐκ ὀλίγον οἶμαι μέρος.

---

1. φθορᾶς M, Bu; O, Te read φορᾶς = "to be rampant."
2. Te in apparatus criticus. There is an ellipse of ὥρα (cf. LSJ s.v. θέρειος II), and no need to add it, as Te does; Bu reads ἡ θέρειος αὐτοῦ and translates "l'été qu'il nous donne."
3. ἐφέλκεται B, G, O, Te; ἀφέλκεται A, Bu.
4. Homer's text has ἀγανοῖς βελέεσσιν.
5. δικάσειν most mss., Bu, who translates "trancher."

exists always between fire and water, these two elements having been allotted mutually opposing natures; and so Poseidon,[1] a watery substance and so named from *posis* ["drink"],[2] fights in opposition to the fiery rays of the sun. Otherwise, what particular reason has he for hating Apollo?

8 This should be enough to explain why I have identified the Sun with Apollo, and what I have been trying to establish. The sun gives plagues their best opportunity to be destructive. For when a soft and mild summer is gently warmed by moderate sunshine, his saving light smiles upon humanity; on the other hand, the scorching of a parched and fiery summer draws pestilential vapors from the earth, and our bodies grow weary and sick because of the unusual changes in the atmosphere, and so perish in visitations of plague. Homer made Apollo the cause of acute epidemics, explicitly connecting the god's name with sudden death, for he says:

Then came Apollo of the silver bow with Artemis,
and with his gentle arrows fell upon and killed them.[3]

So, since Homer assumes the Sun to be one and the same as Apollo, and since disasters of this kind are caused by the Sun, he has made Apollo the physical cause of the plague.

I shall now try to prove that the season when the Greeks fell sick of the plague was the summer, and that the event therefore was not due to Apollo's anger but to a spontaneous corruption of the air. For one thing, the length of the days, extended to its greatest extreme, proves that it was the height of summer "when the days are long."[4] For a single day extends from Agamemnon's heroic exploits to Achilles' going forth without his armor; what is more, it was not even a complete day:

For wide-eyed Lady Hera sent the unwearied sun
unwilling back unto the streams of Ocean—[5]

cheating him, no doubt, of several hours still remaining.

---

1. *Il.* 20.67.

2. The etymology is fanciful but common; cf. Cornutus, *Theol.* ch. 4 = p. 4.12–16 Lang (along with other etymologies), Philo, *Contempl.* 3 (related to *poton*), Ps.-Herodianus, *Partitiones* p. 112, Clement of Alexandria, *Protr.* 5.64.4–5. Athenagoras, *Leg.* 22.4 seems to attribute it to Chrysippus (cf. the etymology of Zeus earlier in the same sentence).

3. *Od.* 15.410.

4. *Od.* 18.367.

5. *Il.* 18.239. The day begins with Agamemnon's *aristeia* in *Il.* 11.

9.1 Αἱ δὲ μεταξὺ πράξεις εἰς ὀκτὼ ῥαψῳδίας μερίζονται. καὶ πρώτη μὲν ἡ ἐπὶ πεδιάδι μάχη, πολλὰς ἀνδραγαθίας ἑκατέρων ἐμπεριέχουσα, μετ' αὐτὴν δὲ ἡ παρὰ τοῖς Ἑλληνικοῖς τείχεσι. **9.2** καὶ τρίτην προστίθημι τὴν ἐπὶ ναυσὶ μάχην ἄχρι τῆς ἀναιρέσεως Πατρόκλου καὶ τῆς δι' ἐκεῖνον Ἀχιλλέως ἐξόδου. πλὴν ὅμως τὸν ἀριθμὸν οὕτω πολὺν ὄντα τῶν ἔργων οὐκ ἄπιστον ἡ θέρειος ὥρα πεποίηκεν. **9.3** Αἵ τε νύκτες ἥκιστα χειμέριοι. Πῶς ἂν κρύους ἐτόλμησεν Ἕκτωρ ταῖς Ἀχαϊκαῖς ἐπινυκτερεῦσαι ναυσίν; **9.4** οὐδ' ἂν "αὐλῶν συρίγγων τ' ἐνοπὴ" διὰ τοῦ βαρβαρικοῦ στρατεύματος ἐπανηγυρίζετο. **9.5** Στιβὰς γὰρ ἀλεεινὴ καὶ στρατόπεδα τοῖς πολεμοῦσι χειμῶνος εὐτρεπίζεται, τῶν δ' ὑπαίθρων ἀγώνων ἐκτός εἰσιν· **9.6** ὥστ' οὐκ ἂν Ἕκτωρ τὴν πόλιν ἐκλιπών, ἐν ᾗ μετ' ἀσφαλείας διέτριβεν, ἐλθὼν ἄν[1] ἐπὶ τῇ θαλάττῃ γυμνὰ τὰ στρατεύματα καθίδρυσε. **9.7** Πῶς δὲ[2] τῶν κατὰ συμμαχίαν ἐληλυθότων ἕκαστος οὕτω ῥιψοκίνδυνος ἦν, ὡς παρ' ὥραν ἐφεδρεύειν τοῖς πολεμίοις, καὶ μάλιστα τῆς Ἴδης ὑπερκειμένης, ὄρους δυσχειμέρου, καὶ ῥεῖθρα ποταμῶν ἄπειρα πηγαζούσης; **9.8** Ἐκρήγνυται γὰρ ἀπὸ τῶν κατὰ μέρη λαγόνων

Ῥῆσός θ' Ἑπτάπορός τε Κάρησός τε Ῥοδίος τε
Γρήνικός τε καὶ Αἴσηπος δῖός τε Σκάμανδρος
καὶ Σιμόεις,

οἳ δίχα τῶν ἀπ' οὐρανοῦ φερομένων ὑετῶν ἱκανοὶ τὸ πεδίον ἦσαν ἐκλιμνάσαι. **9.9** Φέρε δ' οὖν ὑπ' ἀναισθησίας τοὺς βαρβάρους τῶν ἀσυμφόρων ἑλέσθαι τι ποιεῖν·[3] ἀντὶ τίνος οἱ πάντα φρονήσει διαφέροντες Ἕλληνες ἐπιλεξάμενοι τοὺς ἀρίστους ἐπὶ τὴν κατασκοπὴν νύκτωρ ἀποπέμπουσιν, **9.10** ἵν' ἐκ τοῦ κατορθῶσαι τί τηλικοῦτον ὠφεληθῶσιν, ὁπόση βλάβη διαμαρτόντων ἀπήντα; νιφετὸς γὰρ εἷς καὶ χειμερίων ὑδάτων ἐπομβρία ῥᾳδίως ἂν ἀμφοτέρους κατέκλυσε. **9.11** Ἐγὼ μὲν γὰρ αὐτὴν νομίζω τὴν ἀπὸ τῆς πόλεως ἔξοδον ἐπὶ τὴν μάχην οὐκ ἄλλου τινὸς εἶναι καιροῦ σημεῖον ἢ θέρους. Ἅπας γὰρ ἀναπαύεται πόλεμος ἐν χειμῶνι, καὶ τὴν πρὸς ἀλλήλους ἐκεχειρίαν ἄγουσιν, οὔθ' ὅπλα δυνάμενοι βαστάζειν οὔτε τὰς πολεμικὰς ὑπηρεσίας φέρειν. **9.12** Πῶς γὰρ ἢ διῶξαι ῥάδιον ἢ φυγεῖν; πῶς δ' ἂν αἱ χεῖρες εὐστοχίᾳ βάλλοιεν ὑπὸ τοῦ κρύους δεδεμέναι; θέρει δὲ τῷ μεσαιτάτῳ τὰ πλήθη τέτραπται πρὸς τὴν μάχην. **9.13** καὶ τοῦθ' ὅτι τοιοῦτόν ἐστιν, ἀπ' οὐδεμιᾶς εἰκασίας, ἀλλ' ἐναργῶς σκεπτέον.

---

1. Punctuation Russell, following Mehler, who however deleted ἐλθὼν ἄν· διέτριβεν ἐλθὼν ἄν, ἐπὶ τῇ θαλάττῃ Te, Bu = "where he would have gone and been safely established, and stationed his army, etc."

2. Te adds <ἂν>, which is not quite necessary.

3. τῶν ἀσυμφόρων ... τι, Te apparatus criticus; Te, following Mehler, reads τὸ ἀσύμφορον ... [τι], while Bu reads τὸ ἀσύμφορον ... τι; the meaning is unaffected.

9 The intervening actions too are divided among eight books [*rhap-sôidiai*]. First of all comes the battle on the plain, embracing many brave deeds of both parties; next, the battle by the Greek wall; in the third place, I add the battle by the ships, up to the recovering of Patroclus's body and Achilles' return to the battle on his account. The summer season, however, makes this multitude of actions not incredible. The nights, too, are not the nights of winter. If it had been cold, how could Hector have dared to spend the night by the Achaean ships? Nor would there have been any celebratory "sound of flutes and pipes"[1] throughout the barbarian army. Warm bedding and camps are prepared when men go to war in winter: they do not have to campaign without shelter. Hector therefore would not have left the city where he was safely established and gone to station his army, unprotected, by the sea. And why should all those who had come as allies have been so careless of danger as to settle down to besiege the enemy in a bad season, especially in the shadow of Ida, a mountain with a savage climate and the source of innumerable springs of rivers? For from Ida's several flanks burst forth

> Rhesus, Heptaporus, Caresus, Rhodius,
> Granicus, Aesepus, Scamander the divine,
> And Simoeis,[2]

which were quite enough to turn the plain into a lake, even without the rain from heaven. But suppose the barbarians, in their stupidity, did choose to do something contrary to their interests? Why then do the Greeks, who are superior in intelligence in every way, pick their best men to send out on reconnaissance at night—with what conceivable possible success compared with the loss consequent on their failure? A snow shower or a winter rainstorm might easily have drowned them both. My view is that the Trojans' sallying out from the city to do battle is itself a sign that the season can only be summer. War comes to a complete halt in winter, and the combatants maintain a truce, because they can neither carry arms nor carry out the routine tasks of military service. How can it be easy to pursue or to retreat? How can hands aim well if they are stiff with cold? It is in midsummer that great armies turn to battle. The truth of this can be shown very clearly, with no need for conjecture.

---

1. *Il.* 10.13.
2. *Il.* 12.20–22.

10.1 Μετὰ γὰρ τὴν στρατηγικὴν Ἀγαμέμνονος διάπειραν ἐξαναστάντες οἱ Ἕλληνες ἐπὶ τὰς ναῦς κατατρέχουσιν, "ὑπὸ δ᾽ ἤρεον ἕρματα νηῶν," οὐ δήπου [ἢ] κατὰ πρῷραν [ἐναντίων] ἑστηκότων ἀνέμων[1] οὐδ᾽ ἀπειλούσης τῆς θαλάττης· **10.2** τίς γὰρ ἂν ἦν κυβερνήτης ἐπὶ πρόδηλον οὕτω κίνδυνον ἐξιοῦσιν, ἄλλως τε μηδ᾽ ὀλίγην περαιοῦσθαι μέλλουσιν αὐτοῖς θάλατταν; **10.3** οὐ γὰρ εἰς Τένεδον ἀπῆρον οὐδ᾽ ἐπὶ Λέσβου καὶ Χίου παρευτρεπίζοντο τὸν πλοῦν· ἡ δ᾽ Ἑλλὰς ἀπῴκιστο πόρρω, καὶ τὸ πέλαγος ἦν χαλεπόν, ὃ καὶ θέρους ποτὲ πλέοντες ἐσφάλησαν. **10.4** Ἔτι τοίνυν φερομένων ἀπὸ τῆς ἐκκλησίας αὐτῶν ἐγείρεται δαψιλὴς κόνις·

Οἱ δ᾽ ἀλαλητῷ
νῆας ἔπ᾽ ἐσσεύοντο, ποδῶν δ᾽ ὑπένερθε κονίη
ἵστατ᾽ ἀειρομένη,

10.5 τίνι τρόπῳ, τῆς γῆς ἔτι διάβροχον ἐχούσης τοὔδαφος; ἔν τε ταῖς ἐφεξῆς παρατάξεσιν εἴωθε συνεχῶς λέγειν·

λευκοὶ ὕπερθε γένοντο κονισάλῳ, ὅν ῥα δι᾽ αὐτῶν
οὐρανὸν ἐς πολύχαλκον ἐπέπληγον πόδες ἵππων.

10.6 Τί δ᾽ ἐπὶ τοῦ τετρωμένου Σαρπηδόνος; οὐ[2] ῥιπὴ βόρειος

ζώγρει ἐπιπνείουσα κακῶς κεκαφηότα θυμόν,

ἀναψύξεως δεομένου τοῦ σώματος ἐν ἀέρι διαπύρῳ; καὶ πάλιν ἑτέρωθί που

"δίψῃ" καὶ "καρχαλέοι, κεκονιμένοι ἐκ πεδίοιο,"

καὶ

Ἱδρῶ ἀπεψύχοντο πίον τ᾽ ἀκέοντό τε δίψαν.

---

1. Deleting ἢ with Te and Bu, and ἐναντίων (a gloss on κατὰ πρῷραν) with Te (Mehler's addition of τῶν after ἑστηκότων, adopted by Te, is not necessary).
2. So mss., Bu; Te, following Gesner, emends to οὗ, "his" (modifying θυμόν, "spirit").

10 After Agamemnon's strategic "testing," the Greeks rise and make haste to the ships: "and they took away the props from under the ships."[1] The winds, indeed, were not set against them, nor was the sea threatening: for who would have served as steersman to men setting out to such manifest danger, especially as it was not just some narrow stretch of sea that they meant to cross? They were not setting sail for Tenedos or planning a crossing to Lesbos or Chios. Greece lay far away, and the sea was dangerous, as they sometimes found to their cost even in summer voyages. Again: when they moved away from the assembly, a cloud of dust arose:

> shouting they rushed toward the ships, and dust
> rose up from under their feet, and hung in the air.[2]

How could this have happened if the ground had still been wet underfoot? In the subsequent engagements also Homer habitually says:

> white they were with the dust that the feet of their horses
> raised to the brazen sky.[3]

And what happens when Sarpedon is wounded? Did not a blast of the north wind

> blow on him and revive his suffering spirit,[4]

since his body needed to be cooled off in the blazing atmosphere? And again, in other passages:

> all parched with thirst and dusty from the plain,[5]

and

> they wiped the sweat away and drank
> and quenched their thirst.[6]

---

1. *Il.* 2.154.
2. *Il.* 2.149–151.
3. *Il.* 5.503–504.
4. *Il.* 5.698.
5. *Il.* 21.541.
6. *Il.* 22.2.

Ἅπερ ἐν χειμῶνι μὲν ἀμήχανα συμβῆναί τινι, θέρους δὲ μαχομένοις ἦν ἀλεξήματα. **10.7** Τί δεῖ τὰ πολλὰ μηκύνειν; σχεδὸν γὰρ ἀπόχρη, κἂν εἴ τι τῶν εἰρημένων ἓν ἀπεδείξαμεν, ἐκφῆναι τοῦ ἔτους τὸν καιρόν·

Καίοντο πτελέαι τε καὶ ἰτέαι ἠδὲ μυρῖκαι,
καίετο δὲ λωτός τε ἰδὲ θρύον ἠδὲ κύπειρον.

11.1 Εἰ δὲ θέρος μὲν ὁμολογεῖται κατ' ἐκεῖνον εἶναι τὸν χρόνον, αἱ δὲ νόσοι περὶ τὴν θέρειον ὥραν συνίστανται, τῶν δὲ λοιμικῶν παθημάτων προστάτης Ἀπόλλων, τί λοιπὸν ἢ δοκεῖν τὸ συμβεβηκὸς οὐ θεοῦ μῆνιν, ἀλλὰ συντυχίαν ἀέρος γενέσθαι; **11.2** σφόδρα γοῦν πιθανῶς Ἡρόδικος ἀποφαίνεται μηδ' ὅλην τὴν δεκαετίαν ἐν Ἰλίῳ μεμενηκέναι τοὺς Ἕλληνας, ἀλλ' ἐπὶ τέλει τοῦ καθειμαρμένου χρόνου τῆς ἁλώσεως ἐληλυθέναι. **11.3** καὶ γὰρ ἦν ἄλογον εἰδότας ἐξ ὧν προεῖπεν ὁ Κάλχας, ὅτι "τῷ δεκάτῳ" πόλιν αἱρήσουσιν "εὐρυάγυιαν," ἐπ' οὐδενὶ χρησίμῳ τοσούτων ἐτῶν ἀργίαν ἀναλίσκειν, ἀλλ' εἰκὸς ἐν τοῖς μεταξὺ καιροῖς περιπλέοντας ἄνω καὶ κάτω τὴν Ἀσίαν ἅμα τάς τε πολεμιστηρίους ἀσκήσεις ὑπογυμνάζειν καὶ λαφύρων τὸ στρατόπεδον ἐμπιπλάναι, **11.4** τοῦ δεκάτου δ' ἐνστάντος ἔτους, ἐν ᾧ πεπρωμένον ἦν τὸ τῆς ἁλώσεως τέλος, ἀθρόους καταχθῆναι. **11.5** κοῖλα δ' αὐτοὺς τενάγη καὶ τόπος ἑλώδης ἐξεδέχετο, καὶ διὰ τοῦτο θέρους ἐνστάντος ἡ λοιμικὴ νόσος ἐγκατέσκηψε.

12.1 Νῦν τοίνυν καὶ τὰ κατὰ μέρος εἰρημένα περὶ τῆς νόσου διασκεψώμεθα· σχεδὸν γὰρ ἅπαντα συνάδει[1] τοῖς ὑφ' ἡμῶν λεγομένοις. **12.2** Καὶ πρωτήν γε φυσικὴν ὑπεστήσατο τὴν φερομένην ἀπὸ τῶν οἰστῶν φωνήν, οὐ μὰ Δί' οὐ μυθικῶς βέλη φθεγγόμενα τερατευόμενος, ἀλλ' ἔστιν ἐν τῷ στίχῳ θεωρία φιλόσοφος·

---

1. O, Te; συνάψει A, Bu = "will accord with."

These things cannot happen to anyone in winter, but they were comforts for men fighting in summer. Need I say more? It would probably have been enough if I had just cited one passage to demonstrate the season of the year:

> elms, willows, tamarisks were scorched,
> and scorched the lotus, the rushes, and the reeds.[1]

11 If therefore it is agreed that it was summer at that time, and if plagues form in the summer season and Apollo is the lord of pestilences, what choice have we but to believe that this event was due not to the wrath of the god but to a condition of the air? Herodicus[2] shows convincingly that the Greeks did not stay throughout the whole ten years at Troy, but only came there at the end of the period destined for its fall. It would have been irrational for them, when they knew from Calchas's prophecy that they would take "the city of wide streets in the tenth year,"[3] to have spent all those idle years to no useful purpose. It is surely likely that, in the intervening period, they sailed up and down the coast of Asia, practicing military exercises and filling their camp with plunder; then, when the tenth year arrived, in which the capture was destined to be accomplished, they joined forces and landed at Troy.[4] Lowlying swamps and marshy ground awaited them; and so, when summer came, the plague struck.

12 Let us now look in detail at what is said about the plague. It agrees in almost every respect with the view that I am putting forward. First, Homer presents the sound emitted by the arrows as a natural phenomenon. He emphatically does not give us any pretentious myth about talking arrows; on the contrary, there is a philosophical doctrine in the line

---

1. *Il.* 21.350–351.

2. Herodicus of Babylon, probably a disciple of Crates of Mallus, and author of various scholarly works; cited chiefly in Athenaeus, e.g., *Deipn.* 5.215B, 219C, 222, 234D; 8.340E; 13.586A.

3. *Il.* 2.329.

4. Heraclitus seems to mean that the Greeks only descended on Troy in the tenth year of the war, when it was destined to fall. But he may mean that not all the Greeks stayed continually at Troy for the whole ten years, but gathered there in force only in the tenth; it was their camp at Troy that they filled with plunder. Both views seem to be attributed to the *Cypria*, an early epic poem on the Trojan War, by the scholia on Lycurgus's *Alexandra*, citing in part Pherecydes (*FGH* 3F40); see *Cypria* frg. 29 Bernabé.

Ἔκλαγξαν δ' ἄρ' ὀιστοὶ ἐπ' ὤμων χωομένοιο
αὐτοῦ κινηθέντος.

12.3 Εἰσὶ γάρ, εἰσί τινες οὐράνιοι μεθ' ἁρμονίας ἐμμελοῦς[1] ἦχοι κατὰ τὴν
ἀίδιον φορὰν ἀποψαλλόμενοι, μάλιστα δὲ τῆς ἡλιακῆς περιόδου συντόνως
φερομένης. **12.4** Οὐ γὰρ δήπου ῥάβδῳ μὲν ὑγρᾷ πλήξας τις εἰκῇ τὸν ἀέρα καὶ
λίθον ἀπὸ σφενδόνης ἀφεὶς ῥοίζους ἀποτελεῖ καὶ συριγμὸν[2] οὕτω βαρύφθογγον, τηλικούτων δὲ σωμάτων ἡ κυκλοπόρος βία †δρόμοις† ἀπ' ἀνατολῆς εἰς
δύσιν ἁρματηλατουμένη μεθ' ἡσυχίας τὸν σφοδρὸν ὁδοιπορεῖ δρόμον.[3] **12.5**
Τούτους δὲ τοὺς διηνεκῶς ἐν τῷ[4] οὐρανῷ τελουμένους φθόγγους ἀγνοοῦμεν
ἢ διὰ τὴν ἀπὸ πρώτης γονῆς συνήθειαν ἐνδελεχῶς ἐνοικοῦσαν ἡμῖν, ἢ διὰ
τὴν ἄμετρον ὑπερβολὴν τοῦ διαστήματος ἐκλυομένου τοῦ ψόφου τῷ
διείργοντι μέτρῳ.[5] **12.6** Καὶ τοῦθ' ὅτι τοιοῦτόν ἐστιν, ὁ φυγαδεύων Ὅμηρον
ἐκ τῆς ἰδίας πολιτείας συγκαταινεῖ Πλάτων οὕτω λέγων· **12.7**

Ἐπὶ δὲ τῶν κύκλων αὐτοῦ ἄνωθεν ἐφ' ἑκάστου βεβηκέναι Σειρῆνα
συμπεριφερομένην φωνὴν μίαν ἱεῖσαν ἕνα τόνον· ἀπασῶν δ' ὀκτὼ
οὐσῶν μίαν ἁρμονίαν συμφωνεῖν.

12.8 Ὁμοίως δὲ καὶ ὁ Ἐφέσιος Ἀλέξανδρος ἐπεξελθὼν ὅπως κατὰ τάξιν οἱ
πλάνητες ἀστέρες ὁδεύουσιν, ἐπάγει περὶ τῶν ἑκάστου φθόγγων· **12.9**

Πάντες δ' ἑπτατόνοιο λύρης φθόγγοισι συνῳδὸν
ἁρμονίην προχέουσι,[6] διαστάσει[7] ἄλλος ἐπ' ἄλλου.

Δι' ὧν ἂν εἴη γνώριμον, ὡς οὐ κωφὸς οὐδ' ἄφθογγός ἐστιν ὁ κόσμος.

---

1. Homeric scholia, Te; M, Bu read ἐμμελεῖς, modifying "sounds," but this is an excess
of adjectives for a single noun.

2. Te; A, Bu read συριγμούς, which sits ill with the singular βαρύφθογγον.

3. The text is unsure: δρόμοις is superfluous, and could be deleted (as Mehler suggested) but for the resulting hiatus. On the other hand, δρόμον ("journey") is preferable to
νόμον (adopted by Bu: "la route formidable qui leur est assignée," referring to 36.3, which
however has δρόμος). Perhaps one should both delete δρόμοις and transpose βία to
follow ἁρματηλατουμένη (or even to follow ὁδοιπορεῖ: long hyperbata are characteristic
of Heraclitus).

4. ἐν τῷ, Homeric scholia, Te; omitted by M, Bu.

5. μέτρῳ ("space," literally "measure") is suspect after ἄμετρον, "measureless"; perhaps
it has displaced τόπῳ, "space."

6. Bredow, Te; προσέχουσι mss., Bu; στοιχοῦσι or στειχοῦσι mss. of Theon of Smyrna,
who also cites these lines.

7. Te, following Theon of Smyrna (*De utilitate mathematicae*); διαστὰς M, Bu.

the arrows clanged on his shoulder
as he started up in anger.[1]

For there are, there are indeed, certain celestial sounds accompanied by melodious music, a vibration produced by the perpetual motion [sc. of the spheres], especially when the sun's orbit is "tauter."[2] If you beat the air with a pliant stick or discharge a stone from a sling, it makes a whirring sound and a resonant whistling: surely, then, the circular force of such mighty bodies, as it drives on its way from risings to settings, does not accomplish its swift journey in silence! But we are unaware of these musical sounds which are continually produced in the heavens, either because we have a permanent habituation to them from our birth, or else because the immeasurable vastness of the distance from us causes the sound to be dissipated in the intervening space. That this is so is confirmed by Plato, the very man who banishes Homer from his own private Republic. I quote:

And above, on the circles [of the spindle], on each of them stands
a Siren who moves round with it, emitting a single sound on a
single note; and all eight of these together form a single harmony.[3]

Likewise, Alexander of Ephesus, explaining how the planets move in order, says of the sound made by each planet:

They all pour forth a harmony that matches notes
of a seven-stringed lyre, each one of them at different intervals.[4]

It is clear from this that the universe is not dumb or voiceless.

---

1. *Il.* 1.46.

2. *suntonôs*, "tautly," refers both to the rapidity of the sun's course in summer, when it was supposed to be closer to the earth, and to the tightening of a string that produces a high-pitched sound. On the "music of the spheres," see Cicero, *Somnium Scipionis* 18–19, with Boyancé (1936, 104–15); note too that Cicero's comparison to people who cannot hear the noise of a cataract corresponds to Heraclitus's first explanation below ("permanent habituation").

3. *Resp.* 617B.

4. Alexander (first century B.C.), *Phainomena* frg. 21.19–20 *SH*; according to Cicero, Alexander was a *poeta ineptus, non inutilis*; he may have been a source for Varro of Atax and Dionysius Periegetes.

13.1 Ἀρχὴ δὲ ταύτης τῆς δόξης Ὅμηρος, εἰπὼν τὰς ἡλιακὰς ἀκτῖνας ἀλληγορικῶς βέλη, προσθεὶς δ' ὅτι φερόμεναι διὰ τοῦ ἀέρος ἔκλαγξαν, ἤτοι ἡδεῖαν τινα καὶ ἔνθεον φωνὴν ἀπετέλεσαν.¹ **13.2** Τὰ κοινὰ δὲ τῶν φθόγγων παραστήσας ἐπὶ τὸ ἴδιον εὐθὺς τοῦ λόγου μετέβη προσθείς·

ὁ δ' ἤιε νυκτὶ ἐοικώς.

13.3 Οὐ γὰρ ἀκήρατον φῶς οὐδ' ἀμιγὲς ἀχλύος μελαίνης ὑφίσταται τὸ τοῦ ἡλίου, νυκτὶ δ' αὐτὸν ἐθόλωσεν, ὁποία σχεδὸν εἴωθεν ἐν τοῖς λοιμικοῖς πάθεσιν ἐπιπροσθεῖν τῷ δι' ἡμέρας φέγγει. **13.4** Πῶς γε μὴν τοξάζειν ἐσπουδακὼς Ἀπόλλων

ἕζετ' ἔπειτ' ἀπάνευθε νεῶν, μετὰ δ' ἰὸν ἕηκεν,
δεινὴ δὲ κλαγγὴ γένετ' ἀργυρέοιο βιοῖο;

13.5 εἰ γὰρ οὖν δι' ὀργὴν ἐτόξευεν, ἐγγὺς ἔδει τῶν τιτρωσκομένων² ἑστάναι τὸν βάλλοντα. Νῦν δ' ἀλληγορῶν τὸν ἥλιον εἰκότως ἄπωθεν αὐτοῦ τὴν φορὰν τῆς λοιμικῆς ἀκτῖνος ὑπεστήσατο.

14.1 Καὶ μὴν ἐναργέστατον ἐπιφέρει μετὰ τοῦτο σημεῖον εἰπών·

Οὐρῆας μὲν πρῶτον ἐπῴχετο καὶ κύνας ἀργούς.

14.2 Οὐ γὰρ οὕτως ἄκριτον ἦν παρανάλωμα τῆς Ἀπόλλωνος ὀργῆς τὰ ἄλογα τῶν ζῴων οὐδ' ἂν ὁ θυμὸς ἀφρόνως ἡμιόνοις ἐνήκμαζε καὶ κυσίν, ὡς τὸ Θρακικὸν ἀνδράποδον Ὁμήρου κατεξανίσταται, λέγω δὲ τὸν Ἀμφιπολίτην Ζωίλον ἄνω καὶ κάτω τοιούτους τινὰς λήρους φληναφοῦντα. **14.3** Ὅμηρος δὲ καὶ σφόδρα φυσικῶς τὴν περὶ τὰ λοιμικὰ τῶν παθημάτων συντυχίαν διὰ τούτου παρίστησιν· οἱ γὰρ ἐμπειρίαν ἰατρικῆς τε καὶ φιλοσοφίας ἔχοντες³ δι' ἀκριβοῦς παρατηρήσεως ἔγνωσαν ἐν ταῖς λοιμικαῖς νόσοις τὸ δεινὸν τῶν τετραπόδων ζῴων ἀρχόμενον. **14.4** Κατ' ἄμφω δ' ἡ πρόφασίς ἐστιν εὔλογος,

---

1. O, Homeric scholia, Te; M, Bu omit ἤτοι and καί and ἀπετέλεσαν and read ἰδίαν ἔνθεόν τινα φωνήν, "clanged a special divine sound," perhaps rightly: the hiatus is troubling, and ἤτοι is not used in this sense elsewhere in Heraclitus.

2. Homeric scholia, Te; τοῖς τιτρωσκομένοις M, O, Bu.

3. O, Homeric scholia, Te; αἱ γὰρ ἐμπειρίαι ἰατρικῆς τε καὶ φιλοσοφίας ἔχουσαι M, Bu (improbably making "expertise" or "experience" the subject of the sentence).

13 And the origin of the doctrine is in Homer, who calls the sun's rays "arrows," by allegory, and adds that as they sped through the air they "clanged," that is, produced a pleasing and divine sound.

Having set out the general phenomenon of these sounds, Homer proceeds to the particular detail of his present subject, adding

And he moved like the night.[1]

In this he does not present the sun's light as pure or uncontaminated by dark mist, but muddies him with night—the sort of night which commonly obstructs the daylight in times of plague. And how could it be that Apollo, the professional archer,

sat far away from the ships, and shot his arrow; and fearful was the clang of his silver bow?[2]

For if he had been shooting in anger, the archer would have needed to stand near the men who were hit. The fact is that Homer, representing the sun allegorically, naturally sets the trajectory of the ray of pestilence at a distance from him.

14 Indeed, he adds a very plain indication of this by saying:

he fell first on the mules and the swift dogs.[3]

For brute animals were surely not just indiscriminate and incidental victims of Apollo's anger, nor could his fury have raged senselessly against mules and dogs. That is the attack on Homer made by the Thracian slave—Zoilus of Amphipolis,[4] I mean, who throws this sort of nonsense around all over the place. Homer is actually very scientific in representing the circumstances of plagues in this way. Experts in medicine and philosophy know from careful observation that, in epidemics of pestilence, the trouble begins with the four-footed animals. There are two plausible reasons why these should fall victim easily to this peril. On the

---

1. *Il.* 1.47.

2. *Il.* 1.48–49.

3. *Il.* 1.50.

4. Zoilus of Amphipolis (fourth-third century B.C.), the "Scourge of Homer" (*Homeromastix*), wrote several books pointing out foolish things in the epics; our passage = 71F5 *FGH*.

ὥστ' εὐάλωτα πρὸς τὸ δεινὸν εἶναι· τῆς τε γὰρ διαίτης τὸ ἀκριβὲς οὐ θηρᾶται,[1] δι' ἣν ἀταμιεύτως σιτίων τε καὶ ποτῶν πιμπλάμενα[2] διαφθείρεται μηδενὸς λογισμοῦ τὴν ἐπὶ τὸ πλεῖον ὁρμὴν χαλινοῦντος· **14.5** ἔπειθ', ὃ καὶ μᾶλλον ἀληθές ἐστιν, οἱ μὲν ἄνθρωποι μεταρσίοις ταῖς ἀναπνοαῖς τὸν καθαρώτατον ἕλκοντες ἀέρα βραδύτερον ἁλίσκονται τῷ πάθει, τὰ δ' ἐπὶ γῆς ἐρριμμένα ζῷα τοὺς νοσώδεις ἐκεῖθεν ἀτμοὺς εὐμαρέστερον ἕλκει. **14.6** Πάνυ γε μὴν ἀληθῶς οὐκ ἐν ἀρτίοις ἡμέραις τὴν ἀπαλλαγὴν τῆς νόσου δεδήλωκεν, ἀλλ' ἐν περιτταῖς·

Ἐννῆμαρ μὲν ἀνὰ στρατὸν ᾤχετο κῆλα θεοῖο.

μάλιστα γὰρ ἐν τῇ παρ' ἕκαστα πείρᾳ γνώριμόν ἐστι τοῦθ' ὅτι κρίσιμοι τῶν σωματικῶν παθημάτων αἱ περιτταὶ γίγνονται τῶν ἡμερῶν.

15.1 Λυτὴρ δ' Ἀχιλλεὺς τῆς νόσου· Χείρων γὰρ αὐτὸν ἐδίδαξε, "δικαιότατος Κενταύρων," ὃς πάσῃ μὲν ἐκέκαστο σοφίᾳ, περιττῶς δὲ τῇ ἰατρικῇ,[3] ὅπου γνώριμον αὐτῷ φασιν εἶναι καὶ Ἀσκληπιόν. **15.2** Προσέθηκε δ' Ἀχιλλεῖ θεραπεύοντι φυσικῶς ἀλληγορήσας θεὰν Ἥραν·

Τῷ γὰρ ἐπὶ φρεσὶ θῆκε θεὰ λευκώλενος Ἥρη.

15.3 Δύο γὰρ ὄντων κατὰ τοὺς φυσικοὺς τῶν πνευματικῶν στοιχείων, αἰθέρος τε καὶ ἀέρος, τὸν μὲν Δία τὴν πυρώδη φαμὲν οὐσίαν, ἡ δὲ Ἥρα μετ' αὐτόν ἐστιν ἀήρ, μαλακώτερον στοιχεῖον, διὰ τοῦτο καὶ θῆλυ. **15.4** Τὰ δ' ἀκριβῆ περὶ τούτου διαλεξόμεθα μικρὸν ὕστερον· **15.5** νῦν δ' ἀπόχρη τοσοῦτον εἰπεῖν, ὅτι τοῦ πάλαι θολεροῦ διαχυθέντος ἀέρος αἰφνιδίως διεκρίθη τὸ σύμπαν.[4] **15.6** Οὐδὲ γὰρ ἀλόγως λευκώλενον εἶπε τὴν Ἥραν, ἀλλ' ἀπὸ τοῦ

---

1. Retaining οὐ (from the extract in the Homeric scholia), and taking θηρᾶται metaphorically; alternatively, "they do not hunt for just enough." Without οὐ (so Bu), the sense is perhaps "they hunt for scanty sustenance." For the sense of ἀκριβές, cf. Andocides 4.32 τοὺς ἀκριβῶς διαιτωμένους.

2. A, B, G, Bu; ἐμπιπλάμενα O, Homeric scholia; ἐμπιμπλάμενα Te.

3. O, Homeric scholia, Te; περιττὸς δ' ἦν τὴν ἰατρικὴν M, Bu.

4. Reading τὸ σύμπαν (proposed by Heyne) for mss. τὸ συμβάν, retained by Te and Bu (τὸ συμβάν was perhaps influenced by συμβεβηκότος below). Te defends συμβάν by comparing τὸ συμβεβηκός in 8.6 and 11.1 and τὸ συμβαῖνον in 37.6, but the perfect participle has a distinct usage, and in any case neither can properly stand as the subject of διεκρίθη, "separated out," which is a standard presocratic term for the formation of the universe; cf. Anaxagoras, frg. 13, πᾶν τοῦτο διεκρίθη, and Heraclitus himself at 43.3: πρὶν ἢ διακριθῆναι τὰ νῦν βλεπόμενα, νὺξ ἦν τὸ σύμπαν.

one hand, in their diet they do not strive to be sparing, and because of it they stuff themselves with food and drink inordinately, since they have no reasoning power to rein in their greed. Secondly—and this is a truer account—humans inhale a purer air because their breathing is at a higher level, so that they are less quickly infected, whereas animals which are flat on the ground more easily ingest the pestilential vapors that arise from there. Another very real detail is that Homer makes the relief from the disease come in an odd, not an even, number of days:

Nine days the god's darts sped among the host.[1]

For it is a well-known fact of ordinary experience that the odd days are the critical ones in physical illnesses.[2]

15 The healer of the plague is Achilles, because Achilles was taught by Chiron, "most just of Centaurs,"[3] who excelled in all wisdom, but particularly in medicine; Asclepius too is said to have been his pupil.[4] There is scientific allegory also in Homer's association of the goddess Hera with the healing activity of Achilles:

For white-armed Hera put it in his mind.[5]

According to the scientists, there are two "pneumatic" elements, aether and air.[6] Zeus, we say, is the fiery element, and Hera, who comes after him, is air, the softer element, and therefore also the female. I will discuss this matter in detail a little later. For the moment, it is sufficient to say that when the formerly turbulent air was dissipated, the whole universe was immediately separated out. Nor was it without good reason that he

---

1. *Il.* 1.53.

2. Homer's medical knowledge is the subject of Ps.-Plutarch, *Vit. poes. Hom.* 200–211; but the point made by Heraclitus about "critical days" is not there. According to *Epidemics* 1.26, some diseases have crises on even days, and others on odd days; see W. H. S. Jones in the Loeb edition of Hippocrates (1923–1931, 1:liv–v).

3. *Il.* 11.832. Achilles as pupil of Chiron: Ps.-Plutarch, *Vit. poes. Hom.* 202, Plutarch, *Adol. poet. aud.* 26B–C.

4. Asclepius instructed by Chiron: *Il.* 4.218–19, Pindar *Nem.* 3.54–56, etc. Cf. Testimonies 50–62 (our passage = no. 60) in the collection of Asclepius's testimonies by E. J. and L. Edelstein (1945); Servius on *Georgics* 3.550; Cornutus, *Theol.* ch. 33 = p. 70.17–18 Lang.

5. *Il.* 1.55.

6. See also below, ch. 22. Air and aether have similar characteristics (Cicero, *Nat d.* 2.66); both are incapable of changes of shape (Cleomedes 1.5.130 Todd), and *pneuma* is sometimes synonymous with *aêr*. SVF 1.144.26 couples air and fire (= aether) as *pneumatika*.

συμβεβηκότος, ὅτι τὴν νυκτὶ προσεοικυῖαν ἀχλὺν ὁ λευκὸς ἀὴρ ἐπὶ τὸ καθαρώτερον ἐλάμπρυνεν.

15.7 Εἶτ' ἀνεθὲν τῆς νόσου τὸ Ἑλληνικὸν πλῆθος ἐπὶ τὴν συνήθη τοῖς ἀπηλλαγμένοις ὁδὸν ἐτράπη, λέγω δὲ τοὺς ὀνομαζομένους ἀποτροπιασμούς τε καὶ καθαρμούς·

Οἳ δ' ἀπελυμαίνοντο, καὶ εἰς ἅλα λύματ' ἔβαλλον.

16.1 Δοκεῖ δέ μοι καὶ Ὀδυσσεὺς οὐδένα ἄλλον ἢ τὸν Ἥλιον ἱλάσκεσθαι δι' ἧς προσηνέγκατο θυσίας· ἀμέλει

πανημέριοι μολπῇ θεὸν ἱλάσκοντο.
Ἦμος δ' ἠέλιος κατέδυ καὶ ἐπὶ κνέφας ἦλθεν,
δὴ τότε κοιμήσαντο παρὰ πρυμνήσια νηός.

16.2 Πέρας γάρ ἐστι τῆς εὐσεβείας ἡ δύσις, ἕως ἀκούοντα καὶ βλέποντα τὸν θεὸν ἐτίμων· μηκέτι δ' αὐτοῦ τοῖς τελουμένοις παρεῖναι τὸ λοιπὸν δυναμένου τὸ τῆς ἑορτῆς πέπαυται. **16.3** Πρός γε μὴν βαθὺν τὸν ὄρθρον ἀναχθέντων φησὶν ὁ ποιητής·

Τοῖσιν δ' ἴκμενον οὖρον ἵει ἑκάεργος Ἀπόλλων,

τὸ περὶ τὸν ἥλιον ἐσπουδακὼς ἰδίωμα δηλοῦν. **16.4** Ἄχρι γὰρ οὐδέπω φλογώδης οὐδ' ἔμπυρος ἐπὶ μεσημβρίαν ὁ δρόμος αὐτοῦ νένευκεν, ἡ δροσώδης ἰκμάς, ὑγρὸν τὸ περιέχον ἀφεῖσα, ἀμυδρὰ καὶ νωθῆ παραπέμπεται τὰ πρὸς ἔω πνεύματα. Διὰ τοῦτο τὸ ὄρθριον[1] ὁ ἥλιος αὐτοὺς ἐναυστόλησεν, ἴκμενον[2] ἀποστείλας ἄνεμον, τὸν ἐκ τῆς ἰκμάδος πνέοντα.

16.5 Τὴν μὲν οὖν πρώτην ἀλληγορίαν ἐπεδείξαμεν οὐ θυμὸν Ἀπόλλωνος ὀργισαμένου μάτην, ἀλλὰ φυσικῆς θεωρίας φιλοσοφοῦσαν ἔννοιαν.

17.1 Ἐφεξῆς δ' ἡμῖν σκεπτέον ὑπὲρ τῆς ἐφισταμένης Ἀθηνᾶς Ἀχιλλεῖ·

Ἕλκετο γὰρ[3] ἐκ κολεοῖο μέγα ξίφος, ἦλθε δ' Ἀθήνη
οὐρανόθεν· πρὸ γὰρ ἧκε θεὰ λευκώλενος Ἥρη,
ἄμφω ὁμῶς θυμῷ φιλέουσά τε κηδομένη τε.
Στῆ δ' ὄπιθεν, ξανθῆς δὲ κόμης ἕλε Πηλείωνα,

---

1. O, Homeric scholia, Te; A, G, Bu read ὄρθιον, which Bu translates "le soleil qui poussa tout droit leur navire."

2. Pierson, followed by Te; mss., Bu read ἱκανόν, "sufficient" (Bu translates "efficace"); but the point of the adjective is unclear, and the etymological point confirms Pierson's conjecture.

3. The mss. of Homer read δ'; γάρ is Heraclitus's connective and not, strictly speaking, part of the quotation.

called Hera "white-armed"; this reflects what actually happened: the white air brightened and cleared the mist which "resembled night."

Relieved of the plague, the Greek host took the steps usually taken by those who have escaped from trouble: they undertook what are called apotropaic rites and purifications:

they scoured themselves, threw scourings into the sea.[1]

16 I think too that the sacrifice Odysseus performed was specifically to propitiate the sun. At any rate,

All day with song they sought the god's good will...,
and when the sun set and the dark came down,
they rested by the ropes that moored the ship.[2]

The end of their worship comes with sunset. Up to this, the god they were honoring could hear and see them. The festival is brought to an end when he can no longer be present at the ritual. When they put to sea at break of day, the poet says:

Hekaergos Apollo sent them a gentle [ikmenos] wind.[3]

In this he has been careful to show the special contribution of the sun. Before the sun's course turns toward noon, and before it becomes fiery and flaming, the dewy damp [ikmas], giving off moisture in the atmosphere, brings with it dawn breezes that are faint and feeble. This is why the sun sent them to sea at dawn, giving them a gentle [ikmenos] wind, that is to say one that arises from moisture [ikmas]

We have thus disclosed the first allegory. It is not the wrath of an Apollo angry without cause, but a philosophical idea related to scientific speculation.

17 We must next consider Athena standing at Achilles' side:

He was drawing his great sword from the scabbard when
Athena came from heaven: white-armed Hera sent her,
because she loved and cared for both alike.
Athena stood behind and gripped Achilles

---

1. *Il.* 1.314.
2. *Il.* 1.475–476. Odysseus has now returned Chryseis to her father.
3. *Il.* 1.479. There is the same derivation in Eustathius ad loc.

οἴῳ φαινομένη, τῶν δ' ἄλλων οὔ τις¹ ὁρᾶτο.
Θάμβησεν δ' Ἀχιλεύς, μετὰ δ' ἐτράπετ', αὐτίκα δ' ἔγνω
Παλλάδ' Ἀθηναίην· δεινὼ δέ οἱ ὄσσε φάανθεν.

17.2 Τὸ μὲν γὰρ πρόχειρον ἐκ τῶν λεγομένων ἔστιν εἰπεῖν, ὅτι μεταξὺ τοῦ σπωμένου σιδήρου θεά, παντὸς ὀξυτέρα τάχους τὴν οὐράνιον ἐκλιποῦσα διατριβήν, ἐμποδὼν ἔστη τῇ μιαιφονίᾳ, πάνυ γραφικῷ σχήματι τῆς κόμης ἀπρὶξ ὄπισθεν Ἀχιλλέως λαβομένη. **17.3** Λαμπρά γε μὴν καὶ λίαν φιλόσοφος ὑφεδρεύει τοῖς νοουμένοις κατ' ἀλληγορίαν ἐπιστήμη. **17.4** Πάλιν οὖν ὁ πρὸς Ὅμηρον ἀχάριστος ἐν τῇ πολιτείᾳ Πλάτων ἐλέγχεται διὰ τούτων τῶν ἐπῶν τὸ περὶ τῆς ψυχῆς δόγμα νοσφισάμενος ἀπ' αὐτοῦ. **17.5** Τὴν γὰρ ὅλην ψυχὴν διήρηκεν εἰς γένη δύο, τό τε λογικὸν² καὶ τὸ ἄλογον ὑπ' αὐτοῦ προσαγορευόμενον. **17.6** Τοῦ δ' ἀλόγου μέρους εἰδικωτέραν³ ὑφίσταται διαίρεσιν, εἰς δύο μερίζων, καὶ τὸ μὲν ἐπιθυμητικὸν ὀνομάζει, τὸ δ' ἕτερον θυμοειδές. **17.7** Καὶ καθάπερ δὲ οἴκους τινὰς ἑκάστῳ μέρει⁴ καὶ διατριβὰς ἐν τῷ σώματι διένειμεν· **17.8** τὸ μὲν οὖν λογικὸν τῆς ψυχῆς⁵ ἀκρόπολίν τινα τὴν ἀνωτάτω τῆς κεφαλῆς μοῖραν εἰληχέναι νομίζει, πᾶσι τοῖς αἰσθητηρίοις ἐν κύκλῳ δορυφορούμενον, τοῦ δ' ἀλόγου μέρους ὁ μὲν θυμὸς οἰκεῖ περὶ τὴν καρδίαν, αἱ δὲ τῶν ἐπιθυμιῶν ὀρέξεις ἐν ἥπατι. **17.9** Ταῦτα δ' ἀλληγορικῶς ἐν τῷ Φαίδρῳ προσωμοίωσεν ἵπποις τε καὶ ἡνιόχῳ, διαρρήδην λέγων·

Ὁ μὲν τοίνυν αὐτῶν ἐν τῇ καλλίονι στάσει ὢν τό τ' εἶδος ὀρθὸς καὶ διηρθρωμένος, ὑψαύχην, ἐπίγρυπος, λευκὸς ἰδεῖν, μελανόμματος, τιμῆς ἐραστὴς μετὰ σωφροσύνης τε καὶ αἰδοῦς, δόξης⁶ ἑταῖρος, ἄπληκτος, κελεύσματι καὶ λόγῳ μόνῳ⁷ ἡνιοχεῖται.

17.11 Ταῦτα μὲν περὶ θατέρου μέρους τῆς ψυχῆς. περὶ δὲ τοῦ λοιποῦ φησίν·

17.12 Ὁ δ' αὖ σκολιός, πολύς, εἰκῇ συμπεφορημένος, κρατεραύχην, πολυτράχηλος,⁸ σιμοπρόσωπος, μελανόχρως, γλαυκόμματος, ὕφαιμος, ὕβρεως καὶ ἀλαζονείας ἑταῖρος, περὶ ὦτα λάσιος, ὑπόκωφος, μάστιγι μετὰ κέντρων μόλις ὑπείκων.

---

1. So Homer; mss. of Heraclitus have οὔτε, followed by Te, Bu.
2. A, Bu read λογιστικὸν.
3. Mehling, Te; A, O, Bu read ἰδικωτέραν (Bu translates "specifiques")
4. Te; mss., Bu have μερίζει, but note impf. διένειμε.
5. Te inserts ὡς, "as."
6. The Teubner supplies καὶ ἀληθινῆς, "and genuine" glory, from the text of Plato. But Heraclitus may have miscopied, or had a faulty ms.
7. Te adopts μόνον from the text of Plato, which reads μόνον καὶ λόγῳ.
8. Te, following Mehler, reads βραχυτράχηλος, "short-throated," from the text of Plato, perhaps rightly.

by his yellow hair;[1] to him alone she appeared,
no other saw her. Amazed, Achilles turned:
at once he knew Athena: fearful flashed her eyes.[2]

The surface meaning of this passage is that, as Achilles is actually drawing his sword, the goddess, leaving her occupation in heaven with incredible speed, stands there to stop a foul murder. With a graphic gesture, she seizes Achilles from behind by the hair. Yet behind these ideas, in the allegory, lies a very splendid and profound piece of knowledge. And once again Plato, so ungrateful to Homer in his *Republic*,[3] is shown by these lines to have stolen his psychological theory from him. Plato divides the whole soul into two parts, which he calls the rational and the irrational. Within the irrational part, he sets up a more specific division, splitting it into two sections and calling one the "desiderative" and the other the "spirited." He also gives each part a home, as it were, and a residence in the body: he thinks that the rational element of the soul has been assigned the top of the head, as a citadel, surrounded by a protective guard of sense-organs. As for the irrational part, its "spirit" dwells around the heart, while the urges of desires are in the liver. In his *Phaedrus*,[4] he likens this situation, allegorically, to a team of horses and its charioteer. I quote:

> The one that is in the nobler position is upright and clean-limbed, high-necked, hook-nosed, fair-complexioned and black-eyed: a lover of honor, together with temperance and modesty; in other words, a friend of genuine glory, not needing the whip, but guided by command and word alone.

That describes one part of the soul. Of the other, he says:

> The other is crooked, a great jumble of a beast, strong-necked, deep-throated, snub-nosed, dark-complexioned, grey-eyed, bloodshot, a friend of violence and vanity, hairy about the ears, rather deaf, barely yielding to the whip and goad together.

---

1. For an allegorical interpretation of the "yellow hair" as signifying anger, cf. the scholia ad loc. (ed. Erbse, 1.61).

2. *Il.* 1.194–200; cf. Ps.-Plutarch, *Vit. poes. Hom.* 129–130.

3. Cf. Maximus of Tyre, *Or.* 26.4.

4. *Phaedr.* 253D–E.

17.13 Τὸ μέντοι λογικὸν μέρος τῆς ψυχῆς, ὃ ἐν τῇ κεφαλῇ καθίδρυτο, τῶν ὅλων πεποίηκεν ἡνίοχον οὑτωσὶ λέγων·

17.14 Περὶ δὲ τοῦ κυριωτάτου παρ' ἡμῖν ψυχῆς εἴδους διανοεῖσθαι δεῖ τῇδε, ὡς ἄρα αὐτὸ δαίμονα θεὸς ἑκάστῳ δέδωκε, τοῦτο ὃ δὴ φαμὲν οἰκεῖν μὲν ἡμῶν ἐπ' ἄκρῳ τῷ σώματι, πρὸς δὲ τὴν ἐν οὐρανῷ ξυγγένειαν ἀπὸ γῆς ἡμᾶς αἴρειν ὡς ὄντας φυτὸν οὐκ ἐπίγειον, ἀλλ' οὐράνιον.

18.1 Ταῦτα τοίνυν ὥσπερ ἐκ πηγῆς τῶν Ὁμηρικῶν ἐπῶν εἰς τοὺς ἰδίους διαλόγους ὁ Πλάτων μετήρδευσεν. Καὶ πρῶτόν γε περὶ τῶν ἀλόγων μερῶν τῆς ψυχῆς σκεπτέον. **18.2** Ὅτι μὲν γὰρ ὁ θυμὸς εἴληχε τὸν ὑποκάρδιον χῶρον, Ὀδυσσεὺς τοῦτο ποιήσει σαφὲς ἐν τῇ κατὰ μνηστήρων ὀργῇ καθάπερ οἶκόν τινα τῆς μισοπονηρίας θυροκρουστῶν τὴν καρδίαν· **18.3**

Στῆθος δὲ πλήξας κραδίην ἠνίπαπε μύθῳ·
τέτλαθι δή, κραδίη, καὶ κύντερον ἄλλο ποτ' ἔτλης.

18.4 Ἀφ' ἧς γὰρ αἱ θυμικαὶ ῥέουσι πηγαί, πρὸς ταύτην ὁ λόγος ἀποκλίνει.[1] **18.5** Τόν γε μὴν Τιτυὸν ἐρασθέντα τῶν Διὸς γάμων, ἀφ' οὗ μέρους ἤρξατο νοσεῖν,[2] εἰς τοῦτο ὑφίσταται κολαζόμενον· **18.6**

Γῦπε δέ μιν ἑκάτερθε παρημένω ἧπαρ ἔκειρον.

Ἀντὶ τίνος, Ὅμηρε;

Λητὼ γὰρ εἵλκυσε, Διὸς κυδρὴν παράκοιτιν.

18.7 Ὥσπερ δὲ οἱ νομοθέται τοὺς πατροτύπτας χειροκοποῦσιν, τὸ δυσ-σεβῆσαν αὐτῶν μέρος ἐξαιρέτως ἀποτέμνοντες, οὕτως Ὅμηρος ἐν ἥπατι κολάζει τὸν δι' ἧπαρ ἀσεβήσαντα.
18.8 Περὶ μὲν δὴ τῶν ἀλόγων τῆς ψυχῆς μερῶν οὑτωσὶ πεφιλοσόφηκεν.

---

1. O, Te read the participle ἀποκλίνων.
2. Te, following Mehler; Bu, mss. read νοεῖν, i.e., "where the thought originated."

The rational part of the soul, which is situated in the head, he regards as the charioteer who guides the whole system. This is what he says about it:

> As to the most important element of our soul, we should conceive it in the following way: God has given each of us, as our Daimon, that which we say dwells at the top of our body, and lifts us up from earth towards our kindred in heaven; for we are not a plant of earth, but a plant of heaven.[1]

18 All this Plato has drawn off from the fountains of Homer's poetry to water his own dialogues.[2] Let us first consider the irrational parts of the soul. That the "spirit" occupies the area below the heart is made plain by Odysseus, in his anger against the suitors, when he beats on the door of his heart, as it were, and treats it as the home of his hatred of evil:

> He struck his chest, and thus reproved his heart:
> "Bear up, my heart, you have borne worse than this."[3]

Here Reason [*logos*] turns towards the organ[4] from which the springs of anger flow.

Again, Tityos, who was in love with the wife of Zeus, is represented as punished in the organ where his disorder originated:

> Two vultures, one each side, tore at his liver.[5]

What for, Homer?

> For he had assaulted Leto, Zeus's good wife.[6]

So, just as lawgivers amputate the hands of father-beaters,[7] thus cutting off precisely the member that committed the offence, so Homer punishes in the liver the man who offended because of his liver!

So much for Homer's doctrine of the irrational parts of the soul.

---

1. *Tim.* 90A.
2. Cf. Longinus, *Subl.* 13.3.
3. *Od.* 20.17–18; quoted in Plato, *Resp.* 441C, *Phaed.* 94D.
4. Or "These words are addressed to the organ...."
5. *Od.* 11.578.
6. *Od.* 11.580.
7. Cf. Theon, *Progymnasmata* 130.30 Spengel.

19.1 Λοιπὸν οὖν καταλείπεται ζητεῖν, ἐν ᾧ τόπῳ τὸ λογικὸν ἵδρυται μέρος. **19.2** Ἔστι τοίνυν ἡ κεφαλὴ καθ' Ὅμηρον ἐν τῷ σώματι τὴν κυριωτάτην εἰληχυῖα τάξιν· **19.3** ὅλον γοῦν[1] εἴωθεν ὀνομάζειν τὸν ἄνθρωπον ἐξαιρέτως ἀφ' ἑνὸς τοῦ κρατίστου τὰ λοιπὰ δηλῶν·

Τοίην γὰρ κεφαλὴν ἕνεκ' αὐτῶν γαῖα κατέσχε,

τὸν Αἴαντα. **19.4** Καὶ σαφέστερον ἐπὶ τοῦ Νέστορος ἵππου κυριώτατον ἀποφαίνεται τοῦτο <τὸ>[2] μέρος,

ὅθι τε[3] πρῶται τρίχες ἵππων
κρανίῳ ἐμπεφύασι, μάλιστα δὲ καίριόν ἐστι.

19.5 Ταύτην δὲ τὴν δόξαν ἀλληγορικῶς βεβαιῶν τὰ κατὰ τὴν Ἀθηνᾶν ἡμῖν παραδέδωκεν. **19.6** Ἐπειδὴ γὰρ ὁ Ἀχιλλεὺς ὑπόπλεως ὀργῆς γενόμενος ὥρμησεν ἐπὶ τὸν σίδηρον, ἐπισκοτουμένου τοῦ κατὰ τὴν κεφαλὴν λογισμοῦ τοῖς περὶ τὰ στέρνα θυμοῖς, κατ' ὀλίγον ἐκ τῆς ἀγανακτούσης μέθης ὁ νοῦς ἐπὶ τὸ βέλτιον ἀνένηψεν. **19.7** Ἡ δὲ σὺν φρονήσει μετάνοια δικαίως ἐν τοῖς ποιήμασιν Ἀθηνᾶ νομίζεται. **19.8** Σχεδὸν γὰρ ἡ θεὸς οὐκ ἄλλου τινὸς ἢ συνέσεως ἐπώνυμός ἐστιν, ἀθρηνᾶ τις οὖσα καὶ πάντα τοῖς λεπτοτάτοις ὄμμασι τῶν λογισμῶν διαθροῦσα. **19.9** Διὸ δὴ καὶ παρθένον αὐτὴν ἐτήρησαν — ἄφθορον γὰρ ἀεὶ τὸ φρόνημα, οὐδεμιᾷ κηλῖδι μιανθῆναι δυνάμενον —, ἔκ τε τῆς τοῦ Διὸς κεφαλῆς γεγενῆσθαι δοκεῖ· τοῦτον γὰρ ἀπεφηνάμεθα τὸν χῶρον ἰδίως λογισμῶν εἶναι μητέρα.

20.1 Καὶ τί δεῖ τὰ πολλὰ μηκύνειν; οὐδὲν ἢ τελέως φρόνησις αὕτη. **20.2** Τοιγαροῦν ἀπὸ τῶν διαφλεξάντων Ἀχιλλέα θυμῶν ὥσπερ τι σβεστήριον κακοῦ φάρμακον ἐπέστη,

ξανθῆς δὲ κόμης ἕλε Πηλείωνα.

20.3 Παρ' ὃν μὲν γὰρ ὀργίζεται καιρόν, ἐν τοῖς στέρνοις ὁ θυμὸς ἕστηκεν· **20.4** ἕλκων γὰρ τὸ ξίφος,

---

1. M, Bu read οὖν.
2. Te, following Aldine edition.
3. Mehler, Te, from Homer; ταὶ M, Bu.

19 It remains to inquire where he places the rational part. Now according to Homer the head occupies the most important position in the body. Indeed he habitually speaks of the whole person by singling out this one most important part in order to indicate the rest:

For this, the earth has taken such a head—[1]

meaning Ajax. He shows even more plainly that this is the most vital part in the passage about Nestor's horse:

Just where a horse's first hairs grow
upon the skull, there is the vital place.[2]

He gives us the episode of Athena as an allegorical confirmation of this doctrine. For when Achilles, bursting with anger, reached for his sword, and the reason residing in his head was eclipsed by the passions in his breast, his mind was gradually freed from the intoxication that irritated it, and recovered its sobriety and better state. This change of heart due to sane thinking is very properly identified in the poem with Athena. Indeed, that goddess probably owes her name simply to her intelligence, since she is a "seer" [athrêna] and "sees through" [diathrousa][3] all things with the keen eyes of rational thought. This is why they kept her a virgin—for wisdom is ever unsullied and cannot be polluted by any stain—and why she is thought to have been born out of Zeus's head: we have shown that the head is specifically the mother of rational thought.[4]

20 But why say more? She is simply wisdom in perfection. And that is why, when the fire of anger blazed in Achilles, she stood over him, a remedy (as it were) to quench the evil,

and gripped Achilles by his yellow hair.[5]

As long as he was angry, his passion [thumos] remained in his breast, for, as he drew his sword,

---

1. *Od.* 11.549; "for this," i.e., "for the sake of Achilles' armor."
2. *Il.* 8.83. The Stoics cited Homer as witness that the rational part resided rather in the heart; cf. *SVF* 2.884, 886 = Galen, *On the Teachings of Hippocrates and Plato* 3.5, etc. See introduction, p. xv.
3. Cf. Cornutus, *Theol.* ch. 20 = p. 36.1–3 Lang, with Ramelli (2003, 362 n. 162).
4. Cf. Cornutus, *Theol.* ch. 20 = p. 35.1–2 Lang (birth from Zeus's head), ch. 20 = 36.8–9 Lang (virginity).
5. *Il.* 1.197.

στήθεσσιν λασίοισι διάνδιχα μερμήριξεν.

20.5 Ἡνίκα δ' ἡ ὀργὴ πέπειρα γίνεται, μετηλλάχασι[1] δ' αὐτὸν οἱ μετα-
νοοῦντες[2] ἤδη λογισμοί, τῆς κεφαλῆς ἀπρὶξ ἡ φρόνησις εἴληπται. **20.6**

Θάμβησεν δ' Ἀχιλεύς·

τὸ πρὸς πάντα κίνδυνον ἀτρεμὲς αὐτοῦ καὶ ἀκατάπληκτον ὁρῶν ἐφοβήθη τὴν
ἐκ λογισμῶν μετάνοιαν. **20.7** Ἐπιγνοὺς δ' εἰς οἷον κακὸν προκυλισθῆναι παρὰ
μικρὸν ἔμελλεν, ὡς ἡνίοχον εὐλαβήθη τὸν ἐφεστῶτα νοῦν· ὅθεν οὐδὲ παν-
τελῶς ἀπήλλακται τῆς ὀργῆς. **20.8** Ἐπιφέρει γοῦν·

Ἀλλ' ἤτοι ἔπεσιν μὲν ὀνείδισον, ὡς ἔσεταί περ.

20.9 Θεὰ μὲν οὖν βοηθοῦσα πάντως ἂν ὁλόκληρον εἰρήνην τοῦ πάθους κατε-
σκεύασεν· **20.10** ἐπειδὴ δὲ λογισμὸς ἀνθρώπινος ἦν, τὸ ξίφος ἀνεῖρξεν
ἀναγκαίως, καὶ τὸ μὲν ἄχρι τῶν ἔργων τολμηρὸν ἐκκέκοπται, ὑπομένει δὲ ἔτι
λείψανα τῆς ὀργῆς· **20.11** οὐ γὰρ ἀθρόως ὑφ' ἕνα καιρὸν οἱ μεγάλοι θυμοὶ τῶν
παθῶν ἀποκόπτονται.
    20.12 Καὶ τὰ μὲν περὶ Ἀθηνᾶς, ἣν μεσῖτιν ὑπεστήσατο τοῦ πρὸς Ἀγα-
μέμνονα θυμοῦ, ταύτῃ τῆς[3] ἀλληγορίας ἀξιούσθω.

    21.1 Βαρύτατον δ' ἔγκλημα κατὰ Ὁμήρου καὶ πάσης καταδίκης ἄξιον,
εἴπερ ἄρα μεμύθευκεν, ὡς ἐν τοῖς ἐφεξῆς ἔνεστιν εὑρεῖν, ὅτι[4] τῶν ἁπάντων
ἡγεμόνα **21.2**

    ξυνδῆσαι Ὀλύμπιοι ἤθελον ἄλλοι,
    Ἥρη τ' ἠδὲ Ποσειδάων καὶ Παλλὰς Ἀθήνη.
    Ἀλλὰ σὺ τόν γ' ἐλθοῦσα, θεά, ὑπελύσαο δεσμῶν,

---

    1. Te, following Hercher and Ludwich; Bu retains the mss. μετειλήχασι and renders
"ont pris partellement possession de son esprit, déjà comme gagné au repentir" (see following note), but the verb should mean "have a share in."
    2. Te, following Mehler and Hercher; Bu retains the mss. οἷα μετανοοῦντα, on the
grounds that sober thoughts do not themselves change their mind; but neither do they influence someone who has already (ἤδη) repented; cf. 73.9, μετανοοῦντι λογισμῷ.
    3. Te in apparatus criticus; Te reads ταύτης τῆς, i.e., "this allegorized interpretation,"
while Bu retains M's αὐτῆς (the sense of which is unclear).
    4. Russell, following G; Te reads μεμύθευκε <κε>νῶς ... ὅτε ("invented the empty fable
... when"); Bu retains ὅτε.

his thoughts were split two ways
within his hairy breast.[1]

But when his anger softens, and his second thoughts begin to make him
act differently, wisdom takes firm hold of his head:

Amazed, Achilles....[2]

His fearlessness, never dismayed in the face of any danger, took fright at
the vision of a reasoned repentance. Realizing the scale of the disaster
into which he had nearly tumbled, he took good heed of the reason that
stood over him, his "charioteer" as it were. But he was not completely
freed of his anger by this. At any rate, Athena proceeds to say:

Either reproach him in words, how it shall come to pass....[3]

Now a goddess coming to help would surely have contrived a complete
pacification of passion; but since the reason involved was a human one, it
held back the sword (as was necessary), and actual physical violence is
cut out, though there still remain relics of anger; for great outbursts of
passion are not completely done away with in a moment.

The episode of Athena, whom Homer represents as the mediator in
Achilles's anger against Agamemnon, may thus be seen to merit an allegorized interpretation.

21 It is however a particularly heavy charge against Homer, deserv-
ing of every condemnation, if he has indeed invented the fable, as we find
in the next lines, that "the other Olympians sought to bind in chains" the
ruler of them all:

Hera and Poseidon, Pallas Athena too;
but, goddess, you came and freed him from his bonds,

---

1. *Il.* 1.189.
2. *Il.* 1.199.
3. *Il.* 1.211.

ὥχ᾽ ἑκατόγχειρον καλέσασ᾽ ἐς μακρὸν Ὄλυμπον,
ὃν Βριάρεων καλέουσι θεοί, ἄνδρες δέ τε πάντες
Αἰγαίων᾽· ὁ γὰρ αὖτε βίῃ οὗ πατρὸς ἀμείνων.

21.3 Ἐν τούτοις τοῖς στίχοις ἄξιός ἐστιν Ὅμηρος οὐκ ἐκ μιᾶς τῆς
Πλάτωνος ἐλαύνεσθαι πολιτείας, ἀλλ᾽ ὑπὲρ Ἡρακλέους φασὶν ἐσχάτας
στήλας καὶ τὴν ἄβατον Ὠκεανοῦ θάλατταν. **21.4** Ζεὺς γὰρ ὀλίγου δεσμῶν
πεπείραται, καὶ τὴν ἐπιβουλὴν αὐτῷ συνιστᾶσιν οὐχ οἱ Τιτᾶνες οὐδὲ τὸ
κατὰ Παλλήνην θράσος Γιγάντων, **21.5** ἀλλ᾽ Ἥρα, διπλοῦν ὄνομα, φύσεως καὶ
συμβιώσεως, ὅ τ᾽ ἀδελφὸς Ποσειδῶν, ἐξ ἴσου νεμηθεὶς ἅπαντα καὶ οὐχὶ τοῦ
διαμαρτεῖν ἧς ὤφειλε τιμῆς ἠξιῶσθαι κατὰ τοῦ πλεονεκτήσαντος ἠγανακ-
τηκώς, τρίτη δ᾽ Ἀθηνᾶ, διὰ μιᾶς ἐπιβουλῆς εἰς πατέρα καὶ μητέρα
δυσσεβοῦσα. **21.6** Νομίζω δ᾽ ἔγωγε τῆς ἐπιβουλῆς Διὶ τὴν σωτηρίαν
ἀπρεπεστέραν· Θέτις γὰρ αὐτὸν ἀπήλλαξε τῶν δεσμῶν καὶ Βριάρεως·
ἀπρεπεῖς δ᾽ αἱ τοιαῦται ἐλπίδες,[1] ὡς τοιούτων δεηθῆναι συμμάχων.

22.1 Ταύτης τοίνυν τῆς ἀσεβείας ἕν ἐστιν ἀντιφάρμακον, ἐὰν
ἐπιδείξωμεν ἠλληγορημένον τὸν μῦθον· ἡ γὰρ ἀρχέγονος ἁπάντων καὶ πρεσ-
βυτέρα φύσις ἐν τούτοις τοῖς ἔπεσι θεολογεῖται. **22.2** Καὶ τῶν φυσικῶν κατὰ
τὰ στοιχεῖα δογμάτων εἷς ἀρχηγὸς Ὅμηρος, ἑκάστῳ τινὶ τῶν μετ᾽ αὐτὸν ἧς
ἔδοξεν εὑρεῖν ἐπινοίας γεγονὼς διδάσκαλος. **22.3** Θάλητα μέν γε τὸν
Μιλήσιον ὁμολογοῦσι πρῶτον ὑποστήσασθαι τῶν ὅλων κοσμογόνον στοιχεῖον
τὸ ὕδωρ· ἡ γὰρ ὑγρὰ φύσις, εὐμαρῶς εἰς ἕκαστα μεταπλαττομένη, πρὸς τὸ
ποικίλον εἴωθε μορφοῦσθαι. **22.4** Τό τε γὰρ ἐξατμιζόμενον αὐτῆς ἀεροῦται,
καὶ τὸ λεπτότατον ἀπὸ ἀέρος αἰθὴρ ἀνάπτεται, συνιζάνον τε τὸ ὕδωρ καὶ
μεταβαλλόμενον εἰς ἰλὺν ἀπογαιοῦται· **22.5** διὸ δὴ τῆς τετράδος τῶν
στοιχείων ὥσπερ αἰτιώτατον ὁ Θαλῆς ἀπεφήνατο στοιχεῖον εἶναι τὸ ὕδωρ.
22.6 Τίς οὖν ἐγέννησε ταύτην τὴν δόξαν; οὐχ Ὅμηρος, εἰπών·

Ὠκεανός, ὅσπερ γένεσις πάντεσσι τέτυκται,

---

1. Understanding (something like) σωτηρίας with ἐλπίδες, added by Polak; the text,
which need not be altered, says simply "such hopes."

swiftly summoning the hundred-handed to high Olympus,
whom the gods call Briareus, and men Aegaeon,
for he is stronger than his father is.[1]

For these lines, Homer deserves to be banished not just from Plato's
Republic but, as they say, beyond the furthest pillars of Heracles and the
inaccessible sea of Ocean. For Zeus comes very near to being chained up,
and the conspiracy against him is put together not by the Titans or the
audacious Giants at Pallene,[2] but by Hera (who has two titles, one from
her kinship with him, and one from her marriage) and by his brother
Poseidon, who had been allotted an equal share of the universe and bore
no grievance against the greater winner for his missing an honor of which
he ought to have been judged worthy; and, thirdly, by Athena, who by
this one plot sinned against both her father and her mother.[3] For my part,
I fancy Zeus's rescue was more disgraceful to him than the conspiracy,
for it was Thetis and Briareus who freed him from his bonds, and hopes
of rescue that depend on such allies are disgraceful.

22 There is only one remedy for this impiety: to show that the myth
is an allegory. The fact is that we have in these lines a theological account
of the oldest natural substance, which is the origin of all things. Homer is
the sole originator of the scientific doctrine of the elements, and taught all
his successors the ideas which they were held to have discovered. It is
commonly agreed that Thales of Miletus was the first to represent water
as the cosmogonic element of the universe. The liquid substance, which
easily adapts itself to every circumstance, habitually takes various forms.
Vaporized, it becomes air, and the subtlest part of it passes from being air
to being kindled as aether. Again, when water settles and turns to mud it
becomes earth. Thales therefore showed that water was, as it were, the
most causative of the four elements. So who originated this opinion?
Surely Homer, when he says

Ocean, who is all things' origin.[4]

---

1. *Il.* 1.399–404; cf. Cornutus, *Theol.* ch. 17 = p. 27.6–17 Lang, who cites the first verse,
with Ramelli (2003, 345 n. 117).

2. The west promontory of Chalcidice, supposed to be site where the gods and giants
fought; its ancient name, according to Herodotus (*Hist.* 7.123) and others, was Phlegra;
alternatively, Phlegra was thought to be a distinct location in Macedonia; cf. Pseudo-
Apollodorus, *Bibliotheca* 1.34.

3. Since Athena sprang from the head of Zeus, he is her mother as well as her father.

4. *Il.* 14.246; cf. Ps.-Plutarch, *Vit. poes. Hom.* 2.93, with Hillgruber's notes (1994–1999,
2:213–14).

22.7 φερωνύμως μὲν ὠκεανὸν εἰπὼν τὴν ὑγρὰν φύσιν παρὰ τὸ ὠκέως νάειν, τοῦτον δ᾽ ὑποστησάμενος ἁπάντων γενεάρχην; **22.8** Ἀλλ᾽ ὁ Κλαζομένιος Ἀναξαγόρας, κατὰ διαδοχὴν γνώριμος ὢν Θάλητος, συνέζευξε τῷ ὕδατι δεύτερον στοιχεῖον τὴν γῆν, ἵνα ξηρῷ μιχθὲν ὑγρὸν ἐξ ἀντιπάλου φύσεως εἰς μίαν ὁμόνοιαν ἀνακραθῇ. **22.9** Καὶ ταύτην δὲ τὴν ἀπόφασιν πρῶτος Ὅμηρος ἐγεώργησεν, Ἀναξαγόρᾳ σπέρματα τῆς ἐπινοίας χαρισάμενος ἐν οἷς φησίν·

Ἀλλ᾽ ὑμεῖς μὲν πάντες ὕδωρ καὶ γαῖα γένοισθε.

22.10 Πᾶν γὰρ τὸ φυόμενον ἔκ τινων εἰς ταὐτὰ ἀναλύεται διαφθειρόμενον, ὡσπερεὶ τῆς φύσεως ἃ δεδάνεικεν ἐν ἀρχῇ χρέα κομιζομένης ἐπὶ τέλει. **22.11** Διὸ δὴ τοῖς Κλαζομενίοις δόγμασιν ἑπόμενος Εὐριπίδης φησί·

Χωρεῖ δ᾽ ὀπίσω
τὰ μὲν ἐκ γαίας φύντ᾽ εἰς γαῖαν,
τὰ δ᾽ ἀπ᾽ αἰθερίου¹ βλαστόντα γονῆς
εἰς αἰθέρα.

22.12 Καταρώμενος οὖν ὁ ποιητὴς τοῖς Ἕλλησι μίαν εὗρεν εὐχὴν² φιλόσοφον, εἰ πάλιν ὕδωρ καὶ γῆ γένοιντο διαλυθέντες εἰς ταὐτά, ἀφ᾽ ὧν ἐπήχθησαν, ὅτε ἐγεννῶντο.

22.13 Ἐσχάτη τοίνυν ὑπὸ τῶν μεγίστων φιλοσόφων ἡ τελεία τετρὰς ἐν τοῖς στοιχείοις συνεπληρώθη· **22.14** δύο μὲν γὰρ ὑλικά φασιν εἶναι, γῆν τε καὶ ὕδωρ, δύο δὲ πνευματικά, αἰθέρα τε καὶ ἀέρα, τούτων δὲ τὰς φύσεις ἀλλήλαις ἐναντία φρονούσας, ὅταν εἰς τὸ αὐτὸ κερασθῶσιν, ὁμονοεῖν.

23.1 Ἆρ᾽ οὖν, εἴ τις θέλοι³ τἀληθὲς ἐξετάζειν, οὐχὶ καὶ ταῦτα τὰ στοιχεῖα παρ᾽ Ὁμήρῳ φιλοσοφεῖται; **23.2** Καὶ περὶ μὲν τῶν Ἥρας δεσμῶν, ἐν οἷς ἡ τάξις ἠλληγόρηται τῶν τεττάρων στοιχείων, εὐκαιρότερον αὖθις ἐροῦμεν· **23.3** νῦν δ᾽ ἀποχρῶσιν οἱ κατὰ τὴν τρίτην ῥαψῳδίαν ὅρκοι τὸ λεγόμενον ὑφ᾽ ἡμῶν βεβαιῶσαι· **23.4**

---

1. Te, following Nauck; Bu retains the mss. reading αἰθρίου, "bright," but translates "l'éther."
2. O, Te; M has ἀρχήν, "principle"; Bu emends to ἀράν, "curse."
3. Bu, with A, O (cf. ch. 40.6); Te, with G, reads θέλει.

Here he gives the watery substance a meaningful name, *Okeanos*, from *ôkeôs naiein*, "to flow quickly,"[1] and makes it the originator of all things. However, Anaxagoras of Clazomenae,[2] a pupil and successor of Thales, joined earth with water, as a second element, so that the wet, combined with the dry, blended with its opposite to produce a harmonious system. Homer was the first who planted this view too, making Anaxagoras a present of the seeds[3] of the idea, by saying

> may you all turn to water and to earth![4]

For when a thing is destroyed, it is resolved into the constituents from which it grew. Nature, as it were, recovers at the end the debt she lent at the beginning. So Euripides, following the doctrine of Clazomenae, says:

> What came from the earth, goes back to the earth;
> what sprang from the aether, to aether returns.[5]

Homer therefore found this one philosophical prayer to curse the Greeks—may they become water and earth again, dissolved into the constituents from which they were formed at birth.

Finally, the great philosophers filled out the complete set of four elements: two, they say, are material, earth and water; two are "pneumatic," aether and air. The natures of these are mutually hostile, but come together in concord when they are combined in the same thing.

23 If one is willing to consider the truth of the matter, is not the doctrine of these elements found in Homer? The "binding of Hera," which contains an allegorical account of the system of the four elements, will be more conveniently discussed later.[6] It suffices for the time being to cite the oaths in book 3 as confirmation of what I say:

---

1. Cf. Cornutus, *Theol.* ch. 8 = p. 8.13 Lang (cf. ch. 17 = p. 30.18–31.2 Lang), with Ramelli (2003, 315 n. 33); the passage is marked as an interpolation by Lang, but see Ramelli (2003, 105–14).

2. A mistake for Xenophanes of Colophon; the *Vit. poes. Hom.* (loc. cit.) is correct.

3. For the metaphor of seeds, cf. Longinus, *Subl.* 16.3; but in Heraclitus the metaphor is continued in *egeôrgêsen*, "planted." Having mistaken Anaxagoras for Xenophanes, Heraclitus is perhaps punning on the seeds (*spermata*) that were also a feature of Anaxagoras's theory.

4. *Il.* 7.99.

5. Euripides, *Chrysippus* frg. 839 Nauck.

6. In ch. 40.

Ζεῦ κύδιστε, μέγιστε, κελαινεφές, αἰθέρι ναίων,
Ἥλιός θ᾽ ὃς πάντ᾽ ἐφορᾷς καὶ πάντ᾽ ἐπακούεις,
καὶ ποταμοὶ καὶ γαῖα, καὶ οἳ ὑπένερθε καμόντας
ἀνθρώπους τίνυσθον, ὅ τίς κ᾽ ἐπίορκον ὀμόσσῃ.

23.5 Πρῶτον ἐπικαλεῖται τὸν ὀξύτατον αἰθέρα τὴν ἀνωτάτω τάξιν εἰληχότα· πυρὸς γὰρ εἰλικρινὴς φύσις, ἅτ᾽ οἶμαι κουφοτάτη, τὸν ὑψηλότατον ἀποκεκλήρωται χῶρον. **23.6** Εἴη δ᾽ ἂν οἶμαι τοῦτο Ζεὺς ἐπώνυμος, ἤτοι τὸ ζῆν παρεχόμενος ἀνθρώποις ἢ παρὰ τὴν ἔμπυρον ζέσιν οὕτως ὠνομασμένος. **23.7** Ἀμέλει δὲ καὶ ὁ Εὐριπίδης τὸν ὑπερτεταμένον αἰθέρα φησίν·

Ὁρᾷς τὸν ὑψοῦ τόνδ᾽ ἄπειρον αἰθέρα
καὶ γῆν πέριξ ἔχονθ᾽ ὑγραῖς ἐν ἀγκάλαις;
τοῦτον νόμιζε Ζῆνα, τόνδ᾽ ἡγοῦ θεόν.

23.8 Ὁ μὲν οὖν πρῶτος αἰθὴρ καλεῖται μεσίτης τῶν ὁρκίων, ποταμοὶ δὲ καὶ γῆ, τὰ ὑλικὰ στοιχεῖα, μετὰ τὴν πρώτην φύσιν αἰθέρος. **23.9** Τὸν δ᾽ ὑπένερθεν Ἀίδην ἀλληγορικῶς ἀέρα προσαγορεύει· **23.10** μέλαν γὰρ τουτὶ τὸ στοιχεῖον, ὡς ἂν οἶμαι παχυτέρας καὶ διύγρου λαχὸν μοίρας· **23.11** δίχα γοῦν τῶν καταφωτίζειν δυναμένων ἀλαμπής ἐστιν, ὅθεν εὐλόγως αὐτὸν Ἀίδην προσηγόρευσεν. **23.12** Τί οὖν τὸ πέμπτον, Ἥλιος; ἵνα τι καὶ Περιπατητικοῖς φιλοσόφοις χαρίσηται, Ὅμηρος ἐπεκαλέσατο καὶ τοῦτον· ἀξιοῦσιν γὰρ[1] ἑτέραν τοῦ πυρὸς εἶναι ταύτην τὴν φύσιν, ἣν κυκλοφορητικὴν ὀνομάζουσι, πέμπτον εἶναι τοῦτο στοιχεῖον ὁμολογοῦντες. **23.13** Ὁ μὲν γὰρ αἰθὴρ διὰ τὴν κουφότητα πρὸς τοὺς ἀνωτάτω χωρεῖ τόπους, ἥλιος δὲ καὶ σελήνη καὶ τῶν ὁμοδρόμων αὐτοῖς ἕκαστον ἄστρων τὴν ἐν κύκλῳ φορὰν

---

1. Te, following Mehler; Bu retains the mss. ἐπεκαλέσατο· καὶ τοῦτο γὰρ ἀξιοῦσιν, which is difficult to construe (the postponed γάρ is also suspect).

Zeus, mighty god of storm clouds, heaven-dwelling;
O Sun, who seest and hearest everything;
O rivers, earth, and ye who dwell below
and punish the dead, if any man swears falsely.[1]

First he calls upon the dazzling[2] aether, which occupies the highest position; for the pure substance of fire, being (I suppose) the lightest, is
assigned to the highest place. This, I think, is how Zeus acquired his name,
either because he gives life [*zên*][3] to man, or because his name comes from
his fiery "boiling" [*zesin*]. Euripides too speaks of the aether that extends
above us:

See you the infinite aether, up on high,
encircling earth within its soft embrace?
Believe that this is Zeus, and this is God.[4]

The aether is therefore named as the first witness of the oaths. Rivers
and earth, the material elements, come after the first substance of aether.
Hades "below" is Homer's allegorical way of naming "air"; this element
is dark because, presumably, it is assigned to a denser and damper
region; at any rate, it is separated from possible sources of light and does
not shine, and so is quite properly called Hades ("the invisible").[5] Then
why is there a fifth witness, the Sun? Homer has invoked him also in
order to do a favor to the Peripatetic philosophers, who claim that the
substance which they call "rotational" is distinct from fire; they regard it
as a fifth element.[6] Aether, because of its lightness, tends toward the
highest regions; but the sun, the moon, and all the stars that run their
courses with these revolve continually in a circular movement, because

---

1. *Il.* 2.412 + 3.277–279; see above, ch. 3, where 3.276–280 is cited.

2. See LSJ s.v. ὀξύς IIb; Bu however renders "infiniment subtil." Homer's word for
"heaven" in the passage just quoted is "aether."

3. Cf. Plato, *Crat.* 396B; *SVF* 528 = Arius Didymus *apud* Eusebius, *Praep. ev.* 15.15 (p. 817,
6); *SVF* 1021–1022 = Diogenes Laertius 7.147–148; *SVF* 1062 = Stobaeus, *Ecl.* I p. 31, 11 W.;
SVF 1076 = Philodemus, *Piet.* ch. 11; Cornutus, *Theol.* ch. 2 = p. 3.4–6 Lang, with Ramelli
(2003, 302 n. 9).

4. Euripides, frg. 941 Nauck. See Probus on Virgil, *Bucolica* 6.31 (p. 333 Thilo), where the
connection with *zeô* ("boil") is also made.

5. The etymology of Hades (in Greek *Haïdês* or *Aïdês*) from *aïdês*, "invisible," is traditional; see Plato, *Gorg.* 493B, *Phaed.* 81E, *Crat.* 403A, and cf. Cornutus, *Theol.* ch. 5 = p. 5.2–4
Lang (glossing it as *aoratos*, "unseen"), Ps.-Plutarch, *Vit. poes. Hom.* 122. For Hades as air,
cf. Chrysippus in *SVF* 2.1076, Ramelli (2003, 308 n. 18).

6. Cf. Ps.-Aristotle, *Mund.* 392a5–9, b35–36; Allan (1952, 50–52).

δινούμενα διατελεῖ, τῆς πυρώδους οὐσίας ἄλλην τινὰ δύναμιν ἔχοντα. **23.14** Διὰ τούτων ἁπάντων ὑπεσήμηνεν ἡμῖν τὰ πρωτοπαγῆ στοιχεῖα τῆς φύσεως.

24.1 Καὶ περὶ αὐτοῦ μηδεὶς λεγέτω, πῶς μὲν ὁ αἰθὴρ προσαγορεύεται Ζεύς, Ἀίδην δ᾽ ὀνομάζει τὸν ἀέρα καὶ συμβολικοῖς ὀνόμασι τὴν φιλοσοφίαν ἀμαυροῖ· **24.2** παράδοξον γὰρ οὐδέν, εἰ ποιητής γε[1] ὢν ἀλληγορεῖ, καὶ τῶν προηγουμένως φιλοσοφούντων τούτῳ τῷ τρόπῳ χρωμένων. **24.3** Ὁ γοῦν σκοτεινὸς Ἡράκλειτος ἀσαφῆ καὶ διὰ συμβόλων εἰκάζεσθαι δυνάμενα <μόνον προφέρων>[2] θεολογεῖ τὰ φυσικὰ δι᾽ ὧν φησί· **24.4**

Θεοὶ θνητοί· [τ᾽] ἄνθρωποι ἀθάνατοι, ζῶντες τὸν ἐκείνων θάνατον, θνήσκοντες τὴν ἐκείνων ζωήν·

24.5 καὶ πάλιν·

Ποταμοῖς τοῖς αὐτοῖς ἐμβαίνομέν τε καὶ οὐκ ἐμβαίνομεν, εἶμέν τε καὶ οὐκ εἶμεν·

ὅλον τε τὸ περὶ φύσεως αἰνιγματῶδες ἀλληγορεῖ. **24.6** Τί δ᾽ ὁ Ἀκραγαντῖνος Ἐμπεδοκλῆς; οὐχὶ τὰ τέτταρα στοιχεῖα βουλόμενος ἡμῖν ὑποσημῆναι τὴν Ὁμηρικὴν ἀλληγορίαν μεμίμηται;

Ζεὺς ἀργὴς Ἥρη τε φερέσβιος ἠδ᾽ Ἀιδωνεὺς
Νῆστίς θ᾽, ἣ δακρύοις τέγγει κρούνωμα βρότειον.

24.7 Ζῆνα μὲν εἶπε τὸν αἰθέρα, γῆν δὲ τὴν Ἥραν, Ἀιδωνέα δὲ τὸν ἀέρα, τὸ δὲ δακρύοις τεγγόμενον κρούνωμα βρότειον τὸ ὕδωρ. **24.8** Οὐ δὴ παράδοξον, εἰ τῶν προηγουμένως ὁμολογούντων φιλοσοφεῖν ἀλληγορικοῖς ὀνόμασι χρησαμένων ὁ ποιητικὴν ἐπαγγελλόμενος ἐξ ἴσου τοῖς φιλοσόφοις ἠλληγόρησε.

25.1 Λοιπὸν οὖν σκοπῶμεν, εἰ ἡ κατὰ Διὸς ἐπιβουλὴ τῶν στοιχείων ἐστὶν ἀπαρίθμησις καὶ φυσικωτέρας ἅπτεται θεωρίας. **25.2** Φασὶ τοίνυν οἱ

---

1. Te (on the hiatus, see Te p. xxxiv); A and G read τε. Bu, following Polak, reads τις.
2. Supplied by Marcovich on Heraclitus frg. 47 = frg. 62 Diels-Kranz.

they possess a force which is different from that of the fiery substance. In all this, Homer has given us indications of the basic elements of the natural world.

24 Let no one ask of Homer, how it can be that aether is given the name Zeus, while he calls air Hades, obscuring his philosophy by these symbolic names. For there is nothing paradoxical in a poet's using allegory, since even professed philosophers use this way of speaking. Heraclitus the Obscure, <putting forward> unclear matters which can <only> be conjectured by means of symbols, presents his doctrine of nature in the following terms:

Gods, mortals; humans, immortals; living the others' death, dying the others' life.[1]

And again:

In the same rivers we walk and do not walk; we are and are not.[2]

His whole enigmatic account of nature is an allegory. And what of Empedocles of Acragas? Does he not imitate Homeric allegory when he wants to indicate the four elements to us?

Bright Zeus, life-bringing Hera, Aidoneus,
Nestis, who wets with tears a mortal spring.[3]

By Zeus he means aether, by Hera earth, by Aidoneus air, by the mortal spring wet with tears water.[4] It is thus no paradox that, when those who claim philosophy as their main business have used allegorical expressions, a professed poet should allegorize on the same terms as the philosophers.

25 Let us now consider whether the conspiracy against Zeus is a catalog of the elements and touches on deeper scientific speculation. Now

---

1. Frg. 47 Marcovich = frg. 62 Diels-Kranz
2. Frg. 40 Marcovich = frg. 49a Diels-Kranz (cf. frg. 12).
3. Frg. 6 Diels-Kranz.
4. For this interpretation, see Stobaeus 1.10.11b (p. 121 Wachsmuth), believed by some to come from Plutarch. [Plutarch], *Plac. philos.* 878A gives an alternative version, in which Zeus is aether, Hera air, Aidoneus earth, and Nestis "sea and water": this latter version is attributed to Crates (frg. 2a Mette).

δοκιμώτατοι φιλόσοφοι ταῦτα περὶ τῆς διαμονῆς τῶν ὅλων· **25.3** ἕως μὲν ἂν ἀφιλόνεικος ἡ ἁρμονία τὰ τέτταρα στοιχεῖα διακρατῇ, μηδενὸς ἐξαιρέτως ὑπερδυναστεύοντος, ἀλλ᾽ ἑκάστου κατ᾽ ἐμμέλειαν ἣν εἴληχε τάξιν οἰκονομοῦντος, ἀκινήτως ἕκαστα μένειν· **25.4** εἰ δ᾽ ἐπικρατήσάν τι τῶν ἐν αὐτοῖς καὶ τυραννῆσαν εἰς πλείω φορὰν παρέλθοι, τὰ λοιπὰ συγχυθέντα τῇ τοῦ κρατοῦντος ἰσχύι μετ᾽ ἀνάγκης ὑπείξειν. **25.5** Πυρὸς μὲν οὖν[1] αἰφνιδίως ἐκζέσαντος ἁπάντων ἔσεσθαι κοινὴν ἐκπύρωσιν, εἰ δ᾽ ἀθροῦν ὕδωρ ἐκραγείη, κατακλυσμῷ τὸν κόσμον ἀπολεῖσθαι. **25.6** Διὰ τούτων τοίνυν τῶν ἐπῶν μέλλουσάν τινα ταραχὴν ἐν τοῖς ὅλοις Ὅμηρος ὑποσημαίνει· **25.7** Ζεὺς γάρ, ἡ δυνατωτάτη φύσις, ὑπὸ τῶν ἄλλων ἐπιβουλεύεται στοιχείων, Ἥρας μέν, τοῦ ἀέρος, Ποσειδῶνος δέ, τῆς ὑγρᾶς φύσεως, Ἀθηνᾶς δέ, τῆς γῆς, ἐπεὶ δημιουργός ἐστιν ἁπάντων καὶ θεὸς Ἐργάνη. **25.8** Ταῦτα δὴ τὰ στοιχεῖα πρῶτον μὲν συγγενῆ διὰ τὴν ἐν ἀλλήλοις ἀνάκρασιν· **25.9** εἶτα συγχύσεως παρὰ μικρὸν αὐτοῖς γενομένης εὑρέθη βοηθὸς ἡ πρόνοια. **25.10** Θέτιν δ᾽ αὐτὴν εὐλόγως ὠνόμασεν· αὕτη γὰρ ὑπέστη τῶν ὅλων εὔκαιρον ἀπόθεσιν, ἐν τοῖς ἰδίοις τόποις[2] ἱδρύσασα τὰ στοιχεῖα. **25.11** Σύμμαχος δ᾽ αὐτῇ γέγονεν ἡ βριαρὰ καὶ πολύχειρ δύναμις· τὰ γὰρ τηλικαῦτα τῶν πραγμάτων νοσήσαντα πῶς <ἂν>[3] ἄλλως δύναιτο πλὴν μετὰ μεγάλης βίας ἀναρρωσθῆναι;

25.12 Καὶ τὸ μὲν ἄφυκτον ἔγκλημα περὶ τῶν Διὸς ἀσεβῶν δεσμῶν οὕτω φυσικὴν ἀλληγορίας ἔχει θεωρίαν.

26.1 Ἐγκαλοῦσι δ᾽ Ὁμήρῳ περὶ τῆς Ἡφαίστου ῥίψεως τὸ μὲν πρῶτον ὅτι χωλὸν αὐτὸν ὑφίσταται, τὴν θείαν ἀκρωτηριάζων φύσιν, εἶθ᾽ ὅτι καὶ παρὰ μικρὸν ἧκε κινδύνου. **26.2**

"Πᾶν," γάρ φησι, "δ᾽ ἦμαρ φερόμην, ἅμα δ᾽ ἠελίῳ καταδύντι κάππεσον ἐν Λήμνῳ, ὀλίγος δ᾽ ἔτι θυμὸς ἐνῆεν."

---

1. Te, following Homeric scholia; omitted by mss., Bu.
2. Russell (very hesitantly) for νόμοις (mss., Te, Bu) which would mean "ordinances."
3. Te, following Mehler; omitted by Bu.

the most respected philosophers[1] give the following account of the permanence of the universe: so long as uncontentious harmony rules the four elements, and no one of them is especially predominant, but each exercises a due control over the area to which it is assigned, then everything will remain unmoved; but if any one of the elements prevails, seizes power and extends beyond its proper range, the others will be merged in the power of the conqueror and inevitably yield to it. Thus when fire suddenly surges over, there will be a general conflagration of all things; and if water bursts out suddenly, the world will be destroyed by a flood. Homer thus suggests in these lines some future disturbance in the universe. Zeus, the most powerful element, is the object of a conspiracy by the others: by Hera, i.e., air; by Poseidon, i.e., water; and by Athena, i.e., the earth, since she, the Worker Goddess,[2] is the creator of all things. These latter elements were at first kin to one another because they were mixed together; then, when they were almost fused into one, Providence was found to come to the rescue. This Providence Homer appropriately named Thetis, for she undertook the timely settlement [apothesis][3] of the universe, establishing the elements within their own spheres. Her ally in this was massive [briara][4] and many-handed power: for how can the disorder of such mighty things be cured except by great force?

So the inescapable charge relating to the impious "binding of Zeus" admits of a scientific explanation in allegorical terms.

26 Critics also charge Homer in regard to the "throwing down" of Hephaestus, first because he represents him as lame, thereby mutilating his divine nature, and secondly because he came near to danger of death. For he says

> all day I fell, and as the sun went down
> landed on Lemnos, not much breath left in me.[5]

---

1. Evidently the Stoics.

2. Athena Erganê: the appropriate festival at Athens was the Chalkeia; cf. Deubner (1932, 35–36).

3. Or "setting apart." In Cornutus, *Theol.* ch. 16 = p. 27.11 Lang, Thetis is derived from *diatheisa,* "having put in order," and Mehler wished to read *diathesin* in our passage; in Eustathius (122.47) it is derived simply from *thesis,* "placing." The idea seems to be that the fusion of the other elements poses a threat to Zeus because, taken together, they may indeed overpower him; by distributing them in separate spheres, Thetis reestablishes the cosmic order, with Zeus, i.e. heavenly fire, as the most powerful element. But note that *apothesis* may refer to the last stage of setting a dislocation or fracture (LSJ).

4. Alluding to Briareus (*Il.* 1.403); for a different etymology (from *bora,* "food"), cf. Cornutus, *Theol.* ch. 17 = p. 27.15–17 Lang.

5. *Il.* 1.592–593.

26.3 Καὶ τούτοις δ᾽ ὑποκρύπτεταί τις Ὁμήρῳ φιλόσοφος νοῦς· **26.4** οὐ¹ πλάσ-μασι² ποιητικοῖς τοὺς ἀκούοντας τέρπων αὐτίκα χωλὸν ἡμῖν παραδέδωκεν Ἥφαιστον, οὐ τὸν ἐξ Ἥρας καὶ Διὸς μυθούμενον παῖδα· **26.5** τοῦτο γὰρ ἀπρεπὲς ὄντως ἱστορεῖν περὶ θεῶν. **26.6** Ἀλλ᾽ ἐπεὶ ἡ³ πυρὸς οὐσία διπλῆ, καὶ τὸ μὲν αἰθέριον, ὡς ἔναγχος εἰρήκαμεν, ἐπὶ τῆς ἀνωτάτω τοῦ παντὸς αἰωρ<ούμενον χώρ>ας⁴ οὐδὲν ὑστεροῦν ἔχει πρὸς τελειότητα, τοῦ δὲ παρ᾽ ἡμῖν πυρὸς ἡ ὕλη, πρόσγειος οὖσα, φθαρτὴ καὶ διὰ τῆς ὑποτρεφούσης⁵ παρ᾽ ἕκαστα ζωπυρουμένη, **26.7** διὰ τοῦτο τὴν ὀξυτάτην φλόγα συνεχῶς Ἥλιόν τε καὶ Δία προσαγορεύει, τὸ δ᾽ ἐπὶ γῆς πῦρ Ἥφαιστον, ἑτοίμως ἁπτόμενόν τε καὶ σβεννύμενον· **26.8** ὅθεν εἰκότως κατὰ σύγκρισιν ἐκείνου τοῦ ὁλοκλήρου τοῦτο νενόμισται χωλὸν εἶναι τὸ πῦρ. **26.9** Ἄλλως τε καὶ πᾶσα ποδῶν πήρωσις ἀεὶ τοῦ διαστηρίζοντος ἐπιδεῖται βάκτρου· **26.10** τὸ δὲ παρ᾽ ἡμῖν πῦρ, ἄνευ τῆς τῶν ξύλων παραθέσεως οὐ δυνηθὲν ἂν ἐπὶ πλεῖον παραμεῖναι, συμβολικῶς χωλὸν εἴρηται. **26.11** Τὸν γοῦν Ἥφαιστον οὐκ ἀλληγορικῶς ἐν ἑτέροις ἀλλὰ διαρρήδην φησὶν Ὅμηρος εἶναι·

Σπλάγχνα δ᾽ ἄρ᾽ ἀμπείραντες ὑπείρεχον Ἡφαίστοιο·

μεταληπτικῶς ὑπὸ τοῦ Ἡφαίστου τὰ σπλάγχνα φησὶν ὀπτᾶσθαι.

26.12 Καὶ μὴν ἀπ᾽ οὐρανοῦ ῥιπτούμενον αὐτὸν ὑφίσταται φυσικῶς. **26.13** κατ᾽ ἀρχὰς γὰρ⁶ οὐδέπω τῆς τοῦ πυρὸς χρήσεως ἐπιπολαζούσης ἄν-θρωποι χρονικῶς χαλκοῖς τισιν ὀργάνοις κατεσκευασμένοις ἐφειλκύσαντο τοὺς ἀπὸ τῶν μετεώρων φερομένους σπινθῆρας, κατὰ τὰς μεσημβρίας ἐναντία τῷ ἡλίῳ τὰ ὄργανα τιθέντες. **26.14** Ὅθεν οἶμαι δοκεῖ καὶ Προμηθεὺς ἀπ᾽ οὐρανοῦ διακλέψαι τὸ πῦρ, ἐπειδήπερ τέχνης προμήθεια τῶν ἀνθρώπων ἐπενόησε τὴν ἐκεῖθεν ἀπόρροιαν αὐτοῦ. **26.15** Λῆμνον δὲ πρῶτον οὐκ ἀλόγως ἐμύθευσε τὴν ὑποδεξαμένην τὸ θεόβλητον πῦρ· ἐνταῦθα γὰρ ἀνίενται

---

1. Te deletes οὐ, which yields: "wishing to delight his hearers by a poetical fiction, Homer has given us a lame Hephaestus, not of course the son of Hera and Zeus whom we know from mythology...."

2. Te, following the Homeric scholia, inserts γάρ.

3. Te deletes the article to avoid hiatus.

4. Adopting the supplement in Te apparatus criticus; the received text would mean "on the highest swing of the universe."

5. O, Te; M, Bu read ὑποστρεφούσης, "that returns."

6. Te; Bu reads ὑφίσταται· φυσικῶς γὰρ κατ᾽ ἀρχὰς..., which gives poor sense.

Homer conceals a philosophical idea in these lines too. It is not because he wants to delight his hearers by poetical inventions that he has told us of a lame Hephaestus—not of course the son of Hera and Zeus whom we know from mythology: that would indeed be an improper tale to tell of the gods. No: the substance of fire is of two kinds; ethereal fire, as we said just now, <suspended> in the highest <region> of the universe, lacks nothing for perfection, whereas the substance of the fire that we possess, being terrestrial, is destructible and is repeatedly rekindled by the matter that feeds it.[1] This is why Homer regularly calls the most brilliant fire "Sun" or "Zeus," and the fire on earth which is readily kindled and extinguished "Hephaestus." Compared with the complete fire, *this* fire is plausibly regarded as "lame."[2] Moreover, crippled feet always need a stick as support, and the fire we have, which could not last any long time without having wood put on it, is thus symbolically described as "lame."[3] Indeed, Homer elsewhere calls fire Hephaestus in plain words, not allegorically at all:

They held the entrails, spitted, over Hephaestus.[4]

In saying that the entrails are roasted by Hephaestus, he uses metalepsis.

Homer's representation of Hephaestus as "thrown down from heaven" is also scientific. For in the earliest times, when the use of fire was not yet common, men on occasion[5] made use of certain bronze instruments that they had constructed to draw down sparks from above, positioning these instruments to face the sun at midday. This, I take it, is why Prometheus[6] is believed to have stolen fire from heaven, since it was the forethought [*prometheia*] of human skill which contrived the flow of fire from there. Nor was it unreasonable for Homer to make Lemnos the place that first[7] received the fire that came from the gods: for spontaneous

---

1. For the distinction between pure and terrestrial fire, cf. Cornutus, *Theol.* ch. 19 = p. 33.12–14 Lang, with Ramelli (2003, 356 n. 145).

2. Cf. Cornutus, *Theol.* ch. 19 = p. 33.18–34.3 Lang.

3. Cf. Plutarch, *Fac.* 922B.

4. *Il.* 2.426. Quoted as an example of "metonymy" in Trypho, *On Figures* 3.195 Spengel (metonymy and metalepsis, as defined by Trypho, are very similar). See Ps.-Plutarch, *Vit. poes. Hom.* 2.23.2 with Hillgruber's notes (1994–1999, 1:138).

5. If this is what *khronikôs* means. Buffière offers "avec le temps," "à intervalles chroniques," "en accord avec l'époque." The instruments were perhaps "burning-glasses," i.e., bronze mirrors used to concentrate the sun's rays (cf. Theophrastus, *On Fire* 73); Archimedes is said to have employed them to burn the Roman ships at Syracuse (Lucian, *Hippias* 2, John Tzetzes [twelfth century], *Chiliades* 2.103–127, in Thomas 1951, 2:18–20).

6. Cf. Cornutus, *Theol.* ch. 18 = p. 31.19ff. Lang with Ramelli (2003, 355 n. 140).

7. Taking *prôton* with *hupodexamenên* despite the word order.

γηγενοῦς[1] πυρὸς αὐτόματοι φλόγες. **26.16** Δηλοῖ δὲ σαφῶς, ὅτι τοῦτο θεωρητόν[2] ἐστι τὸ πῦρ, ἐξ ὧν ἐπήνεγκεν·

ὀλίγος δ᾽ ἔτι θυμὸς ἐνῆεν.

Ἀπόλλυται γὰρ εὐθέως μαρανθέν, εἰ μὴ λάβοιτο τῆς διαφυλάττειν αὐτὸ δυναμένης προνοίας.

27.1 Καὶ ταῦτα μὲν περὶ Ἡφαίστου φιλοσοφητέον. **27.2** Ἐῶ γὰρ ἐπὶ τοῦ παρόντος ὡς τερατείαν τινὰ τὴν Κράτητος φιλοσοφίαν, ὅτι Ζεὺς ἀναμέτρησιν τοῦ παντὸς ἐσπουδακὼς γενέσθαι δύο πυρσοῖς ἰσοδρομοῦσιν, Ἡφαίστῳ τε καὶ Ἡλίῳ, διετεκμήρατο τοῦ κόσμου τὰ διαστήματα, τὸν μὲν ἄνωθεν ἀπὸ τοῦ βηλοῦ καλουμένου ῥίψας, τὸν δ᾽ ἀπ᾽ ἀνατολῆς εἰς δύσιν ἀφεὶς φέρεσθαι· **27.3** διὰ τοῦτ᾽ ἀμφότεροι καὶ συνεχρόνισαν, "ἅμα" γὰρ "ἠελίῳ καταδύντι κάππεσεν" Ἥφαιστος "ἐν Λήμνῳ." **27.4** Τοῦτο τοίνυν εἴτε κοσμική τις ἀναμέτρησις, εἴθ᾽, ὃ μᾶλλον ἀληθές ἐστιν, ἀλληγορικὴ τοῦ καθ᾽ ἡμᾶς πυρὸς ἀνθρώποις παράδοσις, οὐδὲν ἀσεβὲς ὑπὲρ Ἡφαίστου παρ᾽ Ὁμήρῳ λέλεκται.

28.1 Καὶ μὴν ἐπὶ τῆς δευτέρας ῥαψῳδίας ἀνακομιζομένων τῶν Ἑλλήνων Ὀδυσσεῖ διαποροῦντι παρέστηκεν οὐκ ἄλλη τις, ἀλλ᾽ ἡ θεία φρόνησις, ἣν Ἀθηνᾶν ὀνομάζει. **28.2** Καὶ τὴν ἀποστελλομένην Ἶριν ἄγγελον τοῦ Διὸς τὸν εἴροντα λόγον ὑφίσταται, ὥσπερ Ἑρμῆν τὸν ἑρμηνεύοντα· **28.3** δύο γὰρ ἄγγελοι θεῶν, οὐδενὸς ἄλλου πλὴν ἐπώνυμοι τῆς κατὰ τὸν λόγον ἑρμηνείας.

---

1. Te, following the Homeric scholia on *Od.* 8.284; mss., Bu read ἐγγυγηγενοῦς, translating "presque sorti de terre," but the form is impossible Greek.
2. Mss., Bu, who however translates "visible," which does not make sense; Te, following the excerpt in the Homeric scholia, reads θεώρρυτον, i.e., that this fire flows from the gods.

flames of earth-born fire rise from the ground there.[1] He makes it clear
that this is the fire which is under consideration by adding

"not much breath left in me";[2]

for fire quickly fades and goes out if it does not secure the forethought
that can keep it alive.

27 So much then for the philosophical significance of Hephaestus. I
pass over for the time being, as a mere fantasy, the doctrine of Crates,[3]
according to whom Zeus, desiring to measure the world, estimated the
dimensions of the universe by means of two beacons moving with equal
speed, Hephaestus and the Sun, casting Hephaestus down from what
Homer calls the "threshold" and letting the Sun take its course from
rising to setting. For this reason, the two synchronized, for "as the sun
set" Hephaestus "fell on Lemnos."[4] So, whether we have a sort of cosmic
measuring process, or (the truer view) an allegory of the transmission to
mankind of the fire which we use, Homer has said nothing impious
regarding Hephaestus.

28 Again in book 2, when the Greeks are for returning home and
Odysseus is at a loss, there comes to his aid no other than Divine
Wisdom, which Homer calls Athena. And by Iris, who is sent as a messenger of Zeus, he represents the "speaking" [*eironta*] word, just as by
Hermes he represents the "explicatory" [*hermêneuonta*] word:[5] these two
messengers of the gods simply designate the verbal expression of thought
[*hermêneia*].

---

1. For the language, cf. Longinus, *Subl.* 35.5: *potamous ... tou gêgenous ekeinou kai automa-
tou prokheousi puros.*

2. *Il.* 1.593.

3. This is the only place where Crates is mentioned, however much his work may have
been a source for Heraclitus (e.g., perhaps, in ascribing to Homer a knowledge of the
sphericity of the earth in section 43). Crates came from Mallus in Cilicia (cf. Diogenes Laertius 4.23), and was a contemporary of Aristarchus, with whom he debated points of
grammar. For a full discussion of his interpretations of Homer and their relevance to allegorical criticism, see Ramelli (2004, 171–203).

4. *Il.* 1.592.

5. Other ancient etymologies are known: Iris = *eris*, "strife" (Servius on *Aen.* 9.2); *iris
quasi aeris* ("as though of air," Isidore of Seville, *Etymologies* 13.10.1). For the derivation from
eirô, see Scholia on Hesiod, *Theog.* 266 = *SVF* 2.137: *iris de ho prophorikos logos* ("Iris is the
overt word"). Heraclitus elsewhere (72.15) distinguishes the two kinds of *logos, prophorikos*
and *endiathetos.* Cf. also Cornutus, *Theol.* ch. 16 = p. 20.18–23 Lang, with Ramelli (2003, 331
n. 83 and 336 n. 93).

28.4 Ἀλλ' ἀπρεπῶς Ἀφροδίτη μαστροπεύει πρὸς Ἀλέξανδρον Ἑλένην. **28.5** Ἀγνοοῦσι γὰρ ὅτι νῦν λέγει τὴν ἐν τοῖς ἐρωτικοῖς πάθεσιν ἀφροσύνην, ἣ μεσίτης ἐστὶ καὶ διάκονος ἀεὶ μειρακιώδους ἐπιθυμίας· **28.6** αὕτη καὶ τόπον εὗρεν ἐπιτήδειον, ὅπου τὸν Ἑλένης δίφρον ἀφιδρύσει, καὶ ποικίλοις μαγγάνοις ἑκατέρων κινεῖ τὸν πόθον, Ἀλεξάνδρου μὲν ἐρωτικῶς ἔτι διακειμένου, τῆς δ' Ἑλένης μετανοεῖν ἀρχομένης. **28.7** Διὸ δὴ κατ' ἀρχὰς ἀντειποῦσα τοὔσχατον ὑπείκει, μεταξὺ δυοῖν φερομένη παθῶν, ἔρωτός τε τοῦ πρὸς Ἀλέξανδρον καὶ αἰδοῦς τῆς πρὸς Μενέλαον.

29.1 Ἥ γε μὴν εὐωχουμένοις[1] ὑποδιακονουμένη κατ' ἀρχὰς Ἥβη τίς ἂν εἴη πλὴν ἡ διηνεκῶς ἐν ταῖς εὐφροσύναις νεότης; **29.2** οὐδὲν γὰρ ἐν οὐρανῷ γῆρας, οὐδ' ὕπεστί τι ταῖς θείαις φύσεσιν[2] ἔσχατον βίου νόσημα. **29.3** Πάσης δ' ἐξαιρέτως θυμηδίας ὡσπερεὶ συνεκτικὸν ὄργανόν ἐστιν ἡ τῶν συνεληλυθότων ἐπὶ τὴν εὐφροσύνην ἀκμή.

29.4 Περὶ μέν γε τῆς Ἔριδος οὐδ' ὑπεσταλμένως ἠλληγόρησεν οὐδ' ὥστε δεῖσθαι λεπτῆς τινος εἰκασίας, ἀλλ' ἐκ τοῦ φανεροῦ τὰ κατ' αὐτὴν πεπόμπευκεν·

Ἥ τ' ὀλίγη μὲν πρῶτα κορύσσεται, αὐτὰρ ἔπειτα
οὐρανῷ ἐστήριξε κάρη καὶ ἐπὶ χθονὶ βαίνει.

29.5 Διὰ γὰρ τούτων τῶν ἐπῶν οὐ θεά τις οὕτω παντάπασιν τερατώδης ὑφ' Ὁμήρου μεμόρφωται, τὰς πρὸς ἑκάτερον μεταβολὰς τοῦ σώματος ἀπίστους ἔχουσα καὶ ποτὲ μὲν ἐπὶ γῆς ἐρριμμένη ταπεινή, ποτὲ δ' εἰς ἄπειρον αἰθέρος ἐκτειναμένη μέγεθος, **29.6** ἀλλ' ὃ συμβέβηκεν ἀεὶ τοῖς φιλονεικοῦσι πάθος ἐκ ταύτης τῆς ἀλληγορίας διετύπωσεν· **29.7** ἀρξαμένη γὰρ ἀπὸ λιτῆς αἰτίας ἡ ἔρις, ἐπειδὰν ὑποκινηθῇ, πρὸς μέγα δή τι κακοῦ[3] διογκοῦται.

30.1 Καὶ ταυτὶ μὲν ἴσως μετριώτερα. Πολλὴ δὴ καθ' Ὁμήρου τραγῳδία σκηνοβατεῖται παρὰ τοῖς ἀγνωμόνως αὐτὸν ἐθέλουσι συκοφαντεῖν, ὅτι παρεισάγει κατὰ τὴν πέμπτην ῥαψῳδίαν τιτρωσκομένους θεούς, Ἀφροδίτην τὸ πρῶτον ὑπὸ Διομήδους, εἶτ' Ἄρην. **30.2** Προστιθέασι δὲ τούτοις, ὅσα

---

1. Te inserts τοῖς θεοῖς ("the gods") here from the Homeric scholia, but the meaning is clear enough without the addition.
2. Russell; τῆς θείας φύσεως mss., Te, Bu.
3. A, Bu; Te, other mss. read κακόν; the sense is the same.

"But it is indecent to have Aphrodite procuring Helen for Alexander."[1] This shows a failure to understand that Homer here means the folly [*aphrosunê*] involved in the passion of love, a folly which is always the go-between and servant of boyish desire.[2] Aphrodite also found an appropriate place to set Helen's chair, and she stimulates the desire of both of them by various charms—Alexander being still in love, but Helen beginning to change her mind. This is why she first refused but finally yields, caught between two passions, love for Alexander and respect for Menelaus.

29 Again, what can be meant by Hebe's serving the banqueters at the beginning except youth's perpetual involvement in merriment?[3] For there is no old age in heaven, and divine beings do not suffer this last illness of life. In any specially happy occasion, the instrument, as it were, that holds it all together is the youthful prime of the company who have gathered to enjoy the pleasure.

Turning next to Eris, we find that Homer has not used allegory covertly here, or in a way demanding subtle conjecture; indeed, he has paraded his account of her in plain terms:

Small when she first arms, but later on
her head hits heaven as she walks on earth.[4]

In these lines, it is not a goddess to which Homer has given shape—one so utterly monstrous, capable of incredible changes and reversals of form, one moment cast down upon the ground, and the next reaching up to the infinite grandeur of the aether. Instead, he has used this allegory to portray vividly what always happens to quarrelsome people: strife begins with a trivial cause, but once roused it swells up into what is indeed a great evil.

30 These are perhaps matters of no more than modest importance. But Homer's ignorant traducers mount a great dramatic show against him for introducing, in book 5, wounded gods—Aphrodite first, wounded by Diomedes, and then Ares. They add further accusations against the stories

---

1. See *Il.* 3.424ff.

2. For this etymology, cf. Cornutus, *Theol.* ch. 24 = p. 45.6–7 Lang, with Ramelli (2003, 372 n. 193).

3. *Il.* 4.2–3: our text does not make it clear that this is "the beginning" of book 4, and perhaps some words have fallen out.

4. *Il.* 4.442–443.

κατὰ παρηγορίαν ἡ Διώνη περὶ τῶν ἔτι πρότερον ἠτυχηκότων ἀπαγγέλλει θεῶν. **30.3** Ἐν μέρει δ᾽ ὑπὲρ ἑκάστου τὸν λόγον ἀποδώσομεν ἡμεῖς οὐδεμιᾶς[1] ἐκτὸς ὄντα φιλοσοφίας.

30.4 Διομήδης γὰρ Ἀθηνᾶν ἔχων σύμμαχον, τουτέστι τὴν φρόνησιν, ἔτρωσεν Ἀφροδίτην, τὴν ἀφροσύνην,[2] οὐ μὰ Δία οὐ θεάν τινα, τὴν δὲ τῶν μαχομένων βαρβάρων ἀλογιστίαν. **30.5** Αὐτὸς μὲν γὰρ ἅτε διὰ πάσης ἐληλυθὼς πολεμικῆς μαθήσεως καὶ τοῦτο μὲν ἐν Θήβαις, τοῦτο δ᾽ ἐν Ἰλίῳ δεκαετῆ χρόνον ἐμφρόνως τοῦ μάχεσθαι προϊστάμενος, ἐξ εὐμαροῦς διώκει τοὺς βαρβάρους· **30.6** οἵ δ᾽, ἀναίσθητοι καὶ λογισμῶν ὀλίγα κοινωνοῦντες, ὑπ᾽ αὐτοῦ διώκονται καθάπερ "ὄιες πολυπάμονος ἀνδρὸς ἐν αὐλῇ." **30.7** Πολλῶν οὖν φονευομένων ἀλληγορικῶς Ὅμηρος τὴν βαρβαρικὴν ἀφροσύνην ὑπὸ Διομήδους τετρῶσθαι παρεισήγαγεν.

31.1 Ὁμοίως δ᾽ ὁ Ἄρης οὐδέν ἐστιν ἄλλο πλὴν ὁ πόλεμος, παρὰ τὴν ἀρὴν ὠνομασμένος, ἥπερ ἐστὶ βλάβη. **31.2** Γένοιτο δ᾽ ἂν ἡμῖν τοῦτο σαφὲς ἐκ τοῦ λέγειν αὐτὸν

μαινόμενον, τυκτὸν κακόν, ἀλλοπρόσαλλον·

ἐπιθέτοις γὰρ ἁρμόζουσι πολέμῳ κέχρηται μᾶλλον ἢ θεῷ. **31.3** Μανίας γάρ εἰσι πλήρεις ἅπαντες οἱ μαχόμενοι, πρὸς τὸν κατ᾽ ἀλλήλων φόνον ἐνθουσιαστικῶς ζέσαντες· **31.4** καὶ τὸ ἀλλοπρόσαλλον ἑτέρωθί που διὰ πλειόνων ἐξηγεῖται λέγων·

ξυνὸς Ἐνυάλιος, καί τε κτανέοντα κατέκτα.

31.5 Νεμεσηταὶ γὰρ αἱ πολέμων ἐπ᾽ ἀμφότερα ῥοπαί, καὶ τὸ νικηθὲν οὐδὲ προσαντῆσαν[3] αἰφνιδίως πολλάκις ἐκράτησεν· ὥστε τῆς ἐν ταῖς μάχαις ἀμφιβολίας ἄλλοτε πρὸς ἄλλους μεταφοιτώσης ἐτύμως κακὸν ἀλλοπρόσαλλον εἴρηκε [πρὸς][4] τὸν πόλεμον. **31.6** Ἐτρώθη δ᾽ ὑπὸ Διομήδους Ἄρης οὐ κατ᾽ ἄλλο τι μέρος, ἀλλὰ "νείατον ἐς κενεῶνα," σφόδρα πιθανῶς· **31.7** ἐπὶ γὰρ τὰ κενὰ τῆς μὴ πάνυ φρουρουμένης τῶν ἀντιπάλων τάξεως παρεισελθὼν εὐμαρῶς ἐτρέψατο τοὺς βαρβάρους. **31.8** Καὶ μὴν χάλκεον λέγει τὸν Ἄρην τὰς τῶν μαχομένων πανοπλίας ὑποσημαίνων· σπάνιος γὰρ ἦν ὁ σίδηρος ἐν τῷ τότε πάλαι χρόνῳ, τὸ δὲ σύμπαν ἐσκέποντο χαλκῷ. **31.9** Διὰ τοῦτό φησιν·

---

1. Perhaps read οὐδαμῶς, i.e., "which does not at all depart from...."
2. Te suggests deleting τὴν ἀφροσύνην, perhaps rightly (the Homeric scholia have ἤτοι τὴν ἀφροσύνην; on ἤτοι in this sense, see 13.1 n. 1).
3. Perhaps read οὐδὲ προσδοκῆσαν, "without even expecting it" (Polak).
4. πρὸς is omitted by the Homeric scholia and Te; Bu retains it, and translates "songeant à la guerre."

of still earlier misfortunes of gods which Dione tells to comfort Aphrodite.[1] I shall offer, in regard to each of these episodes in turn, an account which is entirely based on philosophical principles.

Diomedes, with Athena (that is to say, Wisdom) as his ally, wounded Aphrodite—that is, Folly [*aphrosunê*]—not of course a goddess, but the foolishness of his barbarian adversaries. Having had a thorough military education and having been a prudent battle commander both at Thebes and in ten years at Troy, he easily puts the barbarians to flight; and they, foolish as they are and not endowed with much intelligence, are chased by him "like sheep on a rich man's holding."[2] Many are massacred, and Homer has represented this allegorically as barbarian folly wounded by Diomedes.

31 Similarly, Ares simply stands for war. He takes his name from *arê*, which means "harm."[3] This should be clear to us from Homer's calling him

madman, embodied evil, double-faced,[4]

for he here uses adjectives which apply better to war than to a god. All men who fight are full of madness, boiling with zeal for mutual murder. "Double-faced" is explained more fully in another passage, where he says:

Enyalios favors none: he kills the killer.[5]

Wars bring retribution as they swing back and forth, and the defeated side often suddenly prevails without even going on the offensive; so, as the fortune of battle passes now to one side and now to the other [*allote pros allous*], Homer has good reason to call war *kakon alloprosallon*, "evil, double-faced." Ares was wounded by Diomedes in a particular place, "in the hollow of the flank [*keneôn*]."[6] This is plausible, for it was by slipping through the empty [*kena*] part of the ill-defended enemy line that he was able to rout the barbarians easily. Again, Homer calls Ares "brazen," suggesting the full armor of the warriors, for iron was scarce in those old days and they universally protected themselves with bronze. This is why Homer says

---

1. *Il.* 5.382ff.
2. *Il.* 4.433.
3. So Cornutus, *Theol.* ch. 21 = p. 41.4 Lang, with alternative derivations from *hairein*, "seize," and *anairein*, "destroy"; cf. Ramelli (2003, 366 n. 176, 367 n. 177, 368 n. 180).
4. *Il.* 5.831.
5. *Il.* 18.309.
6. *Il.* 5.857.

Ὄσσε δ᾽ ἄμερδεν
αὐγὴ χαλκείη κορύθων ἀπὸ λαμπομενάων
θωρήκων τε νεοσμήκτων.

31.10 Ἀναβοᾷ δὲ τρωθεὶς

ὅσσον τ᾽ ἐννεάχιλοι ἐπίαχον ἢ δεκάχιλοι.

Καὶ τοῦτο δὲ τεκμήριον πολλῶν διωκομένων πολεμίων· οὐ γὰρ ἂν εἷς θεὸς ἀνεβόησε τοσοῦτον, ἀλλ᾽ ἡ φεύγουσα μυρίανδρος οἶμαι τῶν βαρβάρων φάλαγξ. **31.11** Ὥστ᾽ ἐναργέσι τεκμηρίοις καὶ διὰ τῶν κατὰ μέρος ἐδείξαμεν οὐκ Ἄρην τὸν τετρωμένον ὑπὸ Διομήδους, ἀλλὰ τὸν πόλεμον.

32.1 Αὗται δ᾽ ἐν παρεκβάσει τῶν προτέρων ἀλληγοριῶν [δι᾽ ὧν]¹ καὶ τεχνικωτέραν ἔχουσιν ἐμπειρίαν, ἐν οἷς φησί·

Τλῆ μὲν Ἄρης, ὅτε μιν Ὦτος κρατερός τ᾽ Ἐπιάλτης,
παῖδες Ἀλωῆος, δῆσαν κρατερῷ ἐνὶ δεσμῷ.

32.2 Γεννικοὶ γὰρ οὗτοι οἱ κατ᾽ ἀλκὴν² νεανίαι³ ταραχῆς καὶ πολέμου μεστὸν ᾔδεσαν τὸν βίον· **32.3** οὐδεμιᾶς δ᾽ εἰρηνικῆς ἀναπαύσεως μέσης τοὺς παρ᾽ ἕκαστα κάμνοντας ἀνείσης, ἰδίοις ὅπλοις ἐκστρατευσάμενοι τὴν ἐπιπολάζουσαν ἀηδίαν ἀνέστειλαν. **32.4** Ἄχρι μὲν οὖν τρεισκαίδεκα μηνῶν ἀκλινής < τ᾽ ἦν>⁴ καὶ ἀστασίαστος αὐτῶν ὁ οἶκος ἐν ὁμονοίᾳ τε⁵ τὴν εἰρήνην διεστρατήγει· **32.5** μητρυιὰ δὲ παρεισπεσοῦσα, φιλόνεικος⁶ οἰκίας νόσος, ἀνέτρεψε πάντα καὶ διέφθειρε⁷ τὴν προτέραν εὐστάθειαν· **32.6** ἐκ δευτέρου δὲ πάλιν ὁμοίας ταραχῆς ἀναφθείσης ἔδοξεν ὁ Ἄρης ἀπὸ τοῦ δεσμωτηρίου λελύσθαι, τουτέστιν ὁ πόλεμος.

33.1 Ἡρακλέα δὲ νομιστέον οὐκ ἀπὸ σωματικῆς δυνάμεως ἀναχθέντα τοσοῦτον ἰσχῦσαι τοῖς τότε χρόνοις, ἀλλ᾽ ἀνὴρ ἔμφρων καὶ σοφίας οὐρανίου

---

1. Deleted by Russell (dittography).
2. Te inserts ἰσχυροί, "strong," following Homeric scholia.
3. Te, following the Homeric scholia and the Aldine edition, inserts γεγονότες, ἐπειδή, that is, they were noble, strong and valiant "since they knew...," eliminating punctuation after βίον.
4. Inserted by Mehler.
5. Te deletes τε; Bu punctuates with a comma after οἶκος.
6. Mss., Bu read καὶ ("and") before φιλόνεικος; Te, following the Homeric scholia, omits καὶ but places the comma after φιλόνεικος.
7. Te, following Homeric scholia; mss., Bu omit πάντα καὶ διέφθειρε = "[she upset] everything and destroyed...."

Their eyes were dazzled by the brazen glare
from shining helm and polished breastplate.[1]

The wounded Ares cries

as if nine or ten thousand men were shrieking,[2]

and here too is an indication that many of the enemy were routed: a single god would not have given such a shout, but the fleeing host of the barbarians, ten thousand strong, would I imagine. I have thus demonstrated by clear proofs and in detail that it was war, and not Ares, that was wounded by Diomedes.

32 The following, in the digression,[3] demonstrates an even more subtle skill than the preceding allegories. I mean the lines:

Ares endured, when Otus and strong Epialtes,
Aloeus's sons, bound him in powerful bonds.[4]

These noble and valiant young men knew that life was full of confusion and war, and as no peaceful interval of rest relieved their perpetual troubles, they took up arms themselves and went to war to put an end to the distress that lay upon them. For thirteen months their house was undisturbed and untroubled and maintained peace and concord. But then there came a stepmother, a plague that brings strife on a house, and she upset everything and destroyed their old stability. A similar disturbance flared up a second time, and this made it seem that Ares—that is, war—had been let out of prison.

33 I turn to Heracles.[5] We must not suppose that he attained such power in those days as a result of his physical strength. Rather, he was a man of intellect, an initiate in heavenly wisdom, who, as it were, shed

---

1. *Il.* 13.340–342.

2. *Il.* 5.860.

3. I.e., in Dione's speech, which gives examples of gods' sufferings; cf. 30.2.

4. *Il.* 5.385–386.

5. Compare Cornutus, *Theol.* ch. 31 = pp. 62–64 Lang, with Ramelli (2003, 392 nn. 244, 246). For Heracles as a philosopher, see Plutarch, *E Delph.* 387D.

μύστης γεγονὼς¹ ὡσπερεὶ κατὰ βαθείας ἀχλύος ὑποδεδυκυῖαν² ἐφώτισε τὴν φιλοσοφίαν, καθάπερ ὁμολογοῦσι καὶ Στωικῶν οἱ δοκιμώτατοι. **33.2** Περὶ μὲν οὖν τῶν ἄλλων ἄθλων, ὁπόσοι τῆς παρ' Ὁμήρῳ μνήμης ὑστεροῦσι, τί δεῖ παρὰ καιρὸν ἐκμηκύνειν φιλοτεχνοῦντας; **33.3** ὅτι κάπρον μὲν εἷλε, τὴν ἐπιπολάζουσαν ἀνθρώποις ἀκολασίαν, λέοντα δέ, τὴν ἀκρίτως ὁρμῶσαν ἐφ' ἃ μὴ δεῖ φοράν· **33.4** κατὰ ταὐτὸ³ δὲ θυμοὺς ἀλογίστους πεδήσας τὸν ὑβριστὴν ταῦρον ἐνομίσθη δεδεκέναι· **33.5** δειλίαν γε μὴν ἐφυγάδευσεν ἐκ τοῦ βίου, τὴν Κερυνείαν ἔλαφον. **33.6** Καί τις ἀπρεπῶς ὀνομαζόμενος ἆθλος ἐκμεμόχθηται διακαθήραντος αὐτοῦ τὴν <πολύχουν κόπρον τὴν>⁴ ἐπιτρέχουσαν ἀνθρώποις ἀηδίαν. **33.7** Ὄρνεις δέ, τὰς ὑπηνέμους⁵ ἐλπίδας, αἳ βόσκουσι τὸν βίον ἡμῶν, ἀπεσκέδασε· **33.8** [δὲ]⁶ καὶ τὴν [πολύχουν κόπρον καὶ] πολυκέφαλον ὕδραν,⁷ τὴν ἡδονήν,⁸ ἥτις ὅταν ἐκκοπῇ πάλιν ἄρχεται βλαστάνειν, ὥσπερ διὰ πυρός τινος τῆς παραινέσεως ἐξέκαυσεν.⁹ **33.9** Αὐτός γε μὴν ὁ τρικέφαλος δειχθεὶς ἡλίῳ Κέρβερος εἰκότως ἂν τὴν τριμερῆ φιλοσοφίαν ὑπαινίττοιτο· τὸ μὲν γὰρ αὐτῆς λογικόν, τὸ δὲ φυσικόν, τὸ δὲ ἠθικὸν ὀνομάζεται· **33.10** ταῦτα δ' ὥσπερ ἀφ' ἑνὸς αὐχένος ἐκπεφυκότα τριχῆ κατὰ κεφαλὴν μερίζεται.

34.1 Περὶ μὲν δὴ τῶν ἄλλων, ὥσπερ εἶπον, ἄθλων ἐν συντόμῳ δεδήλωται. **34.2** Τετρωμένην δ' Ὅμηρος ὑπεστήσατο τὴν Ἥραν, τοῦτο ἀκριβῶς παραστῆσαι βουλόμενος, ὅτι τὸν θολερὸν ἀέρα καὶ πρὸ τῆς ἑκάστου διανοίας ἐπαχλύοντα πρῶτος Ἡρακλῆς θείῳ χρησάμενος λόγῳ διήρθρωσε, τὴν ἑκάστου τῶν ἀνθρώπων ἀμαθίαν πολλαῖς νουθεσίαις κατατρώσας. **34.3** Ὅθεν ἀπὸ γῆς εἰς οὐρανὸν ἀφίησι τὰ τόξα. Πᾶς γὰρ ἀνὴρ φιλόσοφος ἐν θνητῷ καὶ ἐπιγείῳ τῷ σώματι πτηνὸν ὥσπερ τι βέλος τὸν νοῦν εἰς τὰ μετάρσια διαπέμπεται. **34.4** Τεχνικῶς δὲ προσέθηκεν εἰπών· "ἰῷ τριγλώχινι βαλών,"

---

1. Te, following Homeric scholia; Bu omits γεγονώς (the sense in not affected).
2. Te, following Heyne; Bu, following mss. and Homeric scholia, reads ἐπιδεδυκυῖαν, translating "plongée," but it is doubtful that the compound can bear this meaning.
3. Te in apparatus criticus (cf. Bu in translation); mss., Te, Bu read κατ' αὐτό.
4. Transposed here from below (33.8) by Mehler, followed by Te, Bu.
5. Hemsterhuis, followed by Te; Bu retains the mss. συνηνέμους, which might mean "exposed to the wind."
6. Deleted by Te, followed by Bu.
7. Bu emends to ὕβριν, "hybris" or "arrogance," but this is a poor fit, especially since hybris has already been associated with the bull.
8. Omitted by A, Bu. But the text of this passage is puzzling (whence δέ after ἀπεσκέδασε?), and perhaps a verb meaning "killed" or "finished off" has fallen out, e.g. <κατειργάσατο> δέ.
9. Te, following Homeric scholia; mss., Bu read ὥσπερ ὕδραν τινὰ διὰ πυρὸς ... ἐξέκοψεν, "cut off with fire, as though a hydra" (cf. n. 7) but translates "en la brûlant au feu."

light on philosophy, which had been hidden in deep darkness.[1] The most authoritative of the Stoics agree with this account. As regards those labors which find no place in[2] the Homeric tradition, there is surely no need for me to display my ingenuity in a lengthy but irrelevant disquisition. The boar which he overcame is the common incontinence of men; the lion is the indiscriminate rush towards improper goals; in the same way, by fettering irrational passions he gave rise to the belief that he had fettered the violent bull. He banished cowardice also from the world, in the shape of the hind of Ceryneia. There was another "labor" too, not properly so called, in which he cleared out the mass of dung—in other words, the foulness that disfigures humanity. The birds he scattered are the windy hopes that feed our lives; the many-headed hydra that he burned, as it were, with the fires of exhortation, is pleasure,[3] which begins to grow again as soon as it is cut out. On the other hand, the three-headed Cerberus, whom he brought into the light of day, is probably meant to suggest the three branches of philosophy—logic, physics, and ethics, as they are called—which grow as it were out of a single neck, and divide into three at the head.[4]

34 I have, as I promised, given only a very brief account of these other labors. But in representing the wounding of Hera[5] Homer wants to show us precisely that Heracles was the first to use divine reason in order to bring structure to the confused mist [aer] which clouds every individual's mind; he did this by "wounding" every human being's ignorance by repeated reproofs. Heracles therefore shoots his arrows from ground to heaven, because every philosopher, in his mortal and earthly body, despatches his thought, like a winged arrow, to the realms above. Homer added ingeniously, "striking with three-pointed shaft"—the "three-

---

1. Cf. the "old" scholia to Homer, *Il.* 5.392.

2. Or perhaps "which are later than...."

3. An improbable allegorical signification for the hydra. It may be that hopes are paired with pleasure as two of the four classes of *pathê* defined by the Stoics; the desire for pleasure (rather than pleasure itself) grows again as soon as it is cut off. Other sins compared to the hydra are effeminacy (Plutarch, *Cat. Maj.* 16), avarice (Horace, *Carm.* 2.2.12), and doubt (Boethius, *Consolation of Philosophy* 4 pr. 6).

4. Various ways of describing the relationship between the three branches of philosophy are given in Sextus Empiricus, *Math.* 7.16 and similar passages (*SVF* 2.15–17); cf. Cornutus, *Theol.* ch. 14 = p. 15.1–5 Lang, with Ramelli (2003, 324 n. 66).

5. *Il.* 5.392–394.

ἵνα διὰ συντόμου τὴν τριμερῆ φιλοσοφίαν ὑπὸ[1] τοῦ τριγλώχινος ὑποσημήνη βέλους. **34.5** Μεθ' Ἥραν[2] δὲ τετόξευκε καὶ τὸν Ἀιδην· οὐδεὶς γὰρ ἄβατος φιλοσοφίᾳ χῶρος, ἀλλὰ μετὰ τὸν οὐρανὸν ἐζήτησε τὴν κατωτάτω φύσιν, ἵνα μηδὲ τῶν νέρθεν ἀμύητος ἦ. **34.6** Τὸν οὖν ἀλαμπῆ καὶ πᾶσιν ἀνθρώποις ἄβα-τον Ἀιδην ὁ τῆς σοφίας ὀιστὸς εὔστοχα βληθεὶς διευκρίνησεν. **34.7** Ὣσθ' αἱ Ἡρακλέους χεῖρες ἁγνεύουσι παντὸς Ὀλυμπίου μύσους. **34.8** Ἀρχηγὸς δὲ πάσης σοφίας γενόμενος Ὅμηρος[3] ἀλληγορικῶς παρέδωκε τοῖς μετ' αὐτὸν ἀρύσασθαι κατὰ μέρη πάνθ' ὅσα πρῶτος πεφιλοσόφηκε.

35.1 Νομίζουσι τοίνυν ἔνιοι μηδὲ Διόνυσον εἶναι παρ' Ὁμήρῳ θεόν, ἐπειδήπερ ὑπὸ Λυκούργου διώκεται καὶ μόλις δοκεῖ σωτηρίας τυχεῖν Θέτιδος αὐτῷ παραστάσης. **35.2** Τὸ δ' ἐστὶν οἴνου συγκομιδῆς γεωργοῖς ἀλληγορία, δι' ὧν φησίν·

Ὅς ποτε μαινομένοιο Διωνύσοιο τιθήνας
σεῦε κατ' ἠγάθεον Νυσήιον· αἱ δ' ἅμα πᾶσαι
θύσθλα χαμαὶ κατέχευον, ὑπ' ἀνδροφόνοιο Λυκούργου
θεινόμεναι βουπλῆγι. Διώνυσος δὲ φοβηθεὶς
δύσεθ' ἁλὸς κατὰ κῦμα, Θέτις δ' ὑπεδέξατο κόλπῳ
δειδιότα.

35.3 Μαινόμενον μὲν εἴρηκεν ἀντὶ Διονύσου τὸν οἶνον, ἐπειδήπερ οἱ πλείονι τῷ ποτῷ χρώμενοι τοῦ λογισμοῦ διασφάλλονται· ὥσπερ τὸ δέος εἰ τύχοι χλωρὸν λέγει, καὶ πευκεδανὸν τὸν πόλεμον· ἃ γὰρ ἀπ' αὐτῶν συμβαίνει, ταῦτα ἐκείνοις περιῆψεν, ὅθεν ἄρχεται τὰ πάθη. **35.4** Λυκοῦργος δ' ἀνὴρ εὐαμπέλου λήξεως δεσπότης κατὰ[4] τὴν ὀπωρινὴν ὥραν, ὅτε συγκομιδὴ τῶν Διονυσιακῶν καρπῶν ἐστιν, ἐπὶ τὴν εὐφορωτάτην ἐξεληλύθει Νύσαν· τιθήνας δὲ νομίζειν δεῖ τὰς ἀμπέλους. **35.5** Καὶ μετὰ τοῦτο ἔτι δρεπομένων τῶν βοτρύων φησί· "Διώνυσος δὲ φοβηθείς·" ἐπειδήπερ ὁ μὲν φόβος εἴωθε τρέπειν τὴν διάνοιαν, ὁ δὲ τῆς σταφυλῆς καρπὸς τρέπεται θλιβόμενος εἰς

---

1. Neither ἀπό (Te) nor ὑπό (mss., Bu) seems satisfactory; Heraclitus's normal usage would be διά (perhaps he avoided διά here because of διὰ συντόμου four words earlier; cf. 57.3 μετά, 78.19 διά with acc.).

2. Te, following the Homeric scholia (cf. μετὰ τὸν οὐρανόν [μετ' οὐρανόν mss., Bu] below); mss., Bu read μεθ' ἡμέραν = "by day," which seems pointless.

3. Inserting Ὅμηρος, with the Homeric scholia (omitted in Te, Bu); cf. Hillgruber (1994–1999, 1:31). The insertion may not be necessary: cf. 29.16 for a concluding sentence referring to Homer without naming him. It seems difficult to apply the sentence to Heracles (compare the conclusions to sections 35 and 37), but see Bu p. 107.

4. So Te, comparing 39.2; mss., Bu have μετά ("after the autumn"), perhaps rightly: the vintage comes later than most fruits and other crops.

pointed" missile concisely suggests the three branches of philosophy. After Hera, he also shot Hades, for no place is inaccessible to philosophy, but he, having done with heaven, sought out the lowest region, so as to be initiated into the secrets even of what lies below. Thus the well aimed arrow of wisdom has brought clarity to the darkness of Hades, where no human can tread. Heracles' hands therefore are innocent of any foul deed against Olympus. As the originator of all wisdom, Homer has, by using allegory, passed down to his successors the power of drawing from him, piece by piece, all the philosophy he was the first to discover.

35 Now some believe that Dionysus in Homer is not a god either, because he is pursued by Lycurgus and seems to be saved only with difficulty when Thetis comes to his aid. But this is an allegory of the farmers' wine-harvest.[1] These are the lines:

Who once pursued mad Dionysus's nurses
on holy Nyseïon, and on the ground
they threw their wands, by murderous Lycurgus
struck with the goad; in terror, Dionysus
dived down beneath the sea, and Thetis took him,
frightened, to her bosom.[2]

"Mad" applies not to Dionysus but to wine, because people who drink too much lose their reason;[3] it is like calling fear "pale" or war "piercing":[4] the poet attaches the effects of events to the events themselves from which those effects arise. Lycurgus, who was the owner of an estate good for winegrowing, had gone out in the autumn, when Dionysus's crops are harvested, to the very fertile region of Nysa. By "nurses" we must suppose the vines to be meant. Then, when the bunches are still being gathered [*drepomenôn*], we read that Dionysus was "in terror," because fear turns [*trepei*] the mind, just as the fruit of the grape is

---

1. For the allegory, cf. Cornutus, *Theol.* ch. 30 = p. 62.16–22 Lang. Buffière (1962, xxv) connects this passage with the rationalistic style of exegesis characteristic of Palaephetus.

2. *Il.* 6.132–137.

3. For the connection between Dionysus, wine, and madness, cf. Cornutus, *Theol.* ch. 30 = p. 60.4–9 Lang, with Ramelli (2003, 387 n. 233).

4. *Il.* 6.479, 10.8; cf. also Quintilian, *Inst.* 8.6.27.

οἶνον. **35.6** Ἔθος γε μὴν τοῖς πολλοῖς ἐπὶ φυλακῇ τοῦ διαμένειν ἀκλινῇ τὸν οἶνον[1] ἐπικιρνάναι θαλαττίῳ ὕδατι· **35.7** παρὰ τοῦτο ὁ Διόνυσος "δύσεθ᾽ ἁλὸς κατὰ κῦμα, Θέτις δ᾽ ὑπεδέξατο κόλπῳ," ἡ τελευταία μετὰ τὴν ἀπόθλιψιν τοῦ καρποῦ θέσις· αὕτη γὰρ ἐσχάτη δέχεται τὸν οἶνον. **35.8** "Δειδιότα·" τὸν ἐν ἀρχῇ τοῦ νεοθλιβοῦς γλεύκους παλμὸν καὶ τὴν μεθαρμόζουσαν ὁρμὴν δέος εἶπε καὶ[2] τρόμον. **35.9** Οὕτως Ὅμηρος οὐ φιλοσοφεῖν μόνον ἀλληγορικῶς ἀλλὰ καὶ γεωργεῖν [θεωρεῖν][3] ἐπίσταται.

36.1 Φυσικῆς δ᾽ ἅπτεται θεωρίας καὶ ὅταν ὁ Ζεὺς εἰς τὸ αὐτὸ συναθροίσας τοὺς θεοὺς ἅπαντας ἄρχηται τῶν μεγάλων ἀπειλῶν "ἀκροτάτη κορυφῇ πολυδειράδος Οὐλύμποιο." **36.2** Πρῶτος ἔστηκεν αὐτός, ἐπειδὴ τὴν ἀνωτάτω τάξιν, ὥσπερ ἐδηλοῦμεν, ἡ αἰθεριώδης ἐπέχει φύσις. **36.3** Σειρὰν δ᾽ ἀπήρτησεν ἀπὸ τοῦ αἰθέρος ἐπὶ πάντα χρυσῆν· οἱ γὰρ δεινοὶ τῶν φιλοσόφων περὶ ταῦτα ἀνάμματα πυρὸς εἶναι τὰς τῶν ἀστέρων περιόδους νομίζουσι. **36.4** Τὸ δὲ σφαιρικὸν ἡμῖν τοῦ κόσμου σχῆμα δι᾽ ἑνὸς ἐμέτρησε στίχου·

τόσσον ἔνερθ᾽ Ἀΐδεω, ὅσον οὐρανός ἐστ᾽ ἀπὸ γαίης.

36.5 Μεσαιτάτη γὰρ ἁπάντων ἑστία τις οὖσα καὶ κέντρου δύναμιν[4] ἐπέχουσα καθίδρυται βεβαίως ἡ γῆ πᾶσα. **36.6** Κύκλῳ δ᾽ ὑπὲρ αὐτὴν ὁ οὐρανὸς ἀπαύστοις περιφοραῖς εἰλούμενος ἀπ᾽ ἀνατολῆς εἰς δύσιν τὸν ἀεὶ δρόμον ἐλαύνει, συγκαθέλκεται δ᾽ ἡ τῶν ἀπλανῶν σφαῖρα. **36.7** Πᾶσαί γε μὴν αἱ ἀπὸ τοῦ περιέχοντος ἀνωτάτω κύκλου φερόμεναι πρὸς τὸ κέντρον εὐθεῖαι καὶ κατ᾽ ἀναγωγάς εἰσιν ἀλλήλαις ἴσαι. **36.8** Διὰ τοῦτο γεωμετρικῇ θεωρίᾳ τὸ σφαιρικὸν σχῆμα διεμέτρησεν, εἰπών·

τόσσον ἔνερθ᾽ Ἀΐδεω, ὅσον οὐρανός ἐστ᾽ ἀπὸ γαίης.

37.1 Ἔνιοι δ᾽ εἰσὶν οὕτως ἀμαθεῖς, ὡς αἰτιᾶσθαι τὸν Ὅμηρον καὶ περὶ τῶν Λιτῶν, εἰ τὰς Διὸς γονὰς οὕτως ὕβρισε διάστροφον αὐταῖς περιθεὶς ἀμορφίας χαρακτῆρα·

---

1. Te, following the Homeric scholia; Bu, with the mss., reads καρπόν, "crop," but translates "vin."

2. Te, following Homeric scholia; Bu, following the mss., reads γάρ and punctuates with a raised stop after ὁρμήν, rendering the following clause "d'est ce frémissement qu'Homère a nommé crainte"—but τρόμος is a synonym for fear, not for stirring.

3. Deleting θεωρεῖν (dittography) with Te, following Mehler; retained by Bu = "but also how to speculate about farming." For Homer's knowledge of all matters, cf. Plato, *Ion*; Strabo, *Geogr.* 1.1.2; etc.

4. Te, following Homeric scholia; Bu, with mss., reads δύναμιν κέντρου, accepting the resulting hiatus.

"turned" as it is crushed to make wine. It is also common practice to mix
the wine with sea water to prevent it from going off, and this is why
Dionysus "dived down beneath the sea and Thetis took him to her
bosom," Thetis being the final "laying down" [thesis] after the crushing of
the crop:[1] she is the last to "take" the wine. He is "frightened," because
Homer calls the first agitation of the newly pressed wine, and the activity
which causes it to change, fear and trembling. Thus Homer understands
not only how to philosophize allegorically, but also how to farm.

36 He touches again on scientific speculation when Zeus assembles
all the gods and begins his great threatening speech "on rocky Olympus's
topmost crest."[2] He stands there first himself, because (as I showed) the
aetherial substance holds the highest place. He then suspended a chain
of gold from the aether down onto all things. Philosophers expert in
these matters, let us note, believe that the orbits of the stars are trails of
fire.[3] He has also given us the measure of the sphere of the universe in a
single line:

as far below Hades, as heaven above earth;[4]

for the entire earth is midmost of all things, a kind of hearth, functioning
as the centre, and firmly fixed.[5] Circling above it, turning in unceasing
revolutions, the heaven pursues its perpetual course from rising to setting, and the sphere of the fixed stars is drawn along with it. Yet all the
straight lines leading from the highest surrounding circle to the centre,
and in the reverse direction, are equal to one another. Homer thus gives
the dimension of the sphere on geometrical principles, by saying

as far below Hades as heaven above earth.

37 Some people are so ignorant that they find fault with Homer also
with regard to the Prayers, that he should have insulted the offspring of
Zeus by characterizing them as ugly and deformed:

---

1. See also ch. 25 above.

2. *Il.* 8.3; on the following speech, cf. Ps.-Plutarch, *Vit. poes. Hom.* 94, with Hillgruber's
notes (1994–1999, 2:215–16).

3. Presumably the Stoics are meant: cf. Diogenes Laertius 7.145 = *SVF* 650, of the sun;
but the parallel is not exact, and Heraclitus seems to have invented rather freely here. The
term *anamma* means a burning mass of any kind.

4. *Il.* 8.16.

5. Hades must be at the bottom of the earth for the geometry to work.

Καὶ γάρ τε Λιταί εἰσι Διὸς κοῦραι μεγάλοιο,
χωλαί τε ῥυσαί τε παραβλῶπές τ᾽ ὀφθαλμώ.

37.2 Ἐν δὲ τούτοις τοῖς ἔπεσι τὸ τῶν ἱκετευόντων σχῆμα διαπέπλασται. Πᾶσα γὰρ οὖν συνείδησις ἁμαρτόντος ἀνθρώπου βραδεῖα, καὶ μόλις οἱ δεόμενοι τοῖς ἱκετευομένοις προσέρχονται, τὴν αἰδῶ κατὰ βῆμα[1] μετροῦντες· οὔτε μὴν ἀτρεμὲς δεδόρκασιν, ἀλλ᾽ ὀπίσω τὰς τῶν ὀμμάτων βολὰς ἀποστρέφουσι. **37.3** Καὶ μὴν ἔν γε τοῖς προσώποις[2] οὐδὲν γεγηθὸς τῶν ἱκετευόντων ἡ διάνοια περιτίθησιν ἔρευθος, ἀλλ᾽ ὠχροὶ καὶ κατηφεῖς διὰ τῆς πρώτης ὄψεως ἐκκαλούμενοι[3] τὸν ἔλεον. **37.4** Ὅθεν εὐλόγως οὐ τὰς Διὸς θυγατέρας, ἀλλὰ τοὺς ἱκετεύοντας ἀπεφήνατο "χωλούς τε ῥυσούς τε παραβλῶπάς τ᾽ ὀφθαλμώ," τοὔμπαλιν δὲ τὴν Ἄτην "σθεναράν τε καὶ ἀρτίπουν·" κρατερὸν γὰρ αὐτῆς τὸ ἄφρον. **37.5** Ἀλογίστου γὰρ ὁρμῆς ὑπόπλεως δρομὰς ὣς ἐπὶ πᾶσαν ἀδικίαν ἵεται.[4] **37.6** Παθῶν οὖν ἀνθρωπίνων ὥσπερεὶ ζωγράφος Ὅμηρός ἐστιν, ἀλληγορικῶς τὸ συμβαῖνον ἡμῖν θεῶν περιθεὶς ὀνόμασιν.

38.1 Οἶμαι δ᾽ ἔγωγε καὶ τὸ Ἑλληνικὸν τεῖχος, ὃ πρὸς καιρὸν ἔρυμα τῆς ἰδίας ἀσφαλείας ἐπύργωσαν, οὐχ ὑπὸ τοῦ συμμάχου καθῃρῆσθαι Ποσειδῶνος· **38.2** ἀλλ᾽ ὑφ᾽[5] ὑετοῦ δαψιλοῦς γενομένου καὶ τῶν ἀπ᾽ Ἴδης ποταμῶν πλημμυράντων συνέβη καταρριφῆναι, ὅθεν ἐπώνυμος τοῦ πάθους γέγονεν ὁ τῆς ὑγρᾶς φύσεως προστάτης Ποσειδῶν. **38.3** Εἰκὸς δὲ καὶ σεισμοῖς διατιναχθὲν ὑπονοστῆσαι τὸ κατασκεύασμα· δοκεῖ δὲ ὁ Ποσειδῶν ἐνοσίγαιος καὶ σεισίχθων εἶναι τοῖς τοιούτοις τῶν παθημάτων ἐπιγραφόμενος.[6] **38.4** Ἀμέλει φησίν·

Αὐτὸς δ᾽ Ἐννοσίγαιος ἔχων χείρεσσι τρίαιναν
ἡγεῖτ᾽, ἐκ δ᾽ ἄρα πάντα θεμείλια κύμασι πέμπε
φιτρῶν καὶ λάων, τὰ θέσαν μογέοντες Ἀχαιοί,

---

1. Wettstein's (1751–1752) emendation, in his commentary on Luke 15:20, of mss. ῥῆμα, retained by Te, Bu, which would mean "measuring their shame by their speech." Perhaps read δηλοῦντες (Russell), "showing," for μετροῦντες, "measuring out."

2. Heyne's emendation of πρώτοις, mss., retained by Te, Bu; the meaning would be "at first."

3. So the Homeric scholia and Mehler. Mss. have ὠχρὰ κατηφὴς ... ἐκκαλουμένη, followed by Bu. Te has ὠχρὰ καὶ (so Homeric scholia) κατηφὴς ... ἐκκαλουμένη, but records Mehler's suggestion in the apparatus criticus.

4. Te, following Homeric scholia; Bu retains mss. ᾤετο, but also suggests ᾤχετο, "went."

5. Te, following the Homeric scholia; mss., Bu read ὡς, "since there was a heavy rain," and so on.

6. So Mehler, Te for mss. ἐπιγραψόμενος.

The Prayers are daughters of almighty Zeus;
lame they are and wrinkled and squinting in both eyes.[1]

However, what is actually portrayed in these lines is the appearance of suppliants. The conscience of a wrongdoer is always slow, and suppliants approach those whose help they beg with reluctance, measuring out their embarrassment step by step. Their gaze is not fearless either; they turn their eyes away and look back. Nor do the thoughts of suppliants set any blush of joy on their faces—they are pale and downcast, inviting pity at first glance. Homer has thus good reason for describing suppliants—not the daughters of Zeus!—as "lame and wrinkled and squinting in both eyes." Ate,[2] by contrast, he represents as "powerful and strong of foot": for her foolishness is indeed strong, since she is full of irrational impulse and launches herself like a runner on every kind of injustice. So Homer is, as it were, a painter of human passions, attaching the names of gods allegorically to things that happen to us.

38 I believe also that the Greek wall, which they fortified as a temporary protection for their own safety, was not pulled down by their ally Poseidon,[3] but collapsed as a result of heavy rain and the flooding of the rivers that rise on Ida. Poseidon, as patron of the watery element, simply lent his name to the disaster. It may well be also that the construction collapsed by being shaken in an earthquake: Poseidon is the "earth-shaker" and "land-disturber," and has disasters like this ascribed to him. Homer says, anyway:

And the Earth-shaker, trident in his hand,
went first, and thrust down in the waves
all the supports of log and stone the Greeks
had labored hard to put in place.[4]

---

1. *Il.* 9.502–503.
2. Here roughly = "Rashness" or "Infatuation"; cf. *Il.* 9.505.
3. *Il.* 12.27.
4. *Il.* 12.27–29; cf. Cornutus, *Theol.* ch. 22 = p. 42.1–5 Lang, with Ramelli (2003, 369 n. 182).

σεισμοῦ τινος φορᾷ διαδονήσας ἐκ βάθρων τὰ τοῦ τείχους θεμέλια. **38.5** Δοκεῖ δέ μοι λεπτῶς ἐξετάζοντι τὰ τοιαῦτα μηδὲ τὸ κατὰ τὴν τρίαιναν ἀφιλοσόφητον εἶναι, δι᾽ ἧς ὑφίσταται τοὺς λίθους ἀναμεμοχλεῦσθαι τοῦ τείχους. **38.6** Τρία γάρ τοι σεισμῶν διαφέροντα τοῖς παθήμασιν οἱ φυσικοὶ λέγουσιν <εἴδη>[1] καί τινας ἰδίους χαρακτῆρας ὀνομάτων ἐπιγράφουσιν αὐτοῖς, βρασματίαν τινὰ καὶ χασματίαν καὶ κλιματίαν προσαγορεύοντες. **38.7** Τριπλαῖς οὖν καθώπλισεν ἀκμαῖς τὸν τῶν σεισμῶν αἴτιον θεόν. Ἀμέλει πρὸς βραχὺ κινηθέντος αὐτοῦ

τρέμε δ᾽ οὔρεα μακρὰ καὶ ὕλη,

τὸ τῶν σεισμῶν ἰδίωμα τοῦ ποιητοῦ διασημήναντος ἡμῖν.

39.1 Ἔτι τοίνυν πολλήν τινα χλεύην καὶ μακρὸν ἡγοῦνται καταγέλωτα τοὺς ἀκαίρους Διὸς ὕπνους ἐν Ἴδῃ καὶ τὴν ὄρειον ὥσπερ ἀλόγοις ζῴοις ὑπεστρωμένην εὐνήν, ἐν ᾗ δυσὶ τοῖς ἀφρονεστάτοις πάθεσι δεδούλωται Ζεύς, ἔρωτι καὶ ὕπνῳ. **39.2** Νομίζω τοίνυν ἔγωγε αὐτὰ ταῦτα δι᾽ ἀλληγορίας ἐαρινὴν ὥραν ἔτους εἶναι, καθ᾽ ἣν ἅπαντα φυτὰ καὶ πᾶσα ἐκ γῆς ἀνίεται χλόη τοῦ παγετώδους ἡσυχῇ λυομένου[2] κρύους. **39.3** Ὑφίσταται δὲ τὴν Ἥραν, τουτέστι τὸν ἀέρα, στυγνὸν ἀπὸ τοῦ χειμῶνος ἔτι καὶ κατηφῆ· διὰ τοῦτο οἶμαι πιθανῶς αὐτῆς "στυγερὸς ἔπλετο θυμός." **39.4** Μετὰ μικρὸν δ᾽ ἀποκρουσαμένη τὸ συννεφὲς τῆς ἀηδίας

λύματα πάντα κάθηρεν, ἀλείψατο δὲ λίπ᾽ ἐλαίῳ,
ἀμβροσίῳ ἑδανῷ, τό ῥά οἱ τεθυωμένον ἦεν.

39.5 Ἡ λιπαρὰ καὶ γόνιμος ὥρα μετὰ τῆς τῶν ἀνθέων εὐωδίας ὑποσημαίνεται τοιούτῳ χρίσματι τῆς Ἥρας ἀλειψαμένης. **39.6** Τούς τε πλοκάμους φησὶν αὐτὴν ἀναπλέξασθαι "καλούς, ἀμβροσίους, ἐκ κράατος ἀθανάτοιο,"

---

1. The text is uncertain. Bu, following the mss., reads τὰ γάρ τοι σεισμῶν διαφέροντα ... λέγουσιν εἶναι ἴσα (εἶναι omitted by Homeric scholia), "tell us of types of earthquakes that are equal, differing in..."; but "equal" makes no sense here. Te deletes ἴσα, and on a suggestion by Mehler emends τά to τρία (which the sense demands) and inserts εἴδη after σεισμῶν. Mehler locates εἴδη after τοι; we think it goes best after λέγουσιν.
2. Te, following Homeric scholia; Bu retains mss. δυομένου, "sink," which is unintelligible.

That is to say, he shook the supports of the wall violently from the foundations by the movement of an earthquake. Careful study of this passage leads me to think that even the detail of the trident, by which he represents the stones of the wall as having been levered up, is not without philosophical meaning. Scientists tell us of three types of earthquakes, differing in their characteristics, and give them special names: "shakers," "gapers," and "tippers."[1] And this is why Homer armed the god responsible for earthquakes with three prongs. Note that when he moves just a little way,

the high mountains and the forest trembled,[2]

the poet thereby showing us the particular character of the earthquake.[3]

39 Critics also find much amusement and opportunity for ridicule in Zeus's untimely sleep on Ida, and in the mountain bed made ready for him, like the animals' bed, on which he is shown enslaved to the two most stupid of passions, love and sleep.[4] My view is that this is an allegorical way of speaking of spring, the season when all plants and grasses emerge from the ground as the frost and ice gradually melt. He also represents Hera, that is to say the air, as still glum and gloomy after the winter. That is why, I think, it is plausible to say that her "heart was full of gloom."[5] Soon, however, she shakes off the cloud of her distress and

cleaned off all filth, and rubbed herself with oil,
ambrosial and delightful, richly perfumed.[6]

The rich and fertile season, with its sweet scent of flowers, is suggested by the kind of ointment with which Hera anoints herself. In speaking of her as plaiting the "beautiful ambrosial" hair on her "immortal head,"[7] he

---

1. For these types of earthquakes, see Diogenes Laertius 7.154, and Posidonius, frg. 230 Kidd with Kidd's commentary in Edelstein and Kidd (1988–1999). Seneca (*Nat.* 6.21) has *succussio* (= *brasmatias*), *inclinatio* (= *klimatias*), and *tremor*. Ps.-Aristotle, *Mund.* 396a has a rather different classification. On Poseidon's trident, cf. also Cornutus, *Theol.* ch. 22 = p. 43.2–7 Lang.

2. *Il.* 13.18.

3. I.e., the first type, or shaker.

4. *Il.* 14.347–353. See Ps.-Plutarch, *Vit. poes. Hom.* 95–96, with Hillgruber's notes (1994–1999, 2:218–19); Buffière (1956, 106–15); Lamberton (1986, 208–14 on Neoplatonist interpretations).

5. Cf. 14.158.

6. *Il.* 14.171–172.

7. *Il.* 14.177.

τὴν τῶν φυτῶν αἰνιττόμενος αὔξησιν, ἐπειδὴ δένδρον ἅπαν κομᾷ καὶ θριξὶν ὁμοίως ἀπὸ τῶν κλάδων ἀπαρτᾶται τὰ φύλλα. **39.7** Δίδωσι δ' ἐγκόλπιον τῷ ἀέρι[1] καὶ τὸν κεστὸν ἱμάντα, "ἔνθ' ἔνι μὲν φιλότης, ἐν δ' ἵμερος, ἐν δ' ὀαριστύς·" **39.8** ἐπειδήπερ αὕτη μάλιστα τοῦ ἔτους ἡ ὥρα τὸ τερπνότατον ἐπεκλήρωσατο[2] τῶν ἡδονῶν μέρος· **39.9** οὔτε γὰρ λίαν ὑπὸ τοῦ κρύους πεπήγαμεν, οὔτ' ἄγαν θαλπόμεθα· μεταίχμιον δέ τι τῆς ἑκατέρωθεν δυσκρασίας[3] ἐν τοῖς σώμασιν ἀνεῖται.

39.10 Τοῦτον τοίνυν τὸν ἀέρα συνέμιξεν Ὅμηρος μετὰ μικρὸν τῷ αἰθέρι. **39.11** Διὰ τοῦτο ἐπὶ τῆς ὑψηλοτάτης ἀκρωρείας καταλαμβάνεται Ζεύς, ἐν ᾗ "δι' ἠέρος αἰθέρ' ἵκανεν·" ἐνθάδε κιρνᾶται καθ' ἓν ἀναμιχθεὶς ὁ ἀὴρ τῷ αἰθέρι. **39.12** Ἐμφαντικῶς οὖν τοῖς ὀνόμασιν εἶπεν·

ἦ ῥα, καὶ ἀγκὰς ἔμαρπτε Κρόνου παῖς ἦν παράκοιτιν.

Ἀγκαλίζεται γὰρ ἐν κύκλῳ περιέχων ὁ αἰθὴρ ὑφηπλωμένον αὐτῷ τὸν ἀέρα. **39.13** Τῆς δὲ συνόδου καὶ κράσεως αὐτῶν τὸ πέρας ἐδήλωσε τὴν ἐαρινὴν ὥραν·

Τοῖσι δ' ὑπὸ χθὼν δῖα φύεν νεοθηλέα ποίην
λωτόν θ' ἐρσήεντα ἰδὲ κρόκον ἠδ' ὑάκινθον
πυκνὸν καὶ μαλακόν, ὃς ἀπὸ χθονὸς ὑψόσ' ἔεργεν.

39.14 Ἴδια στέφη ταῦτα τῆς ἀρτιθαλοῦς ὥρας, ἐπειδὰν ἐκ τῶν χειμερίων παγετῶν ἡ στερίφη καὶ μεμυκυῖα γῆ τὰς κυοφορουμένας ἔνδον ὠδῖνας ἐκφήνῃ. **39.15** Προσεπισφραγιζόμενος δὲ τοῦτο τὸν λωτὸν εἶπεν ἐρσήεντα, τὸν δροσερὸν τῆς ἐαρινῆς καταστάσεως ἐμφανέστερον ποιῶν τὸν καιρόν.[4]

Ἐπὶ δὲ νεφέλην ἕσσαντο
καλὴν χρυσείην· στιλπναὶ δ' ἀπέπιπτον ἔερσαι.

39.16 Τίς ἀγνοεῖ τοῦθ', ὅτι χειμῶνος μὲν ἐπάλληλα πυκνώματα τῶν νεφῶν ἐκμελαίνεται, καὶ μετὰ θολερᾶς ἀχλύος κατηφὴς ἅπας ὁ οὐρανὸς ἀμαυροῦται,

---

1. Homeric scholia, followed by Te; mss., Bu read ἔαρι, "spring."
2. Te, following the Homeric scholia; Bu retains the mss. ἐπλήρωσε, "which pays (us) in full."
3. Russell; cf. Strabo, *Geogr.* 6.4.1. Te, Bu retain the mss. εὐκρασίας, i.e. "the middle state of a good mixture of the two extremes" (defining genitive).
4. The text is doubtful, but the sense is clear. Bu retains the mss. τοῦ καιροῦ and interprets "clearer than it need be," which is an unlikely sense of καιρός; Te reads καιρόν with the Homeric scholia (no article) = "the damp weather (or season)." Perhaps delete τοῦ καιροῦ (as a gloss on τῆς ἐαρινῆς) and read τὸ [for τὸν] δροσερὸν (Russell) = "dampness" instead of "damp weather"; or (less likely) keep τὸν καιρόν and read τῷ δροσερῷ, "making the season clearer, by mentioning 'the dewy' nature of spring conditions."

symbolizes the growth of plants, because all trees have "hair," and the leaves are attached to the branches like hairs. He also puts into the lap of air the strap or *kestos* "wherein is love, desire, and company,"[1] because this season of the year has as its portion the greatest delights of pleasure, for we are then not chilled by cold or heated too much, but our bodies enjoy the comfort of a middle ground between the two disagreeable extremes.

A little while later, Homer mingles this air with aether. This is why Zeus is found on the highest point of the mountain, where "through air it reached to aether";[2] here air and aether are combined in a single substance. So Homer says vividly:[3]

> So said the son of Cronus, and in his arms
> embraced his wife,[4]

because aether surrounds and embraces the air spread out beneath it. He shows that the outcome of their union and mingling is the spring:

> Beneath them, holy Earth made new grass grow,
> and dewy lotus, saffron, hyacinth,
> all thick and soft, which raised them off the ground.[5]

These are garlands characteristic of the season of early growth, when the winter frosts are done and the barren and closed earth reveals the birth she has conceived within. To give further confirmation of this, he calls the lotus "dewy," thereby making the damp weather characteristic of spring conditions even clearer.

> And over them they pulled a golden cloud,
> most beautiful, and glistening dew dripped from it.[6]

Everyone surely knows that in the winter dense piles of cloud are black, and the whole sky is dark and gloomy with swirling fog, but when the air

---

1. *Il.* 14.216.
2. *Il.* 14.287. It is really a tall pine that reaches up to aether; cf. *Vit. poes. Hom.* 95, with Hillgruber's notes (1994–1999, 2:217).
3. "Très clairement," Bu; but perhaps the sense is "with special significance."
4. *Il.* 14.346.
5. *Il.* 14.347–349.
6. *Il.* 14.350–351.

τοῦ δὲ ἀέρος¹ ὑποσχίζοντος, ἀργὰ τὰ νέφη μαλακῶς ὑποσπείρεται ταῖς ἡλιακαῖς ἀκτῖσιν ἐναγκαλιζόμενα καὶ παραπλήσιόν τι χρυσαῖς μαρμαρυγαῖς ἀποστίλβει. **39.17** Τοῦτο δὴ τὸ περὶ τὴν Ἴδην κορυφαῖον ἡμῖν νέφος ὁ τῆς ἐαρινῆς ὥρας δημιουργὸς ἐφήπλωσεν.²

40.1 Ἀλλ' ἐφεξῆς ἡ τῶν ἐπιφυομένων αὐτῷ τόλμα τοὺς Ἥρας δεσμοὺς αἰτιᾶται, καὶ νομίζουσιν ὕλην τινὰ δαψιλῆ τῆς ἀθέου πρὸς Ὅμηρον ἔχειν μανίας·

> Ἦ οὐ μέμνῃ, ὅτε τ' ἐκρέμω ὑψόθεν, ἐκ δὲ ποδοῖιν
> ἄκμονας ἧκα δύω, περὶ χερσὶ δὲ δεσμὸν ἴηλα
> χρύσεον, ἄρρηκτον; σὺ δ' ἐν αἰθέρι καὶ νεφέλῃσιν
> ἐκρέμω.

40.2 Λέληθε δ' αὐτούς, ὅτι τούτοις τοῖς ἔπεσιν ἡ τοῦ παντὸς ἐκτεθεολόγηται γένεσις, καὶ τὰ συνεχῶς ἀδόμενα τέτταρα στοιχεῖα τούτων τῶν στίχων ἐστὶ τάξις, καθάπερ ἤδη μοι λέλεκται· **40.3** πρῶτος αἰθὴρ καὶ μετὰ τοῦτον ἀήρ, εἶθ' ὕδωρ τε καὶ γῆ τελευταία, τὰ³ πάντων δημιουργὰ στοιχεῖα· **40.4** ταῦτα δ' ἀλλήλοις ἐπικιρνώμενα ζῳογονεῖ τε⁴ καὶ τῶν ἀψύχων ἀρχέγονα καθίσταται. **40.5** Ζεὺς τοίνυν ὁ πρῶτος ἑαυτοῦ⁵ τὸν ἀέρα κατήρτηκεν, στερεοὶ δ' ἄκμονες ὑπὸ ταῖς ἐσχάταις ἀέρος βάσεσιν ὕδωρ τε καὶ γῆ. **40.6** Καὶ τοῦτο ὅτι τοιοῦτόν ἐστιν, ἐφ' ἑκάστης λέξεως, εἴ τις ἀκριβῶς ἐθέλοι⁶ σκοπεῖν τἀληθές, εὑρήσει. "Ἦ οὐ μέμνῃ, ὅτε τ' ἐκρέμω ὑψόθεν;" **40.7** Ἀπὸ γὰρ τῶν ἀνωτάτων καὶ μετεώρων τόπων φασὶν αὐτὴν ἀπηρτῆσθαι. **40.8** "Περὶ χερσὶ δὲ δεσμὸν ἴηλα χρύσεον, ἄρρηκτον." **40.9** Τί τοῦτο τὸ καινὸν αἴνιγμα τῆς κολακευούσης τιμωρίας; πῶς ὀργιζόμενος Ζεὺς πολυτελεῖ δεσμῷ τὴν κολαζομένην ἠμύνατο, χρυσοῦν ἀντὶ τοῦ κραταιοτέρου σιδήρου τὸν δεσμὸν ἐπινοήσας; **40.10** ἀλλ' ἔοικε τὸ μεταίχμιον αἰθέρος τε καὶ ἀέρος χρυσῷ

---

1. Mss., Bu; Te, following the Homeric scholia, reads ἔαρος ("spring"), and indicates a lacuna.

2. Mehler, followed by Te (the Homeric scholia have ἐδήλωσεν, "clarified" or "explained"); Bu reads ἐφήλωσεν, "a fixé," with A.

3. Te, following Homeric scholia; Bu, with mss., omits the article and punctuates after γῆ, taking τελευταῖα with στοιχεῖα and translating (somewhat improbably) "the ultimate elements."

4. So Muenzel; Te (with the Homeric scholia) reads ζῳογόνα τε; Bu, following the mss., reads ζῳογονεῖται, "se changent en vivants." But the point is rather that the elements are the origin of all things, animate and inanimate, not that they themselves become animate.

5. Heyne, followed by Te; τὸν ἑαυτοῦ ἀέρα, mss., Bu. The change is needed to secure the sense and also avoids hiatus. ἑαυτοῦ depends on κατήρτηκεν, which Heraclitus seems to have used instead of ἀπήρτηκεν (cf. 45.3), perhaps to avoid hiatus.

6. Mss., Bu; Te reads θέλει, comparing 23.1, but the mss. there vary between the indicative and optative.

breaks this up, the clouds, now shining, are gently spread in the embrace of the sun's rays, and glisten like the glitter of gold. So Homer, creator of spring, spreads out for us the cloud that crowns Ida.

40 Next, the audacity of those who fasten on Homer finds fault with the binding of Hera. They think they have here rich material for their impious rage against him:

> Don't you recall, when you hung from the height,
> and I set two anvils on your feet, and on
> your hands a bond of gold, unbreakable,
> and there you hung in the aether and the clouds?[1]

It has escaped their notice that this passage contains a theological account of the creation of the universe, and that the order of these lines corresponds to the constantly celebrated four elements, of which I have already spoken:[2] first, aether; then air; then water; and finally earth: the creative elements of the universe. Combined with one another, these create animals and are the origin of inanimate things. Thus Zeus, who comes first, attaches air to himself, and the solid anvils at the base of air are water and earth. If you look carefully for the true meaning of the passage, word by word, you can see that this is so. "Don't you recall, when you were hung from the height," means that she was attached to the highest regions of the upper world. "And on your hands I set a bond of gold, unbreakable": well, what is the new riddle in this flattering form of punishment? Why did Zeus in his anger use such a costly bond to punish his victim, contriving it of gold rather than of the stronger iron? It would seem that the space between aether and air resembles gold in

---

1. *Il.* 15.18–21. Cf. Cornutus, *Theol.* ch. 17 = p. 26.11–27.2 Lang, with Ramelli (2003, 343 n. 116).

2. In ch. 23.

μάλιστα τὴν χρόαν ἐμφερὲς εἶναι· **40.11** πάνυ δὴ πιθανῶς καθ' ὃ μέρος ἀλλήλοις ἐπισυνάπτουσι — λήγων μὲν[1] ὁ αἰθήρ, ἀρχόμενος δὲ μετ' ἐκεῖνον ὁ ἀήρ — χρυσοῦν ὑπεστήσατο δεσμόν. **40.12** Ἐπιφέρει γοῦν· "σὺ δ' ἐν αἰθέρι καὶ νεφέλῃσιν ἐκρέμω," τὸν ἄχρι νεφῶν τόπον ὁρίσας μέτρον ἀέρος. **40.13** Ἐκ δὲ τῶν τελευταίων μερῶν τοῦ ἀέρος, ἃ καλεῖ[2] πόδας, ἀπήρτησε στιβαρὰ βρίθη, γῆν τε καὶ ὕδωρ· "ἐκ δὲ ποδοῖιν ἄκμονας ἧκα δύω." **40.14** Πῶς <δ'>[3] ἂν εἶπε δεσμὸν "ἄρρηκτον," αὐτίκα τῆς Ἥρας λυθείσης, εἴγε τῷ μύθῳ προσεκτέον; ἀλλ' ἐπειδήπερ ἡ τῶν ὅλων ἁρμονία δεσμοῖς ἀρραγέσι συνωχύρωται καὶ δυσχερὴς ἡ τοῦ παντὸς εἰς τἀναντία μεταβολή, τὸ μὴ δυνηθὲν ἂν διαζευχθῆναί ποτε κυρίως ὠνόμασεν ἄρρηκτον.

41.1 Ταύτην δὲ τὴν τετράδα τῶν στοιχείων καὶ μετὰ μικρὸν ἐν τοῖς ὅρκοις διεσάφησεν Ἥρα·

Ἴστω νῦν τόδε γαῖα καὶ οὐρανὸς εὐρὺς ὕπερθεν
καὶ τὸ κατειβόμενον Στυγὸς ὕδωρ.

41.2 Τρισὶ γὰρ ὅρκοις τὴν ὁμόφυλον αὐτῆς καὶ συγγενῆ φύσιν ὠνόμασεν, ὕδωρ τε καὶ γῆν καὶ τὸν ὕπερθεν οὐρανόν, τουτέστι τὸν αἰθέρα· τέταρτον γὰρ στοιχεῖον ἦν ἡ ὀμνύουσα. **41.3** Διὰ πολλῶν[4] γέ τοι καὶ ἐπ' ἄλλοις[5] ἀλληγορικῶς παριστάναι βουλόμενος ταυτὶ τὰ στοιχεῖα, καὶ μετ' ὀλίγον ἐν τοῖς Ποσειδῶνος πρὸς Ἶριν λόγοις αὐτὰ ταῦθ' ὑφίσταται λέγων· **41.4**

Ἦ τοι ἐγὼν ἔλαχον πολιὴν ἅλα ναιέμεν αἰεὶ
παλλομένων, Ἀίδης δ' ἔλαχε ζόφον ἠερόεντα,
Ζεὺς δ' ἔλαχ' οὐρανὸν εὐρὺν ἐν αἰθέρι καὶ νεφέλῃσιν·
γαῖα δ' ἔτι ξυνὴ πάντων καὶ μακρὸς Ὄλυμπος.

---

1. Te, with G; Bu, with A and Homeric scholia, inserts γάρ.
2. Te, following Homeric scholia; Bu retains mss. καλεῖται and emends πόδας to πόδες.
3. Russell; a connective is needed, since a new point is introduced.
4. Russell, in place of mss. Διευπορῶν, followed by Bu (a *hapax legomenon* that surely cannot mean "plein de son sujet"); Te, following Polak, reads Δι' εὐπόρων = "through easy examples."
5. Russell; the Homeric scholia have ἐπὶ πολλοῖς = "in a variety" of allegorical ways; cf. τῷ διηνεκεῖ τῆς παραδόσεως at the end of the paragraph. Mss., Bu read ἐπὶ καλοῖς, "in an honorable context"; presumably this means that 15.190ff. is thought of as a grander and less objectionable context than that of Hera's oath. Te, following Polak, reads ἐπιπολῆς "superficially," i.e. "plainly allegorical."

color more than anything; it is therefore quite plausible that he should put a golden bond at the point where the two elements meet—aether ending and air beginning. At any rate, he adds, "And there you hung in the aether and the clouds," thereby defining the limits of air as the region extending as far as the clouds. To the lowest parts of the air, which he calls its "feet," he attached solid masses, namely, earth and water: "I put two anvils on your feet." And how could he have spoken of an "unbreakable" bond when Hera was immediately released, if we are to believe the story? Well, since the harmony of the universe is secured by unbreakable bonds and the change of the whole to an opposite state is difficult, he was strictly accurate in calling something which could not have been sundered "unbreakable."

41 Soon after, Hera makes a clear reference to these four elements in her oath:

Be witness, earth and the broad heaven above,
and flowing stream of Styx.[1]

In these three oaths she named the three substances which are her kindred and relations, water and earth and heaven above (that is, aether): the fourth element is the oath-taker herself. At any rate, wishing to represent these elements allegorically at length and in other contexts, Homer also presents the same facts again soon after, in Poseidon's words to Iris:

The lots were drawn; it fell to me to live
in the grey sea forever; Hades won
the misty dark, and Zeus the spreading heaven,
aether and clouds. But earth and high Olympus
are common still to all.[2]

---

1. *Il.* 15.36.
2. *Il.* 15.190–193; the interpretation also covers 187–189.

41.5 Οὐ μὰ Δι᾿ οὐ κλῆρος ὁ μυθευόμενος ἐν Σικυῶνι ταῦτα καὶ διαίρεσις ἀδελφῶν οὕτως ἀνώμαλος, ὡς οὐρανὸν ἀντιθεῖναι θαλάττῃ καὶ ταρτάρῳ. Πᾶς γὰρ ὁ μῦθος ἠλληγόρηται περὶ τῶν ἐπ᾿ ἀρχαῖς[1] τεττάρων στοιχείων. **41.6** Κρόνον μὲν γὰρ ὀνομάζει τὸν χρόνον κατὰ μετάληψιν ἑνὸς στοιχείου· πατὴρ δὲ τῶν ὅλων ὁ χρόνος, καὶ τελέως ἀμήχανόν τι γενέσθαι τῶν ὄντων δίχα χρόνου· διὸ δὴ ῥίζα τῶν τεττάρων στοιχείων οὗτός ἐστι. **41.7** Μητέρα δ᾿ αὐτοῖς ἔνειμεν εἶναι Ῥέαν, ἐπειδὴ ῥύσει τινὶ καὶ ἀεννάῳ κινήσει τὸ πᾶν οἰκονομεῖται. **41.8** Χρόνου δὴ καὶ ῥύσεως τέκνα γῆν τε καὶ ὕδωρ, αἰθέρα τε καὶ ἀέρα σὺν αὐτοῖς[2] ὑπεστήσατο· **41.9** καὶ τῇ μὲν πυρώδει φύσει τόπον ἔνειμεν οὐρανόν, τὴν δ᾿ ὑγρὰν οὐσίαν Ποσειδῶνι προσέθηκε, τρίτον δ᾿ Ἅιδην τὸν ἀφώτιστον ἀέρα δηλοῖ, **41.10** κοινὸν δὲ πάντων καὶ ἑδραιότατον ἀπεφήνατο στοιχεῖον εἶναι τὴν γῆν ὥσπερ ἑστίαν τινὰ τῆς τῶν ὅλων δημιουργίας· **41.11**

γαῖα δ᾿ ἔτι[3] ξυνὴ πάντων καὶ μακρὸς Ὄλυμπος.

41.12 Καὶ[4] διὰ τοῦτο δέ μοι δοκεῖ συνεχῶς ἀλληγορεῖν ὑπὲρ αὐτῶν, ἵν᾿ ἡ δοκοῦσα τοῖς ἔπεσιν ἐφεδρεύειν[5] ἀσάφεια τῷ διηνεκεῖ τῆς παραδόσεως ᾖ γνωριμωτέρα.

42.1 Τά γε μὴν ἐπὶ Σαρπηδόνι δάκρυα λύπην μὲν οὐ καταψεύδεται θεοῦ, ὃ καὶ παρ᾿ ἀνθρώποις νόσημα· τῷ[6] δὲ βουλομένῳ τἀκριβὲς ἐρευνᾶν ἐπινοεῖται τρόπος ἀλληγορουμένης ἀληθείας. **42.2** Πολλάκις γὰρ ἐν ταῖς μεταβολαῖς τῶν μεγάλων πραγμάτων ἱστοροῦσι τεράστια τῷ βίῳ συμφέρεσθαι <καὶ>[7] σημεῖα ποταμῶν τε καὶ πηγῶν[8] ναμάτων αἱμοφορύκτοις ῥεύμασιν ἐκμιαινομένων, ὡς ἐπ᾿ Ἀσωποῦ τε καὶ Δίρκης παραδιδόασιν οἱ παλαιοὶ μῦθοι. **42.3** Λόγος δ᾿ ἔχει καὶ κατὰ νεφῶν ψεκάδας ὕεσθαι φόνου τισὶ

---

1. A, G, Bu; D, Te read ἐν ἀρχαῖς.
2. Konstan (cf. 41.5, 86.15, 98.2) for mss. σὺν αὐτῷ, "alongside him" (i.e., Time), followed by Bu and Te; both sense and the resulting hiatus are against the latter. Te in apparatus criticus proposes συνετῶς, "wisely."
3. Homer, Te; mss., Bu read ἐστί, "are."
4. A, Bu; omitted by G, D, Te.
5. Bu, with A, G, Homeric scholia; D, Te read ὑφεδρεύειν, "underlie."
6. Te, following D, Homeric scholia; Bu, following A, G, reads αὐτῷ, and translates "pour moi."
7. Homeric scholia; for τεράστια as a noun, cf. 42.4, below. On the mss. reading, followed by Bu and Te, the meaning is "men tell of miraculous signs..., with streams of rivers...," etc.
8. Mss., Bu (Te emends to πηγαίων, "spring waters"); cf. Plato, Crit. 111D.

This is not of course the mythical lot drawn at Sicyon,[1] the division among the brothers that was so unequal as to make heaven an alternative to the sea and the underworld. All this story is an allegory of the original four elements. By Kronos, he means Time [*Khronos*],[2] changing just one letter. Time is the father of all things, and it is altogether impossible for anything that exists to come into being without time. Kronos is therefore the root of the four elements. For their mother, Homer has given us Rhea, because the universe is controlled by a flow [*rhysis*][3] and an ever-flowing motion. Thus he made earth and water the children of Time and Flow, and set aether and air by their side. He assigned heaven as the site of the fiery substance, and gave the watery substance to Poseidon. Hades, the third, represents unillumined air, and he shows earth to be the element common to all, completely stable, the hearth, as it were, of the creation of the universe:

> Earth and high Olympus
> are common still to all.[4]

It seems to me that the reason why Homer allegorizes so constantly about these matters is to make the obscurity which seems to threaten his lines more intelligible by continuous inculcation of the lesson.

42 The tears wept for Sarpedon[5] do not misrepresent a god as suffering grief, which is an affliction even for humans; rather, the reader who wishes to be exact in his inquiries perceives in this a form of allegorized truth. Often in revolutions of great affairs, men tell of miracles occurring in life and signs of streams of rivers and fountains befouled with turbid currents of blood, as the old stories tell of Asopus and Dirce.[6] We hear too of rain dropping from the clouds colored with stains of murder. So since the change of fortune in the battle was going to produce the mass flight of

---

1. See Callimachus, frg. 465 Schneider = 119 Pfeiffer; cf. *Hymn to Zeus* 60–67.

2. The identification of Kronos with Khronos is old and widespread: e.g., Cornutus, *Theol.* ch. 6 = p. 4.1ff. Lang, with Ramelli (2003, 311 n. 28); further references in Pease (1955–1958) on Cicero, *Nat. d.* 2.64 (Κρόνος enim dicitur, qui est idem χρόνος, id est spatium temporis).

3. Cf. Plato, *Crat.* 402B, Chrysippus in *SVF* 2.1084, Cornutus, *Theol.* ch. 6 = p. 3.20 Lang, with Ramelli (2003, 309 n. 21).

4. *Il.* 15.193.

5. *Il.* 16.459.

6. Dirce is a spring in Thebes; in mythology, Dirce abused Antiope, the mother of Zethus and Amphion, who took a bloody revenge upon her. Asopus is the name of several

κηλῖσιν ἐπικεχρωσμένας. **42.4** Ἐπεὶ τοίνυν ἡ μεταβολὴ τῆς μάχης ἀθρόαν φυγὴν ἐμποιήσειν ἔμελλε τοῖς βαρβάροις, ἐγγὺς δ᾽ ἦν ὁ τοῦ κατ᾽ ἀλκὴν ἀρίστου Σαρπηδόνος ὄλεθρος, ὡσπερεὶ τεράστια προὐφάνη ταύτης τῆς συμφορᾶς ἀγγελτικά·

αἱματοέσσας δὲ ψιάδας κατέχευεν ἔραζε.

42.5 Τοῦτον δὴ τὸν φόνιον[1] ὄμβρον ἀλληγορικῶς εἴρηκεν[2] αἰθέρος δάκρυα, Διὸς μὲν οὔ — ἄκλαυστος γάρ —, ἐκ δὲ τῶν ὑπεράνω τόπων ὡσπερεὶ θρήνοις μεμιγμένου καταρραγέντος ὑετοῦ.

43.1 Ταυτὶ μὲν ἴσως ἐλάττω τεκμήρια περὶ τῶν ἠλληγορημένων· ἐπὶ μέντοι τῆς ὁπλοποιίας μεγάλη καὶ κοσμοτόκῳ διανοίᾳ τὴν τῶν ὅλων περιείληφε[3] γένεσιν. **43.2** Πόθεν[4] γὰρ αἱ πρῶται τοῦ παντὸς ἔφυσαν ἀρχαὶ καὶ τίς ὁ τούτων δημιουργὸς καὶ πῶς ἕκαστα πληρωθέντα διεκρίθη, σαφέσι τεκμηρίοις παρέστησε, τὴν Ἀχιλλέως ἀσπίδα τῆς κοσμικῆς περιόδου χαλκευσάμενος εἰκόνα. **43.3** Καὶ τὸ πρῶτον ὑπεστήσατο τῆς παντελοῦς δημιουργίας νύκτα καιρόν, ἐπειδήπερ αὕτη χρόνου [πτερὰ][5] πάτρια πρεσβεῖα κεκλήρωται, καὶ πρὶν ἢ διακριθῆναι τὰ νῦν βλεπόμενα, νὺξ ἦν τὸ σύμπαν, ὃ δὴ χάος ποιητῶν ὀνομάζουσι παῖδες. **43.4** Οὐ γὰρ οὕτως ἄθλιόν τινα καὶ κακοδαίμονα παρεισάγει τὸν Ἥφαιστον, ὡς μηδὲ νυκτὸς ἀνάπαυσιν ἔχειν τῆς χειρωνακτικῆς ἐργασίας, ὅπου γε καὶ παρ᾽ ἀνθρώποις ἀθλίοις[6] ἄτοπον εἶναι δοκεῖ τὸ μηδὲ νύκτα τῶν πόνων ἐκεχειρίαν ἄγειν. **43.5** Ἀλλ᾽ οὐκ ἔστι ταῦτα χαλκεύων Ἀχιλλεῖ πανοπλίαν Ἥφαιστος οὐδ᾽ ἐν οὐρανῷ βουνοὶ χαλκοῦ καὶ κασσιτέρου, ἀργύρου τε καὶ χρυσοῦ εἰσιν· **43.6** ἀμήχανον γὰρ τὰς ἀηδεῖς καὶ φιλαργύρους γῆς νόσους ἐπ᾽ οὐρανὸν ἀναβῆναι. **43.7** Φυσικῶς δὲ τῆς ἀμόρφου ποτὲ καὶ μὴ διακεκριμένης ὕλης τὸν καιρὸν ἀποφηνάμενος εἶναι νύκτα, δημιουργόν, ἡνίκα ἔμελλε πάντα μορφοῦσθαι, τὸν Ἥφαιστον ἐπέστησε, τουτέστι τὴν θερμὴν οὐσίαν· "πυρὸς" γὰρ δή, κατὰ τὸν φυσικὸν Ἡράκλειτον, "ἀμοιβῇ[7] τὰ πάντα" γίνεται. **43.8** Ὅθεν συνοικοῦσαν οὐκ

---

1. Heyne, followed by Te, instead of φονέα, "murderer" (mss., Bu).
2. A, G, Bu; Te, following D, Homeric scholia, reads εἶπεν. The sense is not affected.
3. Russell (hesitantly); neither the mss. περιήθροισε ("concentrated," adopted by Bu) nor Hercher's ingenious περιήθρησε ("saw," "scrutinized," adopted by Te) seems satisfactory.
4. Muenzel, followed by Te; Bu retains the mss. Ὅθεν.
5. Deleting πτερά with Te (dittography with πάτρια); Bu retains it, translating: "celle-ci a hérité des ailes du temps, comme des privilèges paternels." Apparently, Night here is the same as Chaos, and Chronos is her father.
6. Mss., Bu; bracketed by Te.
7. Russell, following Diels; ἀμοιβή (mss.) would mean "as an exchange for fire."

the barbarians, and the death of valiant Sarpedon was at hand, a miracle appeared as if to announce the disaster:

He poured down bloody drops upon the ground.[1]

Homer allegorically describes this murderous rain as "tears of aether"— not tears of Zeus, for Zeus cannot weep—but, as it were, tears of rain bursting from the sky above and mingled with lamentation.

43 These are perhaps minor attestations of allegory. In the Making of the Armor, on the other hand, Homer has included the origin of the universe in a grand creative idea. In forging the Shield of Achilles[2] as an image of the revolution of the cosmos, he has shown by clear evidences how the universe originated, who is its creator, and how its different parts were formed and separated. First, he made night the time of the entire creative process, for Night has inherited ancestral privileges from Time; all things were Night—or, as the poets say, Chaos[3]—before the things we now see separated out. He surely does not represent Hephaestus as such a wretched and miserable creature that he has no rest from the labors of his craft even at night, since even among unfortunate humans it is thought very strange to have no truce from toil at night. No, this is not what is meant by Hephaestus forging Achilles' armor; nor are there mountains of bronze and tin, gold and silver in heaven—it is out of the question that earth's horrid disease of avarice should have made its way up to heaven.[4] Rather, having explained in scientific terms that the time when matter was formless and not yet differentiated was a time of night, he comes to the moment when everything was to be given form, and for this he employs Hephaestus (that is, the substance of heat) as creator-craftsman. As the scientist Heraclitus tells us, "all things come to

---

rivers, including one in Boeotia; in one version, Antiope is the daughter of this Asopus (Pausanias 2.6.4; cf. Ps.-Apollodorus 3.43), and this may have led Heraclitus to associate Asopus with Dirce. On rivers stained with blood as a portent, see Pease's commentary (1920–1923) on Cicero, *Div.* 1.98.

1. *Il.* 16.459.

2. *Il.* 18.478–613. See esp. Hardie (1985; 1986, 336–76).

3. See Hesiod, *Theog.* 1ff., and cf. Cornutus, *Theol.* ch. 17 = p. 28.2–4 Lang. For the periphrasis with *paides*, see LSJ s.v. I.3.

4. It would be evidence of divine greed if heaps of precious metals had been accumulated there. Heraclitus's language is contrived: *philargurous* "avaricious" is transferred to the "disease" from (presumably) the sinful humans who suffer from it.

ἀπιθάνως τῷ τῶν ὅλων ἀρχιτέκτονι πεποίηκε τὴν Χάριν· ἔμελλε γὰρ ἤδη τῷ κόσμῳ χαριεῖσθαι τὸν ἴδιον κόσμον. **43.9** Ὗλαι δὲ τίνες αὐτῷ¹ τῆς κατασκευῆς;

Χαλκὸν δ' ἐν πυρὶ βάλλεν ἀτειρέα κασσίτερόν τε.

43.10 Εἰ μὲν Ἀχιλλεῖ κατεσκεύασε πανοπλίαν, πάντα ἔδει χρυσὸν εἶναι· καὶ γὰρ οἶμαι σχέτλιον Ἀχιλλέα μηδὲ Γλαύκῳ κατὰ τὴν πολυτέλειαν ἴσον εἶναι. **43.11** Νῦν δὲ τὰ τέτταρα στοιχεῖα κιρνᾶται· **43.12** καὶ χρυσὸν μὲν ὠνόμασε τὴν αἰθερώδη² φύσιν, ἄργυρον δὲ τὸν αὐτῇ τῇ χρόᾳ συνομοιού-μενον³ ἀέρα· **43.13** χαλκὸς δὲ καὶ κασσίτερος ὕδωρ τε καὶ γῆ προσαγορεύεται διὰ τὴν ἐν ἀμφοτέροις βαρύτητα. **43.14** Πρώτη δ' ἀπὸ τούτων τῶν στοιχείων ἀσπὶς ὑπ' αὐτοῦ χαλκεύεται, σφαιροειδὲς ἔχουσα τὸ σχῆμα, δι' οὗ τὸν κόσμον ἡμῖν ἐμφανῶς ἐσήμηνεν, ὃν οὐκ ἀπὸ τῆς ὁπλοποιίας μόνον ἀλλὰ καὶ δι' ἄλλων τεκμηρίων ἐπίσταται κυκλοειδῆ.

44.1 Συντόμως δ' ἐν παρεκβάσει τὰς ὑπὲρ τούτων φιλοτεχνοῦντες ἀποδείξεις δηλώσομεν. **44.2** Συνεχῶς τοίνυν τὸν ἥλιον "ἀκάμαντα" καὶ "ἠλέκτορα" καὶ "ὑπερίονα" προσαγορεύει, διὰ τῶν ἐπιθέτων οὐκ ἄλλο τι πλὴν τοῦτο τὸ σχῆμα σημαίνων. **44.3** Ὅ τε γὰρ ἀκάμας, ὁ μὴ κάμνων, ἔοικεν ὅρους ἔχειν οὐκ ἀνατολὴν καὶ δύσιν, ἀλλὰ τὴν ἀεὶ περίδρομον ἀνάγκην. **44.4** Ἠλέκτωρ δὲ δυοῖν θάτερον· ἢ ἤλεκτρος ὁ θεὸς ὀνομάζεται μηδέποτε κοίτης ἐπιψαύων, ἢ τάχα πιθανώτερον ἔτι ἑλίκτωρ⁴ τις ὢν καὶ κυκλοτερεῖ φορᾷ δι' ἡμέρας καὶ νυκτὸς ἀναμετρούμενος τὸν κόσμον. **44.5** Ὑπερίονα δὲ νομιστέον αὐτὸν τὸν ὑπεριέμενον ἀεὶ τῆς γῆς, ὥσπερ οἶμαι καὶ Ξενοφάνης ὁ Κολοφώνιός φησιν·

Ἥλιός θ' ὑπεριέμενος γαῖάν τ' ἐπιθάλπων.

---

1. Te, following D, Homeric scholia; A, G, Bu read αὐτοῦ.
2. This form (Homeric scholia, Bu) is better attested in other writers than αἰθεριώδη (mss., Te).
3. Mss., Bu; Te, following Homeric scholia (and comparing 67.6), reads προσωμοι-ωμένον.
4. van Lennep, followed by Te; Bu, following the mss., reads ἐπιελίκτωρ and translates "qui roule en spirale sur nos têtes."

be in exchange for fire."[1] It is not implausible therefore for him to make Grace [*Kharis*] the partner of the architect of the universe, for he was now about to grace the world [*kosmos*] with its own adornment [*kosmos*].[2] And what are the materials of his construction?

He threw tough bronze and tin into the fire.[3]

If he had been making a suit of armor for Achilles, it all ought to have been gold, for it would surely have been intolerable for Achilles not to have been as expensively equipped as Glaucus.[4] In fact, however, we have a mixture of the four elements. By gold he means the aetherial substance, by silver the air, which resembles it in color; water and earth are represented by bronze and tin, because both of these are heavy. From these elements he first forges the shield, spherical in shape; by this, Homer gives us a clear indication of the cosmos, which to judge not only from the Making of the Armor, but from other evidence also, he knows to be round in shape.[5]

44 I shall expound my proofs of these matters in a brief scholarly digression. Homer regularly calls the sun *akamas*, *êlektor*, and *hyperiôn*, and the sole function of these epithets is to suggest this shape. Since he is *akamas*, "unwearied," he is surely not bounded by his rising and setting, but rather by the necessity of perpetual revolution. There are two possible explanations of *êlektor*: either the god is called *alektros*, "unbedded," because he never goes to bed, or (perhaps still more convincingly) he is *heliktor*, "spiraler," because he measures off the world day and night by his circular movement. We must suppose that he is *hyperiôn* because he is always passing over [*hyperiemenon*] the earth, as Xenophanes of Colophon also says:

And the sun that passes over the earth and warms it.[6]

---

1. Heraclitus, frg. 54 Marcovich = 90 Diels-Kranz.

2. On the Graces, cf. Cornutus, *Theol.* ch. 15 = p. 19.1–20.14 Lang, with Ramelli (2003, 330 n. 82).

3. *Il.* 18.382.

4. *Il.* 6.236.

5. See chs. 45–47.

6. Frg. 31 Diels-Kranz. For *akamas*, see *Il.* 18.239; for *êlektor*, *Il.* 19.398; for *hyperiôn* (or rather Hyperion), *Il.* 8.480, etc.; cf. Cornutus, *Theol.* ch. 17 = p. 30.17–18 Lang, with Ramelli (2003, 353 n. 132).

44.6 Εἰ γὰρ πατρωνυμικῶς αὐτὸν ἠθέλησεν ὀνομάζειν, εἶπεν ἂν Ὑπεριονίδην, ὡς Ἀτρείδην εἰ τύχοι τὸν Ἀγαμέμνονα καὶ Πηλείδην τὸν Ἀχιλλέα.

45.1 Ἥ τε "θοὴ νὺξ" οὐκ ἄλλο τι σημαίνει πλὴν τὸ σφαιροειδὲς ὅλου τοῦ πόλου σχῆμα· τὸν γὰρ αὐτὸν ἡλίῳ δρόμον ἡ νὺξ ἀνύει, καὶ πᾶς ὁ καταλειφθεὶς ὑπ' ἐκείνου τόπος εὐθὺς ὑπὸ ταύτης ἐκμελαίνεται. **45.2** Σαφῶς γοῦν ἑτέρωθί που τοῦτο μηνύων φησί·

Ἐν δ' ἔπεσ' Ὠκεανῷ λαμπρὸν φάος ἠελίοιο,
ἕλκων νύκτα μέλαιναν ἐπὶ ζείδωρον ἄρουραν.

45.3 Ὥσπερ γὰρ ἀπηρτημένην ἑαυτοῦ τὴν νύκτα κατόπιν ἐφέλκεται συγχρονοῦσαν τοῖς ἡλίου τάχεσιν. Εἰκότως οὖν αὐτὴν Ὅμηρος εἴρηκε θοήν. **45.4** Δύναταί γε μὴν πιθανώτερόν τις ἐπιχειρῶν θοὴν ὀνομάζειν μεταληπτικῶς οὐ τὴν κατὰ κίνησιν ὀξεῖαν, ἀλλὰ τὴν κατὰ σχῆμα. **45.5** Καὶ γὰρ ἑτέρωθί που φησίν·

Ἔνθεν δ' αὖ νήσοισιν ἐπιπροέηκα θοῇσιν,

45.6 οὐ τὸ τάχος τῶν ἐρριζωμένων νήσων, ἠλίθιον[1] γάρ, δηλώσειν ἐσπουδακώς, ἀλλὰ τὸ σχῆμα πρὸς ὀξεῖαν ἀπολήγουσαν ἀποτελοῦν[2] γραμμήν. **45.7** Εἰκότως οὖν νύκτα θοὴν λέγεσθαι τὴν ἐπ' ὀξὺ τέλος τῆς ἐσχάτης σκιᾶς ἀποτερματίζουσαν.

46.1 Φυσικῶς δὲ διὰ τούτων[3] ὁ λόγος ἀποδείκνυσιν, ὅτι σφαιροειδής ἐστιν ὁ κόσμος. **46.2** Τριχῇ γὰρ οἱ μαθηματικοὶ τὰ σχήματα τῶν σκιῶν φασιν ἀποπίπτειν. **46.3** Ἐπειδὰν γὰρ ἔλαττον ᾖ τὸ περιλάμπον τοῦ καταλαμπομένου, τὴν σκιὰν συμβέβηκε καλαθοειδῶς ἐπὶ τὴν ὑστάτην πλατύνεσθαι βάσιν, ἀπὸ λεπτῆς ἀνισταμένην τῆς κατὰ κορυφὴν ἀρχῆς. **46.4** Ὅταν δὲ μεῖζον ᾖ τὸ καταλάμπον φῶς τοῦ καταλαμπομένου τόπου, κωνοειδῆ συμβέβηκε τὴν σκιὰν ἀπὸ πλατείας τῆς ἀρχῆς εἰς λεπτὸν ἀποστενοῦσθαι πέρας. **46.5** Ἐπειδάν γε μὴν ἴσον ᾖ τῷ καταλαμπομένῳ τὸ καταλάμπον, κυλίνδρου δίκην ἡ σκιὰ πρὸς ἴσον ἐν ταῖς ἑκατέρωθεν ἔχει γραμμαῖς. **46.6** Βουλόμενος οὖν Ὅμηρος τὸν ἥλιον ἄλλως μείζονα τῆς γῆς κατὰ τὴν τῶν πλείστων

---

1. Te, with some mss. of the Homeric scholia; mss., Bu read ἠλιθίως.
2. Te, following the Aldine edition; mss., Bu read ἀποτελεῖν. The text remains unsure, though the general sense is clear.
3. D, Te; Bu, with A, G, and the Homeric scholia, reads περὶ τούτου, "about this."

For if Homer had chosen to name him after his father, he would have
said "Hyperionides," on the analogy of "Atrides" for Agamemnon or
"Pelides" for Achilles.[1]

45 *Thoê*[2] as an epithet of night denotes simply the spherical shape of
the whole heaven, because night runs the same course as the sun and
every area abandoned by him is at once darkened by her. Homer makes
this quite clear in another passage:

> And into ocean fell the sun's bright light,
> drawing black night over the fertile land.[3]

For he draws night behind him, as though she were tied to him, and
she keeps pace with the sun's speed. So Homer very properly calls her
thoê, "swift." However, one may, perhaps more convincingly, argue
that *thoê* is to be taken metaleptically, not of sharp movement but of
sharpness of shape. Homer says elsewhere:

> From there I headed towards sharp-pointed [*thoêisin*] islands.[4]

He had no intention of saying anything about the *speed* of firmly rooted
islands (that would be absurd) but only about their shape, which produces a line terminating in an acute angle. So night could reasonably be
called *thoê*, because the extreme end of its shadow ends in a sharp point.

46 In scientific terms, this passage demonstrates that the universe is
spherical. Mathematicians tell us that the shapes of shadows fall in three
ways. When the source of light is smaller than the object illuminated, the
shadow bulges out like a basket towards its base, rising from the slender
apex in which it originates. When the source of light is greater than the
area it illuminates, the shadow is in the shape of a cone, narrowing down
from a broad beginning to its slender end. When, again, the source of
light and the object illuminated are the same size, the shadow maintains
an equal distance between the lines which define its two sides, like a
cylinder. Homer therefore, wishing to show anyway that the sun is larger

---

1. The sons of Atreus and Peleus, respectively; the father of Helios, the sun god, was
Hyperion.
2. See Ps.-Plutarch, *Vit. poes. Hom.* 21 with Hillgruber's commentary (1994–1999, 1:135);
the meaning of *thoos* was much discussed.
3. *Il.* 8.485–486.
4. *Od.* 15.299.

φιλοσόφων ἔννοιαν ἀποδεῖξαι, εὐλόγως θοὴν τὴν νύκτα προσηγόρευσεν εἰς ὀξὺ τὸ πρὸς τῷ πέρατι σχῆμα λήγουσαν, ἅτ' οἶμαι μήτε κυλινδροειδῶς μήτε καλαθοειδῶς τῆς σκιᾶς πίπτειν δυναμένης, ἀλλὰ τὸν λεγόμενον κῶνον ἀποτελούσης. **46.7** Ὁ δὴ πρῶτος Ὅμηρος ἐκ μιᾶς λέξεως ὑπαινιξάμενος τὰς μυρίας τῶν φιλοσόφων ἀμίλλας ἐπιτέτμηται.

47.1 Καὶ μὴν <καὶ>[1] αἱ φοραὶ τῶν ἐναντίων ἀνέμων δηλοῦσι τὸ τοῦ κόσμου σφαιροειδές. **47.2** Βορέας μὲν γὰρ ἀπὸ τῆς ἄρκτου πνέων μετέωρος "μέγα κῦμα κυλίνδει·" τὴν γὰρ ἀπὸ τοῦ μεταρσίου φορὰν ἐπὶ τὸ ταπεινότερον ἐκ μιᾶς λέξεως κατεκύλισεν ὁ στίχος. **47.3** Τοὔμπαλιν δ' ἐπὶ τοῦ νότου πνέοντος ἀπὸ τῶν κάτω τόπων ἱστόρησεν·

ἔνθα νότος μέγα κῦμα ποτὶ σκαιὸν ῥίον ὠθεῖ,

τὴν ἀπὸ τοῦ ταπεινοτέρου κίνησιν εἰς τὸ μετέωρον ἀνακυλίει. **47.4** Ἔτι γε μὴν μετὰ τῶν ἄλλων "ἀπείρονα γαῖαν" ὀνομάζει καὶ πάλιν ἐπὶ τῆς Ἥρας·

Εἶμι γὰρ ὀψομένη πολυφόρβου πείρατα γαίης,

47.5 οὐ δήπου μαχομέναις δόξαις πρὸς αὐτὸν στασιάζων, ἀλλ' ἐπειδὴ πᾶν σφαιροειδὲς σχῆμα καὶ ἄπειρόν ἐστι καὶ πεπερασμένον· **47.6** τῷ μὲν γὰρ ὅρον τινὰ καὶ περιγραφὴν ἔχειν εὐλόγως αὐτὸ πεπεράσθαι νομιστέον, ἄπειρον δ' ἂν ὁ κύκλος ὀνομάζοιτο δικαίως, ἐπειδήπερ ἀμήχανόν ἐστι δεῖξαι πέρας ἐν αὐτῷ τι· τὸ γὰρ νομισθὲν εἶναι τέλος ἐξ ἴσου γένοιτ' ἂν ἀρχή.

48.1 Ταυτὶ μὲν οὖν ἀθρόα τεκμήρια τοῦ σφαιροειδῆ τὸν κόσμον εἶναι παρ' Ὁμήρῳ, τὸ δ' ἐναργέστατόν ἐστι σύμβολον ἡ τῆς Ἀχιλλέως ἀσπίδος κατασκευή.[2] **48.2** Κυκλοτερὲς γὰρ τῷ σχήματι κεχάλκευκεν ὅπλον Ἥφαιστος, ὥσπερ εἰκόνα τῆς κοσμικῆς περιόδου. **48.3** Μυθικῶς μὲν οὖν ἀσπίδα χαλκευομένην ὑποστησάμενος ἁρμόζουσαν <ἂν>[3] Ἀχιλλεῖ τὴν διὰ πάντων ἐνεχάραξε πορείαν. **48.4** Τίς δ' ἦν αὕτη;

Στησάμενοι δ' ἐμάχοντο μάχην ποταμοῖο παρ' ὄχθας,

---

1. Te, following Polak; omitted by mss., Bu.
2. Te, following D, Homeric scholia; A, G, Bu read τῆς Ἀχιλλέως ἀσπίδος κατασκευῆς (omitting ἡ).
3. Te, rightly, rendering the main clause counterfactual; omitted in mss., Bu.

than the earth, as most philosophers think, very reasonably called the night *thoê* because it terminates in a sharp point at the end: the shadow, to be sure, cannot fall in the shape of a cylinder or a basket, but forms what is called a cone.[1] Homer was the first to suggest this, and the hint given by this one word cuts short the innumerable disputes of the philosophers.

47 The movements of the opposing winds also display the spherical shape of the universe. Boreas, blowing from the north, high up, "rolls a great wave": the line rolls a movement which starts high up down to a lower region by a single word.[2] Conversely, he reports of the south wind, which blows from a lower region:

> where to the headland on the left
> the south wind drives its mighty wave.[3]

This line rolls back a movement from lower to higher. Again, he calls the earth "boundless," as others do, but also makes Hera say

> I go to see the bounds of fertile earth.[4]

He is not contradicting himself here with conflicting views: he says this because every spherical object is both infinite and finite. That it is finite may be plausibly concluded from its having a boundary and a circumference; but a circle can very properly be called infinite, because it is impossible to point to any limit in it: what is taken to be the end might equally well be the beginning.[5]

48 These proofs taken together show that Homer regards the universe as spherical. But the clearest token of this is the construction of Achilles' shield, since Hephaestus forged this weapon in circular form, as an image of the cosmic circle. If he had chosen to present the forging of the shield as a mere story, he would have engraved the whole sequence of scenes in a manner appropriate to Achilles. And what would that have been?

> They stood and fought beside the river bank

---

1. Cf. Cleomedes, *On the Cosmos* 2.2, p. 63 Todd; 2.6, p. 90 Todd.
2. *Od.* 5.296; the word is "rolls." Cf. Ps.-Plutarch, *Vit. poes. Hom.* 109–110, with Hill-gruber's discussion (1994–1999, 2:243–45).
3. *Od.* 3.295.
4. *Il.* 14.200.
5. The idea is a commonplace; cf., e.g., Aristotle, *Phys.* 264b9ff.

βάλλον δ' ἀλλήλους χαλκήρεσιν ἐγχείησιν.
Ἐν δ' Ἔρις, ἐν δὲ Κυδοιμὸς ὁμίλεον, ἐν δ' ὀλοὴ Κήρ,
ἄλλον ζῶὸν ἔχουσα νεούτατον, ἄλλον ἄουτον,
ἄλλον τεθνειῶτα κατὰ μόθον ἕλκε ποδοῖιν.

Ταῦτα γὰρ ἦν ὁ διηνεκὴς Ἀχιλλέως βίος. **48.5** Νῦν δὲ Ὅμηρος ἰδίᾳ τινὶ φιλοσοφίᾳ δημιουργῶν τὸν κόσμον εὐθὺς τὰ μέγιστα τῆς προνοίας ἔργα μετὰ τὴν ἀδιευκρίνητον καὶ κεχυμένην ὕλην ἐχάλκευσεν·

Ἐν μὲν γαῖαν ἔτευξ', ἐν δ' οὐρανόν, ἐν δὲ θάλασσαν
ἠέλιόν τ' ἀκάμαντα σελήνην τε πλήθουσαν.

48.6 Ἡ τῆς κοσμικῆς γενέσεως εἱμαρμένη πρῶτον θεμελιοῦχον ἐκρότησε τὴν γῆν· εἶτα ἐπὶ ταύτῃ καθάπερ τινὰ θείαν στέγην τὸν οὐρανὸν ἐπωρόφωσε καὶ κατὰ τῶν ἀναπεπταμένων αὐτῆς κόλπων ἀθρόαν ἔχεε τὴν θάλατταν· εὐθύς τε ἡλίῳ τε καὶ σελήνῃ τὰ διακριθέντα τῶν στοιχείων ἀπὸ τοῦ πάλαι χάους ἐφώτισεν. **48.7**

Ἐν δὲ τὰ τείρεα πάντα, τά τ' οὐρανὸς ἐστεφάνωται·

δι' οὗ μάλιστα σφαιροειδῆ παραδέδωκεν ἡμῖν τὸν κόσμον. **48.8** Ὥσπερ γὰρ ὁ στέφανος κυκλοτερὴς τῆς κεφαλῆς κόσμος ἐστίν, οὕτω τὰ διεζωκότα τὴν οὐράνιον ἁψῖδα, κατὰ σφαιροειδοῦς ἐσπαρμένα σχήματος, εἰκότως οὐρανοῦ στέφανος ὠνόμασται.

49.1 Διακριβολογησάμενος δ' ὑπὲρ τῶν ὁλοσχερῶν ἀστέρων καὶ κατὰ μέρος <τὰ>[1] ἐπιφανέστατα δεδήλωκεν· οὐ γὰρ ἠδύνατο πάντα θεολογεῖν, ὥσπερ Εὔδοξος ἢ Ἄρατος, Ἰλιάδα γράφειν ἀντὶ τῶν **Φαινομένων** ὑποστησάμενος ἑαυτῷ.

49.2 Μεταβέβηκεν οὖν ἀλληγορικῶς ἐπὶ τὰς δύο πόλεις, τὴν μὲν εἰρήνης, τὴν δὲ πολέμου παρεισάγων, ἵνα μηδ' Ἐμπεδοκλῆς ὁ Ἀκραγαντῖνος ἀπ' ἄλλου τινὸς ἢ παρ' Ὁμήρου τὴν Σικελικὴν ἀρύσηται δόξαν. **49.3** Ἅμα γὰρ τοῖς τέτταρσι στοιχείοις κατὰ τὴν φυσικὴν θεωρίαν παραδέδωκε τὸ νεῖκος καὶ τὴν φιλίαν· **49.4** τούτων δ' ἑκάτερον Ὅμηρος ὑποσημαίνων

---

1. Russell (καὶ τὰ κατὰ μέρος Mehler), taking ἐπιφανέστατα as an adjective; D, Te read καὶ τοὺς κατὰ μέρος, "and has shown us the individual stars with great clarity" (A, G, Bu omit τούς). In any case, we expect some reference to Homer's treatment of particular constellations: cf. Ps.-Plutarch, *Vit. poes. Hom.* 106. Quotation of *Il.* 18.480–489 has probably fallen out.

and struck each other with their bronze-tipped spears;
and Strife was there, and Riot, and dreadful Fate,
who seized a wounded man who yet still lived,
and one unwounded, and another dead,
dragging him feet first through the battle.[1]

That is what Achilles' whole life was like. But in fact Homer fashioned the world according to a philosophy of his own, and forged the greatest works of providence immediately after describing the undifferentiated melted material:

therein he wrought the earth, the heaven, the sea,
the untiring sun and the full rounded moon...[2]

The Destiny of Cosmic Creation first fashioned earth as the foundation, then set heaven above it as a kind of divine roof, and poured the sea altogether into its open lap; and then at once it gave light by means of the sun and the moon to the elements that had been separated out of the ancient chaos.

And all the constellations wherewith heaven is garlanded.[3]

In this, Homer particularly teaches us that the universe [*kosmos*] is spherical. For just as a garland is a circular adornment [*kosmos*] of the head, so too the objects which girdle the vault of heaven, scattered all over its sphere, are plausibly called the garland of heaven.

49 Having given this accurate description of the stars in general, he has also shown us in detail those which are most conspicuous: he could not of course include everything in his theology, like Eudoxus or Aratus, because he intended to write an *Iliad*, not a *Phaenomena*.[4]

He then proceeds in his allegory to the two cities, introducing the city of peace and the city of war. Thus it is from none other than Homer that Empedocles of Acragas[5] derived his doctrine. In his theory of nature, Empedocles tells not only of the four elements but of Strife and Love; and it was to suggest this pair that Homer fashioned

---

1. *Il.* 18.533–537.
2. *Il.* 18.483–484.
3. *Il.* 18.485.
4. The astronomical poem by Aratus based on the researches of Eudoxus.
5. Cf. chs. 24 and 69.

δύο¹ πόλεις ἐνεχάλκευσε τῇ ἀσπίδι τὴν μὲν εἰρήνης, τουτέστι τῆς φιλίας, τὴν δὲ πολέμου, τουτέστι νείκους.

50.1 Πτύχας δ' ὑπεστήσατο τῆς ἀσπίδος πέντε, σχεδὸν οὐκ ἄλλο τι πλὴν τὰς² ἐμπεποικιλμένας τῷ κόσμῳ ζώνας ὑπαινιξάμενος. **50.2** Ἡ μὲν γὰρ ἀνωτάτω περὶ τὸν βόρειον εἰλεῖται πόλον, ἀρκτικὴν δὲ αὐτὴν ὀνομάζουσιν· ἡ δ' ἐφεξῆς εὔκρατός ἐστιν· εἶτα τὴν τρίτην διακεκαυμένην καλοῦσιν· **50.3** ἡ τετάρτη δ' ὁμωνύμως τῇ πρότερον [δευτέρᾳ]³ εὔκρατος ὀνομάζεται· πέμπτη δ' ἐπώνυμος⁴ τοῦ νοτίου μέρους ἡ νότιός τε καὶ ἀντάρκτιος καλουμένη. **50.4** Τούτων αἱ μὲν δύο τελέως ἀοίκητοι διὰ τὸ κρύος, ἥ τε τὸν βόρειον εἰληχυῖα πόλον καὶ ἡ τὸν ἀπαντικρὺ νότιον· ὁμοίως δ' ἐν αὐταῖς ἡ διακεκαυμένη καθ' ὑπερβολὴν τῆς πυρώδους οὐσίας οὐδενὶ βατὴ ζῴῳ. **50.5** Δύο δὲ τὰς εὐκράτους φασὶν οἰκεῖσθαι, τὴν μέσην ἀφ' ἑκατέρας ζώνης κρᾶσιν ἐπιδεχομένας. **50.6** Ὁ γοῦν Ἐρατοσθένης καὶ σφοδρότερον ἐν τῷ Ἑρμῇ ταῦτα⁵ διηκρίβωσεν εἰπών· **50.7**

Πέντε δέ οἱ ζῶναι περιηγέες ἐσπείρηντο·⁶
αἱ δύο μὲν γλαυκοῖο κελαινότεραι κυάνοιο,
50.8 ἡ δὲ μία ψαφαρή τε καὶ ἐκ πυρὸς οἷον ἐρυθρή,
τυπτομένη φλογμοῖσιν, ἐπεί ῥά ἑ μαίραν ὑπ' αὐτήν⁷
κεκλιμένην ἀκτῖνες ἀειθερέες πυρόωσιν·
50.9 αἱ δὲ δύο ἑκάτερθε πόλοις περιπεπτηυῖαι⁸
αἰεὶ κρυμαλέαι, αἰεὶ δ' ὕδατι μογέουσαι.

51.1 Ταύτας οὖν Ὅμηρος πτύχας ὠνόμασεν ἐξ ὧν φησίν·

ἐπεὶ πέντε πτύχας ἤλασε κυλλοποδίων,
τὰς δύο χαλκείας, δύο δ' ἔνδοθι κασσιτέροιο,
τὴν δὲ μίαν χρυσῆν·

---

1. Te, following Mehler (the Homeric scholia put the numeral after πόλεις); Bu, following the mss., omits it (but one would have expected at least the article τάς).
2. Te, following D, Homeric scholia; Bu, following A, G, reads οὐκ, and offers a forced translation (reading ἐμπεποικιλμένοις with A).
3. Russell; A, G, Bu have τῇ πρότερον δευτέρᾳ, which is redundant; Te emends to δευτέρον. D, Homeric scholia read τῇ δευτέρᾳ (this gives a difficult hiatus), probably a gloss indicating that Heraclitus is referring to the second zone.
4. Te; G, Homeric scholia read ἐπωνύμως; A, Bu read the unattested form ἐπονύμως.
5. D, Te; A, G, Bu read ταύτῃ.
6. Te, following the Homeric scholia and Achilles Tatius, *Commentary on Aratus* (ed. Maass 1898); mss., Bu read ἐσπείρηνται.
7. Achilles; mss., Te, Bu read ἐπ' αὐτήν.
8. Te, following Achilles; mss., Bu read the unmetrical πόλοιο περιπεπηγυῖαι.

the two cities on the shield, the city of peace, that is of Love, and the city of war, that is of Strife.

50 Homer set up the five layers of the shield simply to give a hint of the zones that diversify the cosmos. The highest zone revolves around the northern pole, and they call it the arctic zone; the next is temperate; then comes the third, the "burnt" zone; the fourth, like the former, is called "temperate"; and the fifth, taking its name from the southern region, is called "southern" or "antarctic." Two of these—the zone that occupies the northern pole and the opposite zone that occupies the southern—are totally uninhabitable because of the cold. Likewise, the "burnt" zone is inaccessible to any living creature because of its excess of fiery substance. The two temperate zones, however, are said to be inhabited, because they enjoy a mixed climate intermediate between the other two. Eratosthenes has set all this out explicitly in more forceful language in his *Hermes:*

> Five circular zones lay coiled round it,
> two of them darker than blue enamel,
> one dry and red as if burned in fire,
> stricken with heat; for rays ever burning
> set it aflame beneath the Dog-star...
> but the two on either side near to the poles
> are always icy, always plagued by rain.[1]

51 Homer called these zones "layers," in the lines:

> For the lame god had forged five layers,
> two of bronze, and two of tin within,
> and one of gold.[2]

---

1. Eratosthenes frg. 16 Powell = frg. 19 Hiller, but omitting line 6: Ἡ μὲν ἔην μεσάτη, ἐκέκαυτο δὲ πᾶσα περι<πρὸ>, "This was the midmost, it was burnt through and through." There are also other slight changes, e.g. περιηγέες for περιειλάδες in the first verse. The omission of v. 6 may be deliberate, since there was argument over the position of the gold band on the shield; see Buffière (1962, 121) on the order of the five layers, and cf. Virgil, *Georg.* 1.233–239 with Mynors's notes (1990, 325).

2. *Il.* 20.270–272.

51.2 τὰς μὲν ἀνωτάτω κατὰ τοὺς ἀλαμπεῖς μυχοὺς τοῦ κόσμου κειμένας δύο ζώνας χαλκῷ προσεικάσας· ψυχρὰ γὰρ ἡ ὕλη καὶ κρύους μεστή· λέγει γοῦν ἑτέρωθί που·

Ψυχρὸν δ᾽ ἕλε χαλκὸν ὀδοῦσι·

51.3 "τὴν δὲ μίαν χρυσῆν"[1] τὴν διακεκαυμένην, ἐπειδήπερ ἡ πυρώδης οὐσία κατὰ τὴν χρόαν ἐμφερεστάτη χρυσῷ· **51.4** "δύο δ᾽ ἐνδόθι κασσιτέροιο" τὰς εὐκράτους ὑποσημαίνων· ὑγρὰ γὰρ ἡ ὕλη καὶ τελέως εὔτηκτος[2] ἡ τοῦ κασσιτέρου, δι᾽ ἧς τὸ περὶ τὰς ζώνας εὐαφὲς ἡμῖν καὶ μαλθακὸν δεδήλωκεν. **51.5** Τὸ μὲν οὖν ἐν οὐρανῷ σεμνὸν ἐργαστήριον Ἡφαίστου τὴν ἱερὰν φύσιν οὕτως ἐδημιούργησεν.

52.1 Ἀνίσταται δ᾽ εὐθὺς ὁ φρικώδης καὶ χαλεπὸς ἐφ᾽ Ὁμήρῳ τῶν συκοφαντούντων φθόνος ὑπὲρ τῆς θεομαχίας. **52.2** Οὐ γὰρ ἔτι "Τρώων καὶ Ἀχαιῶν φύλοπις αἰνὴ" παρ᾽ αὐτῷ συνέρρωγεν, ἀλλ᾽ οὐράνιοι[3] ταραχαὶ καὶ στάσεις τὸ θεῖον ἐπινέμονται· **52.3**

Ἦ τοι μὲν γὰρ ἔναντα Ποσειδάωνος ἄνακτος
ἵστατ᾽ Ἀπόλλων Φοῖβος ἔχων ἰὰ πτερόεντα,
ἄντα δ᾽ Ἐνυαλίοιο θεὰ γλαυκῶπις Ἀθήνη,
Ἥρῃ δ᾽ ἀντέστη χρυσηλάκατος κελαδεινή
Ἄρτεμις ἰοχέαιρα, κασιγνήτη Ἑκάτοιο,
Λητοῖ δ᾽ ἀντέστη σῶκος ἐριούνιος Ἑρμῆς,
ἄντα δ᾽ ἄρ᾽ Ἡφαίστοιο μέγας ποταμὸς βαθυδίνης.

52.4 Οὐκέτι ταῦθ᾽ Ἕκτωρ πρὸς Αἴαντα μαχόμενος, οὐδ᾽ Ἀχιλλεὺς πρὸς Ἕκτορα καὶ μετὰ Πατρόκλου Σαρπηδών, ἀλλὰ τὸν μέγαν οὐρανοῦ πόλεμον ἀγωνοθετήσας Ὅμηρος οὐδ᾽[4] ἄχρι μελλήσεως τὸ κακὸν ὥπλισεν,[5] ἀλλ᾽ ὁμόσε τοὺς θεοὺς συνέρραξεν ἀλλήλοις. **52.5** "Ἑπτὰ" μὲν γὰρ Ἄρης "ἐπέσχε πέλεθρα πεσών, ἐκόνισε δὲ χαίτας," μετὰ ταῦτα δὲ Ἀφροδίτης "λύτο γούνατα καὶ φίλον ἦτορ." **52.6** Ἄρτεμις δὲ καὶ προσεξύβρισται τοῖς ἰδίοις

---

1. Te, following the Homeric scholia, inserts εἰπών.
2. Te, following Hemsterhuis; Bu, following LSJ (s.v.) reads εὔεικτος, "pliant"; the mss. εὔθικτος would mean "to the point, clever."
3. Te, following D, Homeric scholia; Bu reads οὐράνιαι, with A, G, but this is contrary to Heraclitus's usage.
4. Mss., Te, Bu; but Diels's οὐκ is very likely right.
5. Buffière's translation, "il n'arrête pas la bataille au moment où le fléau va se déchaîner" seems to imply ὥρισεν for ὥπλισεν, an emendation worth considering.

He likens the two upper zones, which correspond to the unilluminated recesses of the cosmos, to bronze, because that material is cold and icy. Note that he says in another passage:

And took the *cold* bronze in his teeth.[1]

By the "one gold" layer, he means the burnt zone, because its fiery substance most resembles gold in coloring. By the "two zones of tin within" he signifies the temperate zones, because the material of tin is malleable and quite easily melted, and so he uses it to denote the accessibility and comfort of these zones to us. And so Hephaestus's noble workshop in heaven created holy Nature.[2]

52 But next there rises up against Homer the fearsome and grievous malice of his accusers, in the matter of his Battle of the Gods. It is no longer "dread strife of Trojans and Achaeans"[3] that breaks out in his text; confusions and contentions in heaven infect the gods themselves:

Phoebus Apollo with his winged arrows
confronts the lord Poseidon; grey-eyed Athena
faces the war-god; and to counter Hera
comes Artemis with golden bow resounding
and showers of arrows, she the Archer's sister;
and Hermes, the strong helper, faces Leto;
against Hephaestus, the great eddying river.[4]

Here is no battle of Hector with Ajax or Achilles with Hector or Patroclus and Sarpedon. No: Homer has organized the great war of heaven; he has not set up this disastrous conflict as a mere threat, but really brought the gods to come to blows with one another. Ares "covered seven acres in his fall, and fouled his hair."[5] Then Aphrodite's "knees and heart failed her."[6] Artemis fared worse: she was shamefully wounded by her own bow, like

---

1. *Il.* 5.75.
2. A strange phrase, perhaps signifying "the substance of the divine universe," rather than a personification of Nature.
3. *Il.* 6.1.
4. *Il.* 20.67–73.
5. *Il.* 21.407.
6. *Il.* 21.425.

τόξοις, ὡς νηπία¹ κόρη σωφρονισθεῖσα, Ξάνθος δὲ παρ' ὀλίγον οὐδὲ ποταμὸς ἐρρύη διὰ Ἥφαιστον.

53.1 Ὅμως δ' οὖν πάντα ταῦτα κατ' ἀρχὰς μὲν οὐδ' ὅλως σφόδρα πείθειν δύναται τοὺς πολλούς. **53.2** Εἰ δ' ἐθελήσει τις ἐνδοτέρω καταβὰς τῶν Ὁμηρικῶν ὀργίων ἐποπτεῦσαι τὴν μυστικὴν αὐτοῦ σοφίαν, ἐπιγνώσεται τὸ δοκοῦν [αὐτῷ]² ἀσέβημα πηλίκης μεστόν ἐστι φιλοσοφίας. **53.3** Ἐνίοις μὲν οὖν ἀρέσκει τὴν τῶν ἑπτὰ πλανήτων ἀστέρων ἐν ἑνὶ ζῳδίῳ σύνοδον ὑφ' Ὁμήρου διὰ τούτων διελεγχθῆναι·³ φθορὰ δὲ παντελής, ὅταν τοῦτο γένηται. **53.4** Σύγχυσιν οὖν τοῦ παντὸς ὑπαινίττεται, συνάγων εἰς ἓν Ἀπόλλωνα, τουτέστιν ἥλιον, καὶ Ἄρτεμιν, ἣν φαμὲν εἶναι σελήνην, τόν τε τῆς Ἀφροδίτης καὶ Ἄρεος ἔτι δὲ καὶ Ἑρμοῦ καὶ Διὸς ἀστέρα. **53.5** Ταύτην μὲν οὖν πιθανότητος μᾶλλον ἢ ἀληθείας ἐχομένην τὴν ἀλληγορίαν ἄχρι τοῦ μὴ δοκεῖν ἀγνοεῖν παρειλήφαμεν. Ἃ δ' ἐστὶν ἐναργέστερα καὶ τῆς Ὁμήρου σοφίας ἐχόμενα, ταύτῃ δὴ σκοπεῖν ἀναγκαῖον.

54.1 Ἀντέταξε γοῦν κακίαις μὲν ἀρετάς, ταῖς δὲ μαχομέναις φύσεσι τὰς ἀντιπάλους. **54.2** Αὐτίκα τῶν θεῶν ἡ ζεῦξις οὕτω πεφιλοσόφηται· τῆς μάχης <ἄρχουσιν>⁴ Ἀθηνᾶ καὶ Ἄρης, τουτέστιν ἀφροσύνη καὶ φρόνησις. **54.3** Ὁ μὲν γάρ, ὥσπερ ἔφην, "μαινόμενός" ἐστι, "τυκτὸν κακόν, ἀλλοπρόσαλλον," ἡ δ' "ἐν πᾶσι" θεοῖς "μήτι τε" κλέεται "καὶ κέρδεσιν." **54.4** Ἀδιάλλακτός γε μὴν ἔχθρα τοῖς τὰ βέλτιστα διευκρινοῦσι λογισμοῖς πρὸς τὴν οὐδὲν ὁρῶσαν ἀφροσύνην. **54.5** Ὡς δὲ μάλιστα τὸν βίον ὀνήσειν ἔμελλεν, οὕτω τὰ τῆς μάχης διευκρίνησεν· οὐ γὰρ ἡ μεμηνυῖα καὶ παραπλὴξ ἀναισθησία τῆς συνέσεως γέγονε κρείττων. **54.6** Ἐνίκησε δ' Ἀθηνᾶ τὸν Ἄρην καὶ κατὰ γῆς ἐξέτεινεν, ἐπειδήπερ ἅπασα κακία χαμαιπετὴς ἐν τοῖς ταπεινοτάτοις ἔρριπται βαράθροις, πατούμενον νόσημα καὶ πρὸς πᾶσαν ὕβριν ὑποκείμενον. **54.7** Ἀμέλει συνεξέτεινεν αὐτῷ τὴν Ἀφροδίτην, τουτέστι τὴν ἀκολασίαν· "τὼ μὲν ἄρ' ἄμφω κεῖντο ἐπὶ χθονὶ πουλυβοτείρῃ," συγγενῆ καὶ τοῖς πάθεσι γειτνιῶντα νοσήματα.⁵

---

1. Te, following D, Homeric scholia; Bu, following A, G, reads ἀνηπία, unattested and unintelligible (he cites a mention in Demetrakos and Spyridonos [1949–1951], but this does not show that the term is classical).

2. Bracketed by Te, to avoid hiatus; alternatively, transpose to follow πηλίκης.

3. Te (cf. D, ἐλεγχθῆναι); Bu, following A, G, and the Homeric scholia, reads δὴ λεχθεῖσαν, "mentioned."

4. Russell, after Bekker (cf. *Il.* 21.392). Te indicates a lacuna after πεφιλοσόφηται (Bu punctuates after τῆς μάχης, "pour le bataille").

5. So Te; τὰ νοσήματα A, G, Bu.

a little girl being punished.[1] Finally, Xanthus, thanks to Hephaestus's efforts, almost ceased to be a running river at all.[2]

53 For all that, all these tales cannot even at first sight be entirely convincing to most people. However, anyone who is prepared to delve deeper into Homer's rites and be initiated in his mystical wisdom will recognize that what is believed to be impiety is in fact charged with deep philosophy. Some think that Homer in this episode has revealed the conjunction of the seven planets in a single zodiacal sign. Now whenever this happens, total disaster ensues. He is therefore hinting at the destruction of the universe, bringing together Apollo (the sun), Artemis (the moon), and the stars of Aphrodite, Ares, Hermes, and Zeus.[3] I have included this allegory, which is plausible rather than true, just so far as not to be thought ignorant of it.[4] But we must now examine a more transparent solution which reflects Homer's wisdom.

54 What he has done in fact is to oppose virtues to vices and conflicting elements to their opposites. For example, the pairing of the gods has the following philosophical significance. Athena and Ares—that is to say, folly and wisdom—<begin> the battle. Ares, as I said,[5] is "mad, finished evil, double-faced," and Athena "is famed among all gods for counsel and for cunning."[6] There is in truth an irreconcilable enmity between reasonings that determine what is best and folly that sees nothing. And Homer has expounded the battle in the way that was most going to help human life. Inane and deranged foolishness has not prevailed over intelligence. Athena defeated Ares and laid him low, because vice always falls to the ground and is cast into the deepest pit, an affliction which is trampled on and exposed to every injury. Note that Athena laid low Aphrodite—that is to say, incontinence—as well: "these both lay on the fruitful earth,"[7] being kindred afflictions and similar in their effects.

---

1. *Il.* 21.490.
2. *Il.* 21.328–380.
3. I.e., Venus, Mars, Mercury, and Jupiter.
4. Compare Plutarch's critique of astrological allegory in *Adol. poet. aud.* 19E–20B; Plutarch too argues that the text invites rather an ethical interpretation.
5. Ch. 31; cf. *Il.* 5.831.
6. Cf. *Od.* 13.298–299.
7. *Il.* 21.426.

55.1 Λητοῖ δ' ἀνθέστηκεν Ἑρμῆς, ἐπειδήπερ ὁ μὲν οὐδὲν ἄλλο πλὴν λόγος ἐστὶ τῶν ἔνδον ἑρμηνεὺς[1] παθῶν, **55.2** λόγῳ δὲ παντὶ μάχεται Λητώ, οἱονεὶ ληθώ τις οὖσα καθ' ἑνὸς στοιχείου μετάθεσιν· **55.3** τὸ γὰρ ἀμνημονούμενον οὐκέτι ἀγγελθῆναι δύναται, διὸ δὴ καὶ μητέρα Μουσῶν Μνημοσύνην ἱστοροῦσι, τὰς προστατίδας λόγου θεὰς ἀπὸ μνήμης[2] γεγενῆσθαι λέγοντες. **55.4** Εἰκὸς οὖν τὴν λήθην πρὸς ἀντίπαλον ἄμιλλαν ἐξωρμηκέναι. **55.5** Δικαίως δ' ὑπεῖξεν αὐτῇ· λόγου γὰρ ἧττα λήθη, καὶ τὸ φανερὸν ὑπ' ἀμνηστίας ἐν κωφῇ νενίκηται σιωπῇ.

56.1 Τῶν γε μὴν ὑπολειπομένων θεῶν ἡ μάχη φυσικωτέρα·

Ἦ τοι μὲν γὰρ ἔναντα Ποσειδάωνος ἄνακτος
ἵστατ' Ἀπόλλων Φοῖβος.

56.2 Ὕδατι πῦρ ἀντέθηκε, τὸν μὲν ἥλιον Ἀπόλλωνα προσαγορεύσας, τὴν δ' ὑγρὰν φύσιν Ποσειδῶνα. **56.3** Τούτων δ' ἑκάτερον ὡς ἐναντίαν ἔχει[3] δύναμιν, τί δεῖ καὶ λέγειν; **56.4** φθαρτικὸν κατ' ἐπικράτειαν ἀεὶ θατέρου θάτερον. **56.5** Καὶ μὴν ὑπὸ λεπτῆς τῆς περὶ τὴν ἀλήθειαν θεωρίας διέλυσεν[4] ἀμφοῖν τὴν μάχην, **56.6** ἐπειδήπερ ἡλίου τροφὴν ἀπεφηνάμεθα τὴν ἔνυγρον οὐσίαν καὶ μάλιστα τὴν ἁλμυράν **56.7** — λεληθότως γὰρ ἀπὸ γῆς τὸ δίυγρον ἀνασπῶν τῆς ἀτμίδος τούτῳ μάλιστα τὴν πυρώδη φύσιν αὔξει —, **56.8** χαλεπὸν δ' ἦν τῷ τρέφοντι τὸ τρεφόμενον ἀνθεστάναι, διὰ τοῦθ' ὑπεῖξαν ἀλλήλοις.

57.1 Ἥρη δ' ἀντέστη χρυσηλάκατος κελαδεινή
Ἄρτεμις ἰοχέαιρα.

57.2 Οὐδὲ τοῦτ' ἀλόγως εἰσήγαγεν Ὅμηρος· ἀλλ' ὥσπερ ἔφην Ἥρα μέν

---

1. Te (inserted by Hercher after παθῶν); mss., Bu read ἐν ἡμῖν, i.e., "represents the report [λόγος] of our inner experiences." The etymological reference is essential; cf. what follows concerning Leto and Letho.
2. ἀπό Mehler; μνήμης D, Homeric scholia, Te; A, G, Bu read ὑπὸ μνήμην.
3. G, D, Te; Bu, following A, reads the ungrammatical ἔχειν.
4. Te in apparatus criticus; διαλύει (Te, D) yields an illicit hiatus; Bu, with A, G, reads διαλύειν (the Homeric scholia have διαλύειν ἔστιν, "one can resolve").

55 Hermes opposes Leto, because Hermes represents speech, which is the interpreter [*hermêneus*] of inner experiences, and Leto (change one letter and she is Letho, "forgetfulness")[1] fights against all speech, because what is not remembered cannot be reported. This is why they say that Memory is the mother of the Muses,[2] meaning that the goddesses who preside over speech are born of remembrance. It is to be expected therefore that forgetfulness should come forth to fight her opponent, and very justly did Hermes yield to her,[3] for forgetfulness is the defeat of speech, and plain truth is vanquished by loss of memory and buried in dumb silence.

56 The battle of the remaining gods on the other hand has a more scientific explanation:

> against the lord Poseidon
> stood Phoebus Apollo.[4]

Here Homer opposes fire to water, calling the sun Apollo and the liquid substance Poseidon. Is it necessary to explain how these two have opposite powers? When one dominates the other it always destroys it. But Homer has resolved the conflict between them by a subtle view of the truth. Since we have shown[5] that the sun is nourished by the liquid element, and especially by that which is salty—for it is by imperceptibly drawing up from the earth the dampness of its vapors that the sun principally increases his fire—and since it would have been difficult for the recipient of nourishment to oppose the giver, these therefore gave way to each other.

57 To counter Hera
came Artemis with golden bow resounding
and showers of arrows.[6]

Homer has not introduced these details either without good reason. As I

---

1. Cf. Plato, *Crat.* 400A.
2. See Hesiod, *Theog.* 54, with West's comment (1966, 174–75).
3. *Il.* 21.498.
4. *Il.* 20.67.
5. Chapters 8 and 36.
6. *Il.* 20.70–71.

ἐστιν ἀήρ, τὴν δὲ σελήνην Ἄρτεμιν ὀνομάζει· **57.3** πᾶν δὲ τὸ τεμνόμενον
ἀεὶ πολέμιόν ἐστι τῷ τέμνοντι· **57.4** διὰ τοῦτο ἐχθρὰν ἀέρι τὴν σελήνην
ὑπεστήσατο τὴν ἐν ἀέρι αὐτῆς φορὰν καὶ τοὺς δρόμους ὑποσημαίνων. **57.5**
Εἰκὸς δὲ ταχέως νενικῆσθαι τὴν σελήνην, **57.6** ἐπειδήπερ ὁ μὲν ἀὴρ πολὺς
καὶ πάντη κεχυμένος, ἡ δ᾽ ἐλάττων καὶ συνεχῶς ὑπὸ τῶν ἀερίων παθημάτων
ἀμαυρουμένη τοῦτο μὲν ἐκλείψεσι, τοῦτο δ᾽ ἀχλύι καὶ ταῖς ὑποτρεχούσαις
νεφέλαις. **57.7** Διὰ τοῦτο τῆς νίκης τὰ βραβεῖα τῷ μείζονι καὶ συνεχῶς
βλάπτοντι προσέθηκεν.

58.1 Ἄντα δ᾽ ἄρ᾽ Ἡφαίστοιο μέγας ποταμὸς βαθυδίνης.

58.2 Ἐν τοῖς ὑπὲρ Ἀπόλλωνος καὶ Ποσειδῶνος λόγοις τὸν οὐράνιον[1] ἡμῖν
αἰθέρα καὶ τὴν ἀκήρατον ἡλίου φλόγα δηλώσας, νῦν μεταβέβηκεν ἐπὶ τὸ
θνητὸν πῦρ καὶ τοῦτο ἀνθώπλισε ποταμῷ, τὴν διάφορον ἑκατέρου φύσιν εἰς
μάχην παροξύνας. **58.3** Πρότερον μὲν οὖν εἴκοντα τὸν ἥλιον Ποσειδῶνι
παρεισάγει, νῦν δὲ τὴν ὑγρὰν οὐσίαν ὑπὸ τῆς πυρώδους ἡττωμένην·
δυνατώτερον γὰρ τόδε τὸ στοιχεῖον θατέρου. **58.4** Τίς οὖν οὕτω μέμηνεν ὡς
θεοὺς μαχομένους ἀλλήλοις παρεισάγειν, Ὁμήρου φυσικῶς ταῦτα δι᾽ ἀλληγορίας θεολογήσαντος;

59.1 Ἐπὶ τέλει οὖν[2] τῆς Ἰλιάδος καὶ σφόδρα τὸν Ἑρμῆν ἐναργῶς ἀκο-
λουθοῦντα Πριάμῳ δεδήλωκεν ἀλληγορήσας. **59.2** Οὐδὲν γὰρ ἔοικεν οὕτω
πειθήνιον ἀνδράσιν ὀργιζομένοις, οὐκ ἄργυρος, οὐ χρυσός, οὐδ᾽ ἡ διὰ δώρων
πολυτέλεια·[3] **59.3** μειλίχιον δὲ καὶ προσηνὲς ἱκεσίας ὅπλον ἐστὶν ἡ διὰ τοῦ
λόγου πειθώ. **59.4** Πάνυ γοῦν ἀληθῶς Εὐριπίδης·

Οὐκ ἔστι Πειθοῦς ἱρὸν ἄλλο πλὴν λόγος.

59.5 Τούτῳ τε Πρίαμος ὥσπερ ὀχυρᾷ παντευχίᾳ καθώπλισται· ᾧ καὶ μάλιστα
τὴν Ἀχιλλέως ἐπέκλασεν ὀργήν, οὐκ ἐν ἀρχῇ δείξας "δώδεκα πέπλους,
δώδεκα δ᾽ ἁπλοΐδας χλαίνας" τά τε λοιπὰ τῶν κομισθέντων δώρων, **59.6** ἀλλ᾽
αἱ πρῶται τῆς ἱκεσίας φωναὶ τοὺς ἄρσενας αὐτοῦ θυμοὺς ἐξεθήλυναν·

---

1. Te, following D, Homeric scholia; A, G, Bu read the rarer form ἐνουράνιον, not found
elsewhere in Heraclitus.

2. οὖν is, as Te notes in apparatus criticus, suspect: not only because of the hiatus, however, but because the connection with what precedes is unclear. Perhaps δ᾽ οὖν—"however
that may be"—a transition formula, introducing a new topic and dismissing the last (cf. Denniston 1954, 460).

3. A, G, Bu; Te, following D and the Homeric scholia, reads οὐ δώρων πολυτέλεια. The
sense is not affected.

have said, Hera is air, and he calls the moon Artemis.[1] Now whatever is cut [*temnomenon*] is always the enemy of the cutter [*temnon*], and this is why he has made the moon the enemy of the air [*aêr*], suggesting thereby the movement and course of the moon through the air. It is natural that the moon should soon be defeated, because the air is abundant and is diffused in every direction, whereas the moon is smaller and is often dimmed by events in the air, sometimes by eclipses, sometimes by mist and clouds that pass beneath her. Homer has therefore awarded the prize of victory to the greater power, the one that so often damages its adversary.

58 Against Hephaestus, the great eddying river.[2]

Having shown us, by his account of Apollo and Poseidon, the aether of heaven and the pure fire of the sun, he now turns to mortal fire and makes it take up arms against the river, rousing these two contrary elements to do battle. He has previously presented the sun as giving way to Poseidon; but now he has the liquid substance defeated by the fiery, because this is the more potent element of the two. So who is mad enough to introduce into the story gods fighting one another, when Homer has here given us a scientific theology in allegorical form?

59 At the end of the *Iliad*, Homer gives a vivid picture of Hermes accompanying Priam. This is an allegory. Nothing else—neither silver, nor gold, nor extravagance in gifts—is so convincing to angry men: verbal persuasion is the peaceable and acceptable instrument of supplication. Euripides was quite right to say:

Persuasion has no sanctuary but words,[3]

and it is with these that Priam arms himself as with a stout suit of armor, and by this means above all that he broke down Achilles' anger. He did not begin by showing him the "twelve robes and twelve single cloaks,"[4] and the rest of the presents he took with him. The first words of his appeal softened Achilles' virile anger:

---

1. *Aêr* = Hera; cf. 15.3, Cornutus, *Theol.* ch. 3 = p. 3.15–16 Lang, with Ramelli (2003, 303 n. 13). Various etymologies of Artemis are in Plato, *Crat.* 406B, Cornutus, *Theol.* ch. 32 = p. 65.19 Lang; but not this one relating it to *temnô*, "cut."
2. *Il.* 20.73.
3. Frg. 170 Nauck, from *Antiope*.
4. *Il.* 24.229.

Μνῆσαι πατρὸς σοῖο, θεοῖς ἐπιείκελ' Ἀχιλλεῦ,
τηλίκου οἷος ἐγών, ὀλοῷ ἐπὶ γήραος οὐδῷ.

59.7 Δι' ὀλίγου προοιμίου τῶν λόγων συνήρπασεν Ἀχιλλέα καὶ σχεδὸν ἀντὶ Πριάμου γέγονε Πηλεύς. **59.8** Διὰ τοῦτο ἠλέηται μὲν ἄχρι τραπέζης, λουτροῖς δὲ κοσμηθὲν ἀποδίδοται τὸ Ἕκτορος σῶμα. **59.9** Τοσοῦτον ἴσχυσεν ὁ τῶν παθῶν ἑρμηνεὺς λόγος, ὃν ἀπέστειλεν Ὅμηρος αὐτῷ τῆς ἱκετείας παράκλητον.

60.1 Ἆρ' οὐκ ἀπόχρη δι' ὅλης τῆς Ἰλιάδος συνάδουσα καὶ διηνεκὴς ἡ Ὁμήρου φιλοσοφία, ἐν ᾗ τὰ περὶ θεῶν ἠλληγόρησε; ζητοῦμεν δὲ τούτων τι περιττότερον καὶ μετὰ τοσαύτας ἀποδείξεις ἐνδεῖν ἔτι τὰ κατὰ τὴν Ὀδύσσειαν ἡγούμεθα; **60.2** πλὴν ὅμως, ἀκόρεστον γὰρ ἅπαν τὸ καλόν, ἀπὸ τῆς ἐναγωνίου καὶ πολεμικῆς Ἰλιάδος ἐπὶ τὴν ἠθικὴν μεταβῶμεν Ὀδύσσειαν. **60.3** Οὐδὲ γὰρ αὕτη τελείως ἀφιλοσόφητος· ἀλλ' ἐν ἑκατέροις τοῖς σωματίοις ὅμοιον εὑρίσκομεν Ὅμηρον, μηδὲν περὶ θεῶν ἀπρεπὲς ἱστοροῦντα, διὰ[1] δὲ τῆς τοιαύτης ἐμπειρίας αἰνιττόμενον.

61.1 Αὐτίκα τοίνυν ἐν ἀρχῇ τὴν Ἀθηνᾶν ὑπὸ Διὸς ἀποστελλομένην πρὸς Τηλέμαχον εὑρίσκομεν εὐλόγως, ἐπειδὴ ἐκ τῆς ἄγαν νεότητος ἤδη τὴν εἰκοσαετῆ ἡλικίαν ὑπερκύπτων μετέβαινεν εἰς ἄνδρας[2] **61.2** καί τις αὐτὸν ὑπέδραμε τῶν γιγνομένων λογισμός, ὡς οὐκέτι χρὴ διακαρτερεῖν ἐπὶ τῇ τετραετεῖ τῶν μνηστήρων ἀσωτίᾳ. **61.3** Τοῦτον οὖν τὸν ἀθροιζόμενον ἐν Τηλεμάχῳ λογισμὸν Ἀθηνᾶς ἐπιφάνειαν ἠλληγόρησεν. **61.4** Ὁμοιωθεῖσα γὰρ γέροντι ἥκει· παλαιὸς γοῦν ὁμολογεῖται ξένος Ὀδυσσέως ὁ Μέντης εἶναι. **61.5** Πολιὰ δὲ καὶ γῆρας ἱεροὶ τῶν τελευταίων χρόνων λιμένες, ἀσφαλὲς ἀνθρώποις ὅρμισμα, καὶ ὅσον ἡ τοῦ σώματος ἰσχὺς ὑποφθίνει, τοσοῦτον ἡ τῆς διανοίας αὔξεται ῥῶσις.

---

1. Russell; for δίχα "apart from" (mss., Te, Bu); cf. 6.1, etc. If δίχα is kept, Gale's ἀπρεπείας is the best conjecture: "giving enigmatic hints without any such impropriety."
2. Te, following the Homeric scholia; Bu, following the mss., reads τὸν ἄνδρα, comparing Ps.-Lucian, *Am.* 24, but the sense there is different; cf. 76.7 below.

Godlike Achilles, remember your own father,
a man of my years, at the dread door of age.[1]

He captured Achilles by this brief prooemium; he has almost become
not Priam, but Peleus. This is why Achilles took pity on him so far as to
entertain him at his table, and why Hector's body was restored to him,
washed and made decent. Such was the strength of speech, the interpreter [*hermêneus*] of feelings, sent by Homer to help Priam in his
supplication.[2]

60 Is it not enough for us that, throughout the *Iliad*, the philosophy
with which Homer allegorizes the affairs of the gods remains harmonious
and consistent? Do we ask for something more? After all these demon-
strations, do we think that an account of the *Odyssey* is still needed? Yet
one can never have too much of good things: let us therefore move from
the poem of strife and war that is the *Iliad* to the poem of moral character
that is the *Odyssey*.[3] This too is not quite without philosophical meaning.
Homer, we discover, is much the same in both epics, not telling disrep-
utable tales of the gods, but giving enigmatic hints by means of the
technique we have been studying.

61 For example, right at the beginning we find Athena despatched to
Telemachus by Zeus—quite properly, because Telemachus, no longer
very young, was on the verge of his twentieth year, and becoming a man.
A reasoned understanding of the situation had entered his mind: he saw
that he must not continue to tolerate the suitors' debaucheries, which had
gone on for four years. Homer represents this developing rationality in
Telemachus as the appearance of Athena. She comes in the likeness of an
old man, for Mentes is admitted to be an old friend of Odysseus. Grey
hairs and age are the sacred haven of our last days, a safe anchorage for
humankind,[4] where the strength of the mind increases as the force of the
body wanes.

---

1. *Il.* 24.486–487.
2. *Il.* 24.333.
3. Cf. Longinus, *Subl.* 9.14.
4. Compare Epicurus, *Vat. Sent.* 17 (Arrighetti): ὁ δὲ γέρων καθάπερ ἐν λιμένι τῷ γήρᾳ
καθώρμικεν, "a man enters old age like a harbor."

62.1 Τίνα τοίνυν παρεισελθὼν ὁ νοῦς ἐξεπαίδευσε τὸν Τηλέμαχον, οὐ θεὰ παρακαθημένη καὶ ταῦθ' ἃ λέγει παραινοῦσα[1] διαπεττεύοντος;[2] **62.2** Ἄγε δή, φησίν, ὦ Τηλέμαχε, μειρακίου γὰρ ἤδη τι φρονεῖς πλέον·

Νῆ' ἄρσας ἐρέτῃσιν ἐείκοσιν, ἥ τις ἀρίστη,
ἔρχεο πευσόμενος πατρὸς δὴν οἰχομένοιο·

62.3 Πρῶτος εὐσεβὴς καὶ δίκαιος ἐκ βαθείας τῆς διὰ τὴν ἡλικίαν ἀφροσύνης ὑπεισῆλθε λογισμός, ὡς οὐκ ἄξιόν ἐστιν ἀργοὺς ἐν Ἰθάκῃ κατατρίβειν χρό-νους ἀμνηστίαν ἔχοντα[3] τοῦ γεγεννηκότος, **62.4** ἀλλ' ἀναγκαῖον ἤδη ποτὲ τὸν φιλοπάτορα ναῦν εὐτρεπισάμενον ἐπὶ τὰς διαποντίους ἐκδραμεῖν κληδόνας, ἵνα τὴν Ὀδυσσέως ἀπόδημον ἄγνοιαν[4] ἀνιχνεύσῃ. **62.5** Δεύτερον δ' ἐπὶ τούτοις διεσκέψατο, ὅπου μάλιστα δεῖ τὴν πατρῷαν ἐρευνῆσαι τύχην. **62.6** Ὑπηγόρευσε δ' ἡ φρόνησις ἐγγὺς αὐτοῦ καθεζομένη·

Πρῶτα μὲν ἐς Πύλον ἐλθὲ καὶ εἴρεο Νέστορα δῖον,
κεῖθεν δὲ Σπάρτηνδε παρὰ ξανθὸν Μενέλαον.

62.7 Ὁ μὲν γὰρ εἶχε τὴν ἀπὸ γήρως ἐμπειρίαν, ὃ δ' ἀπὸ τῆς ὀκταετοῦς πλάνης ἐπανεληλύθει νεωστί·

"δεύτατος" γὰρ "ἦλθεν Ἀχαιῶν χαλκοχιτώνων."

Ἔμελλεν οὖν ὠφέλιμος αὐτῷ παραινῶν γενήσεσθαι Νέστωρ, τἀληθῆ δὲ περὶ τῆς Ὀδυσσέως πλάνης ἐρεῖν Μενέλαος.

63.1 Ἅμα δὲ ταῦτ' ἐννοούμενος ὡσπερεὶ παρακροτῶν ἑαυτὸν εἶπεν·

οὐδέ τί σε χρή
νηπιάας ὀχέειν, ἐπεὶ οὐκέτι τηλίκος ἐσσί.

63.2 Ὡσπερεὶ παιδαγωγὸς καὶ πατὴρ ὁ λογισμὸς αὐτοῦ τὸ μεθεκτικὸν τῶν φροντίδων ἀνήγειρεν· εἶτα καθ' ὁμοίωσιν ἡλικιώτιδος ἀρετῆς εἰς τὴν ἴσην φρόνησιν αὐτὸν παρακέκληκεν· **63.3**

---

1. Te, following A, D (D only for παραινοῦσα); G, Bu read θεᾶς παρακαθημένης ... παραινούσης; but the sequence of genitive absolutes is inelegant.
    2. Mss., Bu; Hercher, followed by Te, transposes διαπεττεύοντος to follow πλέον ("you have more sense now than a boy playing dice") but there seems to be no advantage in the change.
    3. D, Te; Bu, with A, G, reads ἔχοντας, agreeing with χρόνους: "the idle times have no thought of Odysseus."
    4. An extraordinary expression, literally "traveling ignorance," and possibly corrupt; Te in apparatus criticus, after Mehler, suggests ἀποδημίαν ἄγνωστον, "unknown travels."

62 So what did reason, when it arrived, teach Telemachus—reason, not a goddess sitting down beside him and giving him her advice as he plays at dice?[1] "Come, Telemachus," says Reason, "you have more sense than a boy now:

> launch your best ship, crew her with twenty rowers,
> and go to seek your long departed father."[2]

The first pious and just thought to emerge from the deep folly of Telemachus's youth is that it is unworthy of him to spend time idly in Ithaca with no thought of his father. The dutiful son must now get ready a ship and pursue rumors overseas, to find the track of Odysseus's unknown travels. Secondly, he also considered where he should best inquire after his father's fate. Wisdom sat at his side and made a suggestion:

> Go first to Pylos and ask godlike Nestor,
> and thence to Sparta, to fair haired Menelaus.[3]

Now Nestor had the experience of old age, and Menelaus had lately reached home after his eight years' wandering:

> he came home last of the bronze-corseleted Achaeans.[4]

Nestor was therefore in a position to give him valuable advice, and Menelaus to tell the true story of Odysseus's wanderings.

63 With these thoughts in mind, he gives himself[5] a tap on the shoulder, as it were, and says

> Nor is it right for you
> to keep your childish ways: you are a child no more.[6]

His reason, you see, behaved as a tutor or a father and aroused in him a readiness to undertake responsibility. It then drew on the example of another young man's courage to exhort Telemachus to show the same good sense:

---

1. At *Od.* 1.106–107 it is the suitors who are playing dice.
2. *Od.* 1.280–281.
3. *Od.* 1.284–285.
4. *Od.* 1.286; cf. the scholia to *Od.* 1.284.
5. Mentes (= Athena) is the speaker; but since he represents Telemachus's reason, he may perhaps be said to reproach himself (*heauton*).
6. *Od.* 1.296–297.

ἢ οὐκ ἀίεις, οἷον κλέος ἔλλαβε δῖος Ὀρέστης
πάντας ἐπ' ἀνθρώπους, ἐπεὶ ἔκτανε πατροφονῆα;

63.4 Τοιούτοις ἐπαρθεὶς λογισμοῖς εὐλόγως μετέωρον αὐτοῦ τὴν διάνοιαν ἐλαφρίζει· διὸ καὶ[1] προσείκασεν αὐτὴν Ὅμηρος ὄρνιθι λέγων·

ὄρνις δ' ὣς ἀνοπαῖα διέπτατο.

63.5 Μεταρσία γὰρ ἡ φρόνησις ὡς ἂν οἶμαι τηλικοῦτον ὄγκον ἐν αὐτῇ πραγμάτων κυοφοροῦσα[2] διανέστηκεν. **63.6** Ἀμέλει ταχέως ἐκκλησία συναθροίζεται, καὶ πατρῴοις λόγοις ἐνρητορεύει. **63.7** Τὸν δ' ἀπόπλουν εὐτρέπιζεν ὁ τῆς ἀλληγορίας ἐπώνυμος, Φρονίου μὲν υἱός, Νοήμων δὲ τοὔνομα· δι' ὧν ἀμφοτέρων οὐδὲν ἄλλο πλὴν τοὺς ὑπογυίους αὐτοῦ λογισμοὺς ὑπεσήμαινεν. **63.8** Ἐμβαίνοντι δ' αὐτῷ τῆς νεὼς συνεμβέβηκεν Ἀθηνᾶ, Μέντορι τὴν μορφὴν εἰκασμένη πάλιν, ἀνδρὶ πρὸς φροντίδας τὴν διάνοιαν ἔχοντι, φρονήσεως μητέρα. **63.9** Δι' ὧν ἁπάντων ἡ κατ' ὀλίγον ἐν τῷ Τηλεμάχῳ τρεφομένη σύνεσις ἐν τοῖς ἔπεσιν ἱστόρηται.

64.1 Καὶ μὴν ὁ περὶ Πρωτέως λόγος[3] οὕτω πολὺς ἐκταθεὶς ὑπὸ Μενελάου τὴν ἐξαπατῶσαν εὐθὺς ἔχει φαντασίαν **64.2** πάνυ μυθώδη,[4] γεγονέναι τῆς ἐν Αἰγύπτῳ νησῖδος ἄθλιον ἔποικον εἰς ἀθανάτου μέτρα τιμωρίας παρελκόμενον, ᾧ βίος ἠπείρου καὶ θαλάττης κοινὸς ἀτυχεῖς ὕπνους μετὰ φωκῶν κοιμωμένῳ,[5] ἵν' αὐτοῦ κολάζηται καὶ τὸ τερπνόν. **64.3** Θυγάτηρ δ' Εἰδοθέα διὰ πατρὸς ἀδικίας ξένον εὖ ποιοῦσα καὶ γινομένη προδότις αὐτοῦ, δεσμοὶ μετὰ τοῦτο καὶ Μενέλαος ἐνεδρεύων, **64.4** εἶθ' ἡ πολυπρόσωπος εἰς ἅπαντα ἃ βούλεται Πρωτέως μεταμόρφωσις ποιητικοὶ καὶ τεράστιοι μῦθοι δοκοῦσιν, εἰ μή τις οὐρανίῳ ψυχῇ τὰς ὀλυμπίους Ὁμήρου[6] τελετὰς ἱεροφαντήσειε.

---

1. Te, following the Aldine edition; διὸ καί omitted by mss., Bu.
2. Perhaps read κουφοφοροῦσα, "lightly lifting the bulk…"; cf. Sextus Empiricus, *Math.* 9.71, of souls rising (intransitive).
3. <ὅς> after λόγος added by Te in apparatus criticus (haplography); Bu, Te punctuate variously.
4. Russell; μυθώδης mss., Te, Bu.
5. D, Te; A, G, Bu read κοιμώμενος, agreeing with βίος.
6. Perhaps delete Ὁμήρου, or read Ὅμηρος, and translate "if it were not a Homer with heavenly soul who is the hierophant of Olympian mysteries."

Have you not heard how Orestes won renown
among all men, for killing his father's killer?[1]

Roused by such reasonings, it is no wonder that he lets his mind fly lightly upwards. Homer therefore compared it to a bird, saying:

And like a bird flew up and through the roof.[2]

Telemachus's wisdom, it seems to me, as if pregnant with the bulk of such mighty deeds, now rises to its full height. The assembly soon gathers, and Telemachus exhibits his father's rhetorical skills. His departure is arranged by a person with an allegorical name, Noemon son of Phronios:[3] these two names simply indicate the ideas that come spontaneously into Telemachus's mind. As he goes on board ship, Athena meets him, once again, as Mentor,[4] a man who brings intelligence, the mother of wisdom, to bear on his anxieties. All this enables the gradual growth of understanding in Telemachus to be related in the poem.

64 Again, the story of Proteus, set out at such length by Menelaus, immediately exhibits a deceptive picture which is thoroughly fabulous:[5] namely, that Proteus was the poor inhabitant of the tiny island in Egypt, dragging out the term of his eternal punishment, with his life divided between land and sea, and taking his unhappy slumbers in the company of seals, so that even his pleasures are tormented. There is his daughter Eidothea, helping a stranger by wronging her father and turning traitress; there is Proteus's subsequent bondage and Menelaus setting his ambush; and finally Proteus's many metamorphoses into whatever shapes he chooses. All these seem to be poetical and miraculous fables, unless some hierophant with heavenly soul can reveal to us Homer's[6] Olympian mysteries.

---

1. *Od.* 1.298–299.

2. *Od.* 1.320. The line was much discussed: Crates saw a reference to the hole in the roof (*an' opaia*); others thought *anopaia* was a kind of bird. Heraclitus's *meteôron* and *metarsia* suggest he thought the word just meant "upwards," but he may have followed Crates' view.

3. *Od.* 2.386.

4. *Od.* 2.401.

5. The story of Proteus (*Od.* 4.351ff.) was the subject of elaborate allegorical interpretation (Buffière 1956, 179–86).

6. In ch. 76 init., Homer is the hierophant who reveals mysteries; here, apparently, the writer himself claims that role, though it is strange that he should claim a "heavenly soul." See note on the Greek text.

65.1 Τὴν γοῦν προμήτορα τῶν ὅλων ὑφίσταται γένεσιν, ἀφ᾽ ἧς τὸ πᾶν ῥιζωθὲν εἰς ὃ νῦν βλέπομεν ἥκει κατάστημα. **65.2** Παλαιοὶ γὰρ ἦσάν ποτε χρόνοι, καθ᾽ οὓς ἀτύπωτος ὕλη μόνον[1] ἦν, οὐδέπω κεκριμένοις χαρακτῆρσιν εἰς τέλειον ἤκουσα μορφῆς· **65.3** οὔτε γὰρ γῆ, τῇ[2] τῶν ὅλων ἑστία, κέντρον ἐπεπήγει βέβαιον οὔτ᾽ οὐρανὸς περὶ <αὐτὴν>[3] τὴν ἀίδιον φορὰν ἱδρυμένος ἐκυκλεῖτο, πάντα δ᾽ ἦν ἀνήλιος ἠρεμία καὶ κατηφοῦσα σιγή, καὶ πλέον οὐδὲν ἦν ἢ[4] κεχυμένης ὕλης **65.4** ἄμορφος[5] ἀργία, πρὶν ἡ δημιουργὸς ἁπάντων καὶ κοσμοτόκος ἀρχὴ σωτήριον ἑλκύσασα τῷ βίῳ τύπον τὸν κόσμον ἀπέδωκε τῷ κόσμῳ· **65.5** διεζεύγνυ τὸν μὲν οὐρανὸν γῆς, ἐχώριζε δὲ τὴν ἤπειρον θαλάττης, τέτταρα δὲ στοιχεῖα, τῶν ὅλων ῥίζα καὶ γέννα, ἐν τάξει τὴν ἰδίαν μορφὴν ἐκομίζετο· **65.6** τούτων δὲ προμηθῶς κιρναμένων ὁ θεὸς μηδεμιᾶς οὔσης διακρίσεως περὶ τὴν ἄμορφον ὕλην <.....>[6].

66.1 Πρωτέως δὲ θυγάτηρ Εἰδοθέα· δικαίως, εἴδους ἑκάστου γενομένη θέα. Διὰ τοῦτο, μία τὸ πρὶν ὢν φύσις, ὁ Πρωτεὺς εἰς πολλὰς ἐμερίζετο μορφὰς ὑπὸ τῆς προνοίας διαπλαττόμενος· **66.2**

Ἤτοι μὲν πρώτιστα λέων γένετ᾽ ἠυγένειος,
αὐτὰρ ἔπειτα δράκων καὶ πάρδαλις ἠδὲ μέγας σῦς,
γίνετο δ᾽ ὑγρὸν ὕδωρ καὶ δένδρεον ὑψιπέτηλον.

66.3 Διὰ μὲν οὖν τοῦ λέοντος, ἐμπύρου ζῴου, τὸν αἰθέρα δηλοῖ. **66.4** Δράκων δ᾽ ἐστὶν ἡ γῆ· τὸ γὰρ αὐτόχθον αὐτοῦ καὶ γηγενὲς οὐδὲν ἄλλο πλὴν τοῦτο σημαίνει. **66.5** Δένδρον γε μήν, ἅπαν αὐξανόμενον καὶ τὴν ἀπὸ γῆς ὁρμὴν μεταρσίαν ἀεὶ λαμβάνον, συμβολικῶς εἶπεν ἀέρα. **66.6** Τὸ μὲν γὰρ ὕδωρ εἰς ἀσφαλεστέραν ὧν προηνίξατο δήλωσιν ἐκ τοῦ φανερωτέρου παρέστησεν εἰπών·

---

1. Te in apparatus criticus (the text is uncertain); Te, Bu, read ἀτύπωτον ἢ ὑπόλιμνον (as corrected by a second hand in G; A, G read ὑπόλημνον). Despite Buffière's efforts, no sense can be found in ὑπόλιμνον (translated "limoneuse"), and ἤκουσα implies a feminine noun, which is surely ὕλη.
2. Omitted in Bu.
3. Russell (or perhaps περὶ <αὐ>τὴν ἀίδιον: the article is not necessary with φοράν). Te inserts γῆν instead of αὐτήν; Bu retains the mss. reading, but revolving around (περί) a motion (φοράν) is odd.
4. Mss. (D omits ἦν), Te; Bu brackets ἤ.
5. D, Te; Bu, following A, G, reads ἄμορφος γάρ, punctuating with raised stop after ὕλης: "there was nothing there but confused matter; for there was shapeless inertness, until...."
6. Russell (Te, Bu place the lacuna after θεός); sc., e.g., <ἅπανθ᾽ ἃ νῦν ὁρῶμεν διέκρινεν>.

65 In fact, he is presenting to us the primordial origin of the universe,[1] whence the whole system on which we now look has its roots. There was a time long ago when there was nothing but shapeless matter, which had not yet attained perfection of form by acquiring distinct characteristics. Earth, the hearth of the universe, had as yet no firm center, nor was heaven established to revolve around <it> with unending motion. Everything was sunless emptiness and gloomy silence, there was nothing there but the shapeless inertness of confused matter—until the principle that crafted all things and gave birth to the universe fashioned the form that brought security to life, and gave the universe [kosmos] its adornment [kosmos].[2] That principle divided earth from heaven and parted dry land from sea, while the four elements, the root and birth of all things, received their several forms in their proper turn. When these were providentially combined, while there was yet no distinction in the formless matter, God <separated out all that we now see>.[3]

66 Proteus's daughter is Eidothea—justly so called, for she is the vision[4] [thea] of every form [eidos]. This is why Proteus, originally a single being [phusis], was divided into many forms, being so fashioned by providence:

First he became a lion with fine mane,
a snake next, then a panther, and a mighty boar;
and water he became, and a tall green tree.[5]

By "lion," a fiery animal, Homer means aether. The "snake" is the earth: the notion that it is indigenous and earth-born signifies precisely this. By the tree, the whole of which grows and continually thrusts upwards from the earth, he symbolizes air. When he comes to water, he gives a more transparent statement, so as to assure us of the meaning of the preceding riddles:

---

1. See Buffière (1956, 179–91) and Spoerri (1959, 69–71).

2. The term kosmos basically means "order," and is used both of decorative ornaments (cf. "cosmetic") and the heavens; there is a play on the two senses of the word.

3. The supplement needed can only be guessed.

4. Bu translates "puisqu'elle est la divinité qui préside à l'apparition des diverses formes," evidently alluding both to θέα = "vision" and θεά = "goddess." For other interpretations of the name, see Buffière (1962, 124).

5. Od. 4.456–458.

γίνετο δ' ὑγρὸν ὕδωρ.

66.7 Ὥστ' εὔλογον τὴν μὲν ἄμορφον ὕλην Πρωτέα καλεῖσθαι, τὴν δ' εἰδωλο-
πλαστήσασαν ἕκαστα πρόνοιαν Εἰδοθέαν, ἐξ ἀμφοῖν δὲ πᾶν διακριθὲν εἰς τὰ
συνεχῆ καὶ συστατικὰ¹ τῶν ὅλων σχισθῆναι. **66.8** Πιθανῶς δὲ καὶ τὴν νῆσον,
ἐν ᾗ ταῦτα διέπλασε, Φάρον ὠνόμασεν, ἐπειδήπερ ἐστὶ τὸ φέρσαι² γεννῆσαι,
66.9 καὶ τὴν γῆν ἀφάρωτον ὁ Καλλίμαχος εἶπε τὴν ἄγονον·

ἀφάρωτος οἷον γυνή.

66.10 Φυσικῶς οὖν τὸν ἀπάντων πατέρα χῶρον ὠνόμασε Φάρον, ἐκ τῆς
γονίμου προσηγορίας ὃ μάλιστα ἐβούλετο σημῆνας.

67.1 Τίσι γε μὴν ἐπιθέτοις καὶ τὸν Πρωτέα κεκόσμηκεν, ἤδη σκοπῶμεν·

πωλεῖταί τις δεῦρο γέρων ἅλιος νημερτής.

67.2 Τὸ μὲν γὰρ οἶμαι τῆς ἀρχεγόνου καὶ πρώτης οὐσίας σημαίνει³ <τὸ>⁴
γεραίτερον, ὥστε ἀποσεμνῦναι τῇ πολιᾷ τοῦ χρόνου τὴν ἄμορφον ὕλην. **67.3**
Ἅλιον δ' ὠνόμασεν οὐ μὰ Δί' οὐ θαλάττιόν τινα δαίμονα καὶ κατὰ κυμάτων
ζῶντα, τὸ δ' ἐκ πολλῶν καὶ παντοδαπῶν συνηλισμένον, ὅπερ ἐστὶ συνηθροισ-
μένον. **67.4** Νημερτὴς δ' εὐλόγως εἴρηται· τί γὰρ ταύτης τῆς οὐσίας
ἀληθουργέστερον, ἐξ ἧς ἅπαντα γεγενῆσθαι νομιστέον;

---

1. Gesner; mss., Te, Bu read προστακτικά, i.e., "directing" the whole. For συστατικά,
cf., e.g., *SVF* 2.136.19 (Chrysippus quoted in Stobaeus). There are four elements, which are
"continuous" and also "constitute" everything: cf. *SVF* 2.155.2–36 (Alexander of Aphro-
disias) on the way in which the lighter elements permeate the heavier ones, but without
either group losing its own φύσις and συνέχεια (identity and continuity).
2. φαρῶσαι Mehler, perhaps rightly (φαρόω or φαράω seems to mean "to plough": see
Callimachus, frg. 287 Pfeiffer); φέρσαι is an unknown form.
3. D, Te; Bu, following A, G, omits σημαίνει, and translates "c'est, je pense, le caractère
de la substance originelle d'être plus ancienne."
4. Inserted by Te.

and liquid water he became.

It is reasonable then that formless matter should be called Proteus, that the providence which formed everything should be called Eidothea, and that everything which derives from these two principles, once separated out, should be divided into continuous masses which are constitutive[1] of the universe. Plausible too is the naming of the island in which he[2] fashioned these different forms as Pharos, because *phersai* means "to generate": when Callimachus calls earth *apharôtos,* he means "barren":

like a barren woman.[3]

Homer therefore has a scientific reason for calling the land that is the father of all things Pharos: the name, with its implication of generation, indicates his real meaning.

67 But let us now consider the epithets with which he honors Proteus also:

Here often comes an old man of the sea [*halios*],
teller of truth [*nêmertês*].[4]

The first description,[5] I think, indicates the antiquity of the first, originary substance: he thus dignifies formless matter by giving it the grey hairs of age. By *halios,* he means not of course some divinity of the sea who lives beneath the waves, but something *sunhêlismenon,*[6] that is, "aggregated" out of many things of all kinds. Proteus is properly called "teller of truth"; for what can be more productive of truth than the substance of which all things must be believed to have been born?

---

1. See note to Greek text.

2. Presumably Homer, but the action of his character Proteus is identified with the poet's.

3. Callimachus, frg. 555 Pfeiffer; unless Heraclitus's text is corrupt, this is not a line of verse, and presumably (as Pfeiffer thinks) comes from a commentary on the *Iambi* that explained the use of the epithet in reference to the earth. The passage remains puzzling; see note to Greek text.

4. *Od.* 4.384.

5. I.e., "old man."

6. Heraclitus connects *halios* with *halizô* ("gather together"), from which this form is derived.

67.5 Καὶ μὴν καὶ ἡ Καλυψὼ τὴν πειθὼ τῶν ποικίλων παρ' Ὀδυσσέως λόγων Ἑρμῆν προσηγόρευσε, μόγις μέν, ἀλλ' ὅμως καταθέλξαντος αὐτοῦ τὸν ἔρωτα τῆς νύμφης, ἵν' εἰς Ἰθάκην προπεμφθείη. **67.6** Διὰ τοῦτ' ὄρνιθι προσωμοιωμένος Ἑρμῆς ἐλήλυθεν ἀπ' Ὀλύμπου· **67.7** "πτερόεντα" γὰρ τὰ ἔπη κατὰ τὸν Ὅμηρον καὶ τάχιον οὐδὲν ἐν ἀνθρώποις λόγου.

68.1 Δεῖ δὲ ἡμᾶς οὐδὲ τὰ μικρὰ παροδεύειν, ἀλλὰ καὶ δι' ἐκείνων τὴν λεπτὴν ἐξετάζειν Ὁμήρου φροντίδα. **68.2** Τὸν γὰρ Ἡμέρας καὶ Ὠρίωνος ἔρωτα, πάθος οὐδ' ἀνθρώποις εὔσχημον, ἠλληγόρησεν·

Ὣς μέν, ὅτ' Ὠρίων' ἕλετο ῥοδοδάκτυλος Ἠώς.

68.3 Παρεισάγει γὰρ αὐτὸν ἔτι νεανίαν ἐν ἀκμῇ τοῦ σώματος ὑπὸ τοῦ χρεὼν πρὸ μοίρας συνηρπασμένον. **68.4** Ἦν δὲ παλαιὸν ἔθος τὰ σώματα τῶν καμνόντων,[1] ἐπειδὰν ἀναπαύσηται τοῦ βίου, μήτε νύκτωρ ἐκκομίζειν μήθ' ὅταν ὑπὲρ γῆς τὸ μεσημβρινὸν ἐπιτείνηται θάλπος, ἀλλὰ πρὸς βαθὺν ὄρθρον ἀπύροις ἡλίου <ταῖς>[2] ἀκτῖσιν ἀνιόντος. **68.5** Ἐπειδὰν οὖν εὐγενὴς νεανίας ἅμα καὶ κάλλει προέχων τελευτήσῃ, τὴν ὄρθριον ἐκκομιδὴν ἐπευφήμουν Ἡμέρας ἁρπαγὴν ὡς οὐκ ἀποθανόντος ἀλλὰ δι' ἐρωτικὴν ἐπιθυμίαν ἀνηρπασμένου. **68.6** Καθ' Ὅμηρον δὲ τοῦτό φασιν.

68.7 Ἰασίων, ἀνὴρ γεωργίας ἐπιμελούμενος καὶ δαψιλεῖς[3] τοὺς ἀπὸ τῶν ἰδίων ἀγρῶν καρποὺς λαμβάνων, εἰκότως ὑπὸ τῆς Δήμητρος ἔδοξεν ἠγαπῆσθαι.

68.8 Δι' ὧν Ὅμηρος οὐκ ἀσελγεῖς ἔρωτας ἱστορεῖ θεῶν οὐδ' ἀκολασίας, σημαίνων[4] δὲ τὰς εὐαγεστάτας Ἡμέραν τε καὶ Δημήτραν **68.9** τοῖς εὐσεβῶς ἐρευνᾶν ἐθέλουσι φυσικῆς ἀκριβῆ θεωρίας ἀφορμὴν χαρίζεται.

---

1. καμόντων, proposed by Toussaint, would mean "the dead."
2. Te (avoids hiatus).
3. D, Te; Bu, with the other mss. and the Homeric scholia, reads the adverb δαψιλῶς.
4. Te, adopting Mehler's emendation; mss., Bu read σημαίνει. Alternatively, read <καὶ> τοῖς (Heyne) or τοῖς <δ'> in the following line. Bu punctuates with raised stop after Δήμητραν (so mss.; Te corrects to Δήμητρα), but a particle is still needed in the following clause.

Again, Calypso[1] gives the name Hermes to the persuasiveness of Odysseus's subtle words, when he succeeds, though with difficulty, in cajoling the amorous nymph into letting him go on his way to Ithaca. This is why Hermes has come from Olympus in the likeness of a bird;[2] for words are "winged" in Homer, and nothing in human life flies swifter than a word.[3]

68 We must not overlook even small episodes, but use these also to study Homer's subtle thinking. For example, he has made an allegory of the love of Day (Dawn) and Orion, an affair which would be discreditable even in a human context:

When rosy-fingered Dawn possessed Orion...[4]

He introduces Orion as still a young man, at the height of his physical powers, snatched away by necessity before his destined time. Now it was the ancient practice with the bodies of the mortally ill, as soon as life was extinct, not to carry them out for burial by night or when the heat of noon extends over the earth, but only at first light, when the rays of the rising sun do not burn. So whenever a well born and outstandingly beautiful young man died, people euphemistically spoke of his dawn funeral as "capture by Day," as though he had not died but had been snatched away because of a passionate love affair. When they say this, they are in accord with Homer.[5]

Iasion, a professional farmer who secured good returns from his own lands, is plausibly believed to have been loved by Demeter.[6]

In these episodes, Homer is not relating improper loves or indecent behavior of the gods, but, by pointing to the most chaste goddesses, Day and Demeter, he offers a clear starting-point for scientific inquiry for anyone who wishes to pursue this in a pious spirit.

---

1. *Od.* 5.87. This has nothing to do with what precedes. Heraclitus is presumably just following the order of the poem, but it may be that something has been lost before this abrupt transition.

2. *Od.* 5.52.

3. Cornutus, *Theol.* ch. 16 = p. 22.3–5 Lang connects winged words with Hermes' winged sandals; cf. Ramelli (2003, 336 n. 92).

4. *Od.* 5.121.

5. Or "they say this is in accordance with Homer." This sentence is an odd addition; Te suggests that it is an interpolation.

6. *Od.* 5.124.

69.1 Νῦν τοίνυν ἅπαντα τἆλλα ἀφέντες ἐπὶ τὴν διηνεκῆ καὶ χαλεπῶς θρυλουμένην ὑπὸ τῶν συκοφαντῶν κατηγορίαν τραπώμεθα.[1] **69.2** Ἄνω γὰρ οὖν[2] καὶ κάτω τραγῳδοῦσι τὰ περὶ Ἄρεος καὶ Ἀφροδίτης ἀσεβῶς διαπεπλάσθαι λέγοντες· **69.3** ἀκολασίαν γὰρ ἐμπεπολίτευκεν οὐρανῷ, καὶ τὸ παρ' ἀνθρώποις, ὅταν γένηται, θανάτου τιμώμενον[3] οὐκ ἐδυσωπήθη παρὰ θεοῖς ἱστορῆσαι, λέγω δὲ μοιχείαν· **69.4**

Ἀμφ' Ἄρεος φιλότητος ἐϋστεφάνου τ' Ἀφροδίτης,
ὡς τὰ πρῶτα μίγησαν ἐν Ἡφαίστοιο δόμοισιν.

69.5 εἶτα μετὰ τοῦτο δεσμοὶ καὶ θεῶν γέλωτες ἱκεσία τε πρὸς Ἥφαιστον Ποσειδῶνος· **69.6** ἅπερ εἰ[4] θεοὶ νοσοῦσιν, οὐκέτι τοὺς παρ' ἀνθρώποις ἀδικοῦντας ἔδει κολάζεσθαι. **69.7** Νομίζω δ' ἔγωγε καίπερ ἐν Φαίαξιν, ἀνθρώποις ἡδονῇ δεδουλωμένοις, ᾀδόμενα ταῦτα φιλοσόφου τινὸς ἐπιστήμης ἔχεσθαι· **69.8** τὰ γὰρ Σικελικὰ δόγματα καὶ τὴν Ἐμπεδόκλειον γνώμην ἔοικεν ἀπὸ τούτων βεβαιοῦν, Ἄρην μὲν ὀνομάσας τὸ νεῖκος, τὴν δὲ Ἀφροδίτην φιλίαν. **69.9** Τούτους οὖν διεστηκότας ἐν ἀρχῇ παρεισήγαγεν Ὅμηρος ἐκ τῆς πάλαι φιλονεικίας εἰς μίαν ὁμόνοιαν κιρναμένους. **69.10** Ὅθεν εὐλόγως ἐξ ἀμφοῖν Ἁρμονία γεγένηται τοῦ παντὸς ἀσαλεύτως καὶ κατ' ἐμμέλειαν ἁρμοσθέντος. **69.11** Γελᾶν δ' ἐπὶ τούτοις εἰκὸς ἦν καὶ συνήδεσθαι τοὺς θεούς, ἅτε δὴ τῶν εἰδῶν <τῶν> ἀρχικῶν[5] οὐκ ἐπὶ φθοραῖς διϊσταμένων, ἀλλ' ὁμονοοῦσαν εἰρήνην ἀγόντων. **69.12** Δύναταί γε μὴν καὶ περὶ τῆς χαλκευτικῆς τέχνης ἀλληγορεῖν. **69.13** Ὁ μὲν γὰρ Ἄρης εἰκότως ἂν ὀνομάζοιτο σίδηρος, τοῦτον δὲ ῥᾳδίως Ἥφαιστος ἐχειρώσατο· **69.14** τὸ γὰρ πῦρ, ἅτ' οἶμαι σιδήρου κραταιοτέρας δυνάμεως μετειληχός, εὐκόλως ἐν αὐτῷ τὴν ἐκείνου στερρότητα θηλύνει. **69.15** Δεῖ δὲ τῷ τεχνίτῃ πρὸς τὸ κατασκευαζόμενον καὶ Ἀφροδίτης· ὅθεν οἶμαι διὰ πυρὸς μαλάξας τὸν σίδηρον ἐπαφροδίτῳ τινὶ τέχνῃ τὴν ἐργασίαν κατώρθωσε. **69.16** Ποσειδῶν δ' ἐστὶν ὁ ῥυόμενος παρ' Ἡφαίστου τὸν Ἄρη πιθανῶς, ἐπειδήπερ ἐκ τῶν βαύνων διάπυρος ὁ τοῦ σιδήρου μύδρος ἑλκυσθεὶς ὕδατι βαπτίζεται καὶ τὸ φλογῶδες ὑπὸ τῆς ἰδίας[6] φύσεως κατασβεσθὲν ἀναπαύεται.

---

1. Te, following D, Homeric scholia; A, G, Bu read τραπῶμεν.
2. A, G, Bu; D, Te read γοῦν.
3. G, D, Te; A, Bu read τιμωρούμενον.
4. Te, following the Homeric scholia and D; Bu, following A, G, reads οἱ, i.e., "human wrongdoings should not be punished for the failings of the gods," etc.
5. Russell (tentatively; cf. Te in apparatus criticus); τῶν ἰδίων χαρίτων = "the individual graces" (mss., Te, Bu) is impossible (ἀγόντων implies a masculine or neuter noun).
6. Mehler's ὑγρᾶς ("liquid") for ἰδίας ("special") is attractive.

69 So let us now pass over everything else, and concentrate on the continued grievous accusations which Homer's traducers notoriously make. For up and down they go with their pretentious talk of the "impious" fiction concerning Ares and Aphrodite. "He has given immorality citizenship in heaven, he has felt no shame about attributing to the gods a crime punishable by death in human societies, adultery:

> The love of Ares and garlanded Aphrodite,
> and how they came together in Hephaestus's house.[1]

And then the binding, and the gods' laughter, and Poseidon's plea to Hephaestus! If such are the failings of the gods, there is no longer need for human wrongdoers to be punished!" My own view is that, though this song was sung to the Phaeacians, a people dominated by pleasure, it none the less has some philosophical relevance. Homer seems here to be confirming Sicilian doctrine (the views of Empedocles), calling strife Ares and love Aphrodite. He therefore represents these old adversaries as giving up their former contention and coming together in concord. Naturally therefore the child born of these two is Harmonia, because the universe is unshakably and harmoniously put together.[2] That the gods should laugh and take pleasure in all this is also probable, because the original forms are not destructively separated, but maintain concord and peace. It may also, however, be an allegory relating to the art of the bronzeworker. Ares may reasonably denote iron, and Hephaestus easily subdues him, because fire, having (as I see it) a power superior to that of iron, softens the stubbornness of the metal in its flames. But the craftsman also needs Aphrodite for his construction: so he softens the iron with fire and brings his work to a successful conclusion by delicate [*epaphroditos*] art.[3] Poseidon plausibly represents the force that rescues Ares from Hephaestus, because, when the mass of iron is withdrawn red-hot from the furnace, it is plunged into water, and its fire is extinguished and laid to rest by the special nature of that element.

---

1. *Od.* 8.266ff. See, e.g., Ps.-Plutarch, *Vit. poes. Hom.* 101, 214 with Hillgruber's notes (1994–1999, 2:225–27, 431); also Proclus, *Commentary on Plato's Republic* 1.141–143.

2. Cf. Cornutus, *Theol.* ch. 19 = p. 34.20 Lang, with Ramelli (2003, 358 n. 149).

3. Cornutus, *Theol.* ch. 25 = p. 48.5–6 Lang connects *epaphroditos* with Eros.

70.1 Καθόλου δὲ τὴν Ὀδυσσέως πλάνην, εἴ τις ἀκριβῶς ἐθέλει σκοπεῖν, ἠλληγορημένην εὑρήσει· **70.2** πάσης γὰρ ἀρετῆς καθάπερ ὄργανόν τι τὸν Ὀδυσσέα παραστησάμενος ἑαυτῷ διὰ τούτου¹ πεφιλοσόφηκεν, ἐπειδὴ τὰς ἐκνεμομένας τὸν ἀνθρώπινον βίον ἤχθηρε κακίας. **70.3** Ἡδονὴν μέν γε, τὸ Λωτοφάγων χωρίον, ξένης γεωργῶν² ἀπολαύσεως, [ἣν]³ Ὀδυσσεὺς ἐγκρατῶς παρέπλευσεν. **70.4** Τὸν δ᾽ ἄγριον ἑκάστου θυμὸν ὡσπερεὶ καυτηρίῳ τῇ παραινέσει τῶν λόγων ἐπήρωσε· **70.5** Κύκλωψ δὲ οὗτος ὠνόμασται, ὁ τοὺς λογισμοὺς ὑποκλωπῶν.⁴ **70.6** Τί δ᾽; οὐχὶ πρῶτος εὔδιον πλοῦν δι᾽ ἐπιστήμης ἀστρονόμου τεκμηράμενος ἔδοξεν ἀνέμους δεδεκέναι;⁵ **70.7** Φαρμάκων τε τῶν παρὰ Κίρκης γέγονε κρείττων, ὑπὸ πολλῆς σοφίας πεμμάτων⁶ ἐπεισάκτων κακῶν λύσιν εὑρόμενος. **70.8** Ἡ δὲ φρόνησις ἕως Ἅιδου καταβέβηκεν, ἵνα μηδέ τι τῶν νέρθεν ἀδιερεύνητον ᾖ. **70.9** Ἔτι⁷ δὲ Σειρήνων ἀκούει, τὰς πολυπείρους ἱστορίας παντὸς αἰῶνος ἐκμαθών.⁸ **70.10** Καὶ Χάρυβδις μὲν ἡ δάπανος⁹ ἀσωτία καὶ περὶ πότους ἄπληστος εὐλόγως ὠνόμασται· **70.11** Σκύλλαν δὲ τὴν πολύμορφον ἀναίδειαν ἠλληγόρησε, διὸ δὴ κυνῶν οὐκ ἀλόγως ὑπέζωσται προτομάς, ἁρπαγῇ, τόλμῃ καὶ πλεονεξίᾳ πεφραγμένη.¹⁰ **70.12** Αἱ δ᾽ ἡλίου βόες ἐγκράτεια γαστρός εἰσιν, εἰ μηδὲ λιμὸν¹¹ ἔσχεν ἀδικίας ἀνάγκην. **70.13** Ἃ δὴ μυθικῶς μέν ἐστιν εἰρημένα παρὰ¹² τοὺς ἀκούοντας, εἰ δέ <τις>¹³ ἐπὶ τὴν ἠλληγορημένην σοφίαν καταβέβηκεν,¹⁴ ὠφελιμώτατα τοῖς μεμυημένοις¹⁵ γενήσεται.

---

1. Te, following D, Homeric scholia; Bu, following A, G, reads διὰ τοῦτο, which means "because of this," but translates "par son intermédiaire" = διὰ τούτου.
2. Te; Bu, with mss., reads Λωτοφάγον and γεωργόν, "ce pays lotophage qui cultive," etc.
3. Deleted by Te; retained, with mss., by Bu.
4. This is Hase's emendation; the mss. and the scholia read the nonsensical ὑπολωπῶν.
5. Te, following D, Homeric scholia; A, G, Bu: δεδωκέναι, "given" (cf. δῶκε, *Od*. 10.19).
6. Hesitantly retained, with Bu, A, and G, but taken in a wider sense than "pastries"; πομάτων = "brews" (Te, following D, Homeric scholia) is attractive, because a κυκεών is drunk, and does not, *pace* Buffière, have "plutôt le caractère d'une pâtisserie que d'une boisson." For this and the remainder of the paragraph, cf. Old Scholia to *Od*. 10.549.
7. D, Te; Bu, following A, G, reads Τίς, "Who," and punctuates with a question mark.
8. Perhaps read ἐκμανθάνων (Russell) for ἐκμαθών, "having learned"; the present participle seems more suitable, and the corruption is a common one.
9. A, G, Bu; Te, following D and Homeric scholia, reads πολυδάπανος.
10. Heyne, followed by Te. Bu retains mss. κύνας ... προτομαῖς ... πεφραγμέναις.
11. Mss., Bu; Te adopts Polak's λιμός = "since not even hunger is under compulsion to do wrong."
12. D, Te; A, G, Bu read περί = "about the audience."
13. Heyne; mss., Te, Bu read εἰ δ᾽.
14. A, G, Bu; D, Te read μεταβέβηκεν = "if they take the form of allegorical wisdom," which strains the Greek. Allegorical wisdom is deep, and you have to descend into it; cf. 3.2, 53.1.
15. Russell, in place of μιμουμένοις (mss., Te, Bu) = "those who imitate them" (or "him" = Odysseus). Cf. 53.2, καταβὰς ... μυστικὴν ... σοφίαν.

70 Odysseus's wanderings as a whole, if carefully studied, will be found to be allegorical. Homer has produced in Odysseus a sort of instrument of every virtue, and has used him as the vehicle of his own philosophy, because he hated the vices which ravage human life. Pleasure is represented by the land of the Lotophagi, cultivators of exotic delights: Odysseus sails staunchly past it. He cripples our fierce anger by cauterizing it, as it were, with verbal advice: the name for this anger is Cyclops, he who "steals away" [*hupoklôpôn*] our powers of reasoning.[1] Again, was not Odysseus, who is supposed to have tied up the winds,[2] really the first person to foretell good sailing weather by his knowledge of astronomy? He prevailed also over Circe's drugs, using the depth of his wisdom to find a remedy for the ill effects of exotic delicacies. His wisdom descends to Hades, so that nothing even of what lies below us goes unexplored. He listens also to the Sirens, learning from them the varied history of all ages. Charybdis is a natural name for extravagant luxury and insatiable drinking. Scylla is his allegory for the many forms of shamelessness, and so she naturally has a girdle of of dogs' heads, since she is fenced around with rapacity, audacity, and greed.[3] The cattle of the sun represent temperance in eating, for Odysseus did not even regard hunger as a compelling reason to do wrong. These things are told as fables for the sake of the audience; but if one penetrates deeply into the wisdom which they represent allegorically, they will be found very useful to the initiated.

---

1. Up to this point, the paragraph = Old Scholia to *Od.* 9.89, which is introduced as "from Heraclitus" (the latter part also = Old Scholia to *Od.* 9.388, again ascribed to Heraclitus).

2. Heraclitus apparently assimilates Odysseus to Aeolus, who kept the winds tied up in a bag and gave it to Odysseus (*Od.* 10.19ff.). Buffière (1956, 237) points out that Aeolus is sometimes regarded as instructing Odysseus about the winds (Palaephatus 17).

3. Heraclitus seems here to diverge from Homer, who does not give Scylla dogs, only a dog's bark (*Od.* 12.86).

71.1 Τὸν μὲν γὰρ Αἴολον ἐξαιρέτως ἔγωγε νομίζω τὸν ἐνιαυτὸν εἶναι, ταῖς δωδεκαμήνοις τοῦ χρόνου περιόδοις ἐνδεδεμένον. **71.2** Ὠνόμασται γοῦν Αἴολος, τουτέστι ποικίλος, ἐπειδήπερ οὐκ ἰσοχρόνῳ καὶ μονοειδεῖ κατὰ πᾶσαν ὥραν τῇ φύσει συνήνωται, διάφοροι δ᾽ αὐτὸν αἱ παρ᾽ ἕκαστα μεταβολαὶ ποικίλλουσιν. **71.3** Ἔκ τε γὰρ ἀργαλέου κρύους εἰς πραεῖαν ἡδονὴν ἔαρος γαληνοῦται, **71.4** καὶ τὸ νοτερὸν τῆς ἐαριζούσης καταστάσεως ἔμπυρος ἡ τοῦ θέρους βία πυκνοῖ· **71.5** μετόπωρον δέ, φθινὰς ὥρα καρπῶν ἐτησίων, τὸ θέρειον ἐκλύσασα[1] θάλπος ὥραις χειμερίαις προοιμιάζεται. **71.6** Ταύτης δὲ τῆς ποικιλίας ὁ ἐνιαυτὸς ὢν πατὴρ εἰκότως Αἴολος ὠνόμασται. **71.7** Παῖδα δ᾽ αὐτὸν ὠνόμασεν Ἱππότου· τί γὰρ ὀξύτερον χρόνου; τί δ᾽ οὕτω ποδῶκες, ἀεὶ φερομένῳ καὶ ῥέοντι τῷ τάχει τοὺς ὅλους αἰῶνας ἐκμετρουμένου; **71.8** Δώδεκα δ᾽ αὐτοῦ παῖδές εἰσιν οἱ μῆνες,

ἓξ μὲν θυγατέρες, ἓξ δ᾽ υἱέες ἡβώοντες.

71.9 Τὸ μὲν εὔκαρπον καὶ γόνιμον τῶν τὸ θέρος ἐκπιμπλάντων μηνῶν θηλείᾳ γονῇ προσείκασε, τὸ δὲ στερρὸν καὶ πεπηγὸς τῶν χειμερίων ἠρρένωσεν. **71.10** Οὐκ ἀσεβὴς δ᾽ οὐδ᾽ ὁ περὶ τῶν γάμων μῦθος, ἀλλὰ τοὺς ἀδελφοὺς ἀνέμιξε ταῖς ἀδελφαῖς, ἐπειδήπερ ὑπ᾽ ἀλλήλων συμβέβηκε τὰς ὥρας ὀχεῖσθαι. **71.11** Ταμίας δ᾽ ἐστὶν ἀνέμων,

ἠμὲν παυέμεναι ἠδ᾽ ὀρνύμεν ὅν κ᾽ ἐθέλησιν·

ἔμμηνοι γὰρ αἱ τούτων φοραὶ καὶ κατὰ προθεσμίαν πνέουσαι, δεσπότης δ᾽ ἁπάντων ὁ ἐνιαυτός.

72.1 Καὶ τὰ μὲν ὑπὲρ Αἰόλου τοιαύτης ἠξίωται φυσιολογίας.

72.2 Ὁ δὲ Κίρκης κυκεὼν ἡδονῆς ἐστιν ἀγγεῖον, ὃ πίνοντες οἱ ἀκόλαστοι διὰ τῆς ἐφημέρου πλησμονῆς συῶν ἀθλιώτερον βίον ζῶσι. **72.3** Διὰ τοῦτο οἱ μὲν Ὀδυσσέως ἑταῖροι, χορὸς ὄντες ἠλίθιος, ἥττηνται τῆς γαστριμαργίας,

---

1. Te, following D and Homeric scholia; ἑλκύσασα A, G, Bu, who translates "tire," presumably "withdraw."

71 Aeolus, I believe, specially represents the year, which is bound up with time's twelve-month cycle. He is called Aeolus, which means "variegated," because he does not have a single, equally timed[1] and consistent character throughout all the seasons, but is made "various" by the particular changes that they bring. Thus when the bitter frosts are done he settles calmly into the mild pleasure of spring; the fiery heat of summer then condenses the moisture of springtime conditions; and autumn, the waning season of the annual harvest, loosens the grip of summer's heat and is the prelude to winter. And of all this variety the year is the father: it is quite right that he should be called Aeolus. Homer calls him son of Hippotes, "the horseman," for what is quicker than time, and what is so swift of foot? Time measures out whole ages with ever-moving, ever-flowing speed. Aeolus's twelve children are the months:

Six daughters and six lusty sons.[2]

Homer likens the fruitful and fertile nature of the months that make up summer to Aeolus's female offspring, and makes the stiffness and rigidity of the winter months masculine. There is no impiety either about the story of their marriages. He joins brothers and sisters together because the seasons are supported by one another. And Aeolus is the manager of the winds,

to halt or rouse whatever wind he will.[3]

This is because the movements of the winds are governed by the months, and they blow at duly appointed times. The year is master of them all.

72 Such is the proper scientific explanation of the story of Aeolus.

Circe's[4] *kukeôn* ["draught"] is a cup of pleasure, by drinking which the intemperate, for the sake of a momentary satisfaction, come to live a life more wretched than that of pigs. Odysseus's comrades, a foolish band,[5] therefore fell victim to gluttony, whereas Odysseus's wisdom

---

1. *Ouk isokhronôi* presumably indicates the fact that the days vary in length as the year proceeds.

2. *Od.* 10.6.

3. *Od.* 10.22.

4. On the Circe episode (*Od.* 10.133–574), see Buffière (1956, 506ff.), Hillgruber (1994–1999, 2:276; on *Vit. poes. Hom.* 126), Plutarch, frg. 200 Sandbach (= Stobaeus 1.445 Wachsmuth).

5. There is perhaps a pun here on *choros* and *choiros*, "pig."

ἡ δ' Ὀδυσσέως φρόνησις ἐνίκησε τὴν παρὰ Κίρκη τρυφήν. **72.4** Ἀμέλει τὸ πρῶτον ἐκ τῆς νεὼς ἀνιόντι καὶ πλησίον ὄντι τοῖς προθύροις Ἑρμῆς ἐφίσταται, τουτέστιν ὁ ἔμφρων λόγος. **72.5** Ὑφιστάμεθα γοῦν ἐτύμως αὐτὸν Ἑρμῆν λέγεσθαι παντὸς τοῦ νοουμένου κατὰ ψυχὴν ἑρμηνέα τινὰ ὄντα. **72.6** Τετράγωνόν τε ζωγράφων καὶ λιθοξόων χεῖρες αὐτὸν ἐλείαναν, ὅτι πᾶς ὀρθὸς λόγος ἑδραίαν ἔχει τὴν βάσιν οὐκ ὀλισθηρῶς ἐφ' ἑκάτερα κυλινδούμενος. **72.7** Καὶ μὴν καὶ πτεροῖς ἀνέστεψαν αὐτόν, αἰνιττόμενοι τὸ παντὸς λόγου τάχος. **72.8** Εἰρήνη τε χαίρει· πόλεμοι γὰρ οὐχ¹ ἥκιστα λόγων ἐνδεεῖς, τὸ γὰρ πλεῖστον ἐν αὐτοῖς κράτος εἰλήχασι χεῖρες. **72.9** Ὅμηρος δὲ καὶ διὰ τῶν ἐπιθέτων τοῦτ' ἔοικεν ἡμῖν σαφέστερον ποιεῖν. **72.10** "Ἀργειφόντην" τε γὰρ ὀνομάζει τὸν θεόν, οὐ μὰ Δί' οὐχὶ τοὺς Ἡσιοδείους μύθους ἐπιστάμενος, ὅτι τὸν βουκόλον Ἰοῦς ἐφόνευσεν, **72.11** ἀλλ' ἐπειδὴ μία παντὸς λόγου φύσις ἐκφαίνειν² ἐναργῶς τὸ νοούμενον, διὰ τοῦτο εἶπεν αὐτὸν ἀργειφόντην· **72.12** <καὶ>³ "Ἐριούνιον" καὶ "σῶκον·" ἔτι δ' "ἀκάκητα," <ὃ>⁴ λόγων ἐμφρόνων τὸ τελειότατόν ἐστι μαρτύριον· **72.13** ἐκτός τε γὰρ κακίας ὁ λογισμὸς ᾤκισται, σῴζει δὲ πάντα τὸν χρώμενον αὐτῷ καὶ μεγάλ'⁵ ὠφέλησεν. **72.14** Τί οὖν δὴ διπλᾶς καὶ διχρόνους διένειμε τῷ θεῷ τιμάς, τὴν μὲν ὑπὸ γῆν χθονίαν, τὴν δ' ὑπὲρ ἡμᾶς οὐράνιον; ἐπειδὴ διπλοῦς ὁ λόγος. **72.15** Τούτων δ' οἱ φιλόσοφοι τὸν μὲν ἐνδιάθετον καλοῦσι, τὸν δὲ προφορικόν. **72.16** Ὁ μὲν οὖν τῶν ἔνδον λογισμῶν ἐστι διάγγελος, ὃ δ' ὑπὸ τοῖς στέρνοις καθεῖρκται. **72.17** Φασὶ δὲ τούτῳ χρῆσθαι καὶ τὸ θεῖον· μηδενὸς γὰρ ὄντες ἐνδεεῖς τῆς φωνῆς τὴν χρείαν⁶ ἐν αὐτοῖς στέργουσι.⁷ **72.18** Διὰ τοῦτ' οὖν Ὅμηρος τὸν μὲν ἐνδιάθετον εἶπε χθόνιον, ἀφανὴς γὰρ ἐν τοῖς τῆς διανοίας βυθοῖς ἀπεσκότωται, τὸν δὲ προφορικόν, ἐπειδὴ πόρρωθέν ἐστι δῆλος, ἐν οὐρανῷ κατῴκισεν. **72.19** Γλῶττα δ' αὐτῷ θυσία, τὸ μόνον λόγου μέρος, καὶ τελευταίῳ κατὰ κοίτην ἰόντες Ἑρμῇ σπένδουσιν, ἐπειδὴ πάσης φωνῆς ἐστιν ὅρος ὕπνος.

---

1. Mss., Bu; Te, following Mehler, deletes οὐχ, in which case the sense is "for wars have very little need of speech."

2. Te (cf. D, ἐμφαίνειν); A, Bu read ἐκφαίνει, "displays," which gives a hiatus.

3. Russell (cf. τε γάρ at the beginning of 72.10).

4. Konstan, Russell; ἀκάκητα is nominative (accusative, only found in late texts, is ἀκακήτην), whereas Ἐριούνιον and σῶκον are accusative. Te posits a lacuna, Bu retains the mss. text (punctuating with full stop after ἀργειφόντην and comma after σῶκον).

5. Te (cf. μεγάλα in Homeric scholia); Bu, following A, D, reads μέγα (μέγ' is perhaps preferable).

6. Te; mss., Bu read τὴν φωνὴν τῆς χρείας, "the voice of use (or need)."

7. Mss., Bu; Te emends to στέγουσι, "they cover up."

prevailed over the luxury of Circe's dwelling. Note that Odysseus is just coming up from the ships and approaching the goddess' door when Hermes—that is to say, wise speech—meets him. Hermes, we take it, is appropriately so called as a kind of interpreter [*hermêneus*] of everything conceived in the mind. The hands of painters and sculptors make him a square figure, because every upright discourse has a stable basis and does not slip and roll from one side to the other.[1] They have however also given him wings, as a symbol of the speed of speech. He loves peace too: for wars are particularly short of speech, because the chief power in them belongs to the strong arm. Homer seems to make this even clearer to us by the god's epithets. He calls him *argeiphontes*, not of course because he knew Hesiod's story that he killed Io's herdsman [i.e., Argos], but because the one common characteristic of all speech is to display [*ekphainein*] thought plainly [*enargôs*]—that is why he names him Argeiphontes.[2] He also calls him *eriounios*, *sôkos*, and furthermore *akakêta*; this is the most complete evidence of words of wisdom, for reason dwells apart from evil [*kakia*] and preserves [*sôzei*] all who use it, and gives them great help [as if from *eri-*, "great" and *oninêmi*, "help"].[3] Why then did Homer assign the god two kinds of honor at two different times, the one chthonic, below the earth, the other heavenly, high above us?[4] It is because speech [*logos*] is of two kinds: the philosophers call one kind internal [*endiathetos*] and the other overt [*prophorikos*]. The overt is the reporter of our inner thoughts, the internal is held within our breast. (The latter, they say, the gods also employ:[5] for, lacking nothing, they are content with the use of voice within themselves.) Homer therefore called internal speech "chthonic," as being hidden in the dark depths of the mind, whereas he located overt speech in heaven, because it is plain from afar. The sacrifice to Hermes is a tongue, the sole organ of speech;[6] and the last libation at bedtime is to Hermes, because sleep is the end of all speech.

---

1. Cf. Cornutus, *Theol.* ch. 16 = p. 23.12 Lang, with Ramelli (2003, 338 n. 100).

2. Similar etymology in Cornutus, *Theol.* ch. 16 = p. 21.11 Lang; cf. Ramelli (2003, 334 n. 89). For the reference to Hesiod, see frg. 126 Merkelbach and West.

3. Cf. Cornutus, *Theol.* ch. 16 = p. 21.4ff. Lang, with Ramelli (2003, 333 n. 18).

4. Hermes is messenger of the Olympian gods and as psychopomp guides the souls of the dead to Hades.

5. It seems that the gods have only *endiathetos logos*, "internal speech": cf. *SVF* 3.135 = Sextus Empiricus, *Math.* 8.275; *SVF* 2.144 (Galen), where Circe is held to be *audêessa*, "speaking," because she has human form, gods in themselves having no *prophorikos logos* ("overt speech"); Galen, *Protrepticus* 1–2.

6. Cf. Cornutus, *Theol.* ch. 16 = p. 21.4 Lang, with Ramelli (2003, 340 n. 106).

73.1 Οὗτος οὖν Ὀδυσσεῖ παρέστηκε σύμβουλος ἐπὶ Κίρκην βαδίζοντι. **73.2** Καὶ κατ' ἀρχὰς μὲν ὑπ' ὀργῆς τε καὶ λύπης ὧν ἐπύθετο φερόμενος ἀκρίτως ἐνθουσιᾷ. **73.3** Κατὰ μικρὸν δ' ἐκείνων τῶν παθῶν μαραινομένων ὑπαναδύεται[1] τὸ μετὰ τοῦ συμφέροντος εὐλόγιστον, ὅθεν " Ἑρμείας χρυσόρραπις" ἀντεβόλησεν αὐτῷ. **73.4** Τὸ μέν γε χρυσοῦν ἀντὶ τοῦ καλοῦ παρείληπται, τὸ δὲ ῥάπτειν μεταφορικῶς ἀντὶ τοῦ συντιθέναι τε καὶ δια- νοεῖσθαι. **73.5** Λέγει γοῦν ἐν ἑτέροις·

κακὰ ῥάπτομεν ἀμφιέποντες.

73.6 Διὰ τοῦτο καὶ μύθους εἶπεν πλοκίους, ἐπειδὴ λόγος ἐκ λόγου γινόμενος καὶ ἑαυτῷ συρραφεὶς [γινόμενος][2] εὑρίσκει τὸ συμφέρον. **73.7** Οὐκοῦν χρυσόρραπιν εἶπε τὸν λόγον ἐκ τοῦ δύνασθαι καλῶς βουλεύεσθαί τε καὶ ῥάπτειν πράγματα. **73.8** Παραστὰς οὖν οὗτος ὁ λογισμὸς ἀπὸ τῆς ἀκρατοῦς ὀργῆς ἐπέπληξεν αὐτῷ μάτην κατασπεύδοντι·

Τίφθ' αὔτως, δύστηνε, δι' ἀκρίας ἔρχεαι οἶος,
χώρου ἄιδρις ἐών;

73.9 Ταῦτα πρὸς αὐτὸν ἐλάλησεν Ὀδυσσεὺς μετανοοῦντι λογισμῷ τὴν πρότερον ὁρμὴν ἀναχαλινώσας. **73.10** Τὴν δὲ φρόνησιν οὐκ ἀπιθάνως μῶλυ προσεῖπεν,[3] μόνους[4] ἀνθρώπους ἢ μόλις εἰς ὀλίγους ἐρχομένην· **73.11** φύσις δ' αὐτῆς ῥίζα μέλαινα, "γάλακτι δὲ εἴκελον ἄνθος·" **73.12** Πάντα γὰρ οὖν συλλήβδην τὰ τηλικαῦτα τῶν ἀγαθῶν τὰς μὲν ἀρχὰς προσάντεις καὶ χαλεπὰς ἔχει, γεννικῶς δ' ὅταν ὑποστῇ τις ἐναθλήσας τῷ κατ' ἀρχὰς πόνῳ, τηνικαῦτα γλυκὺς ἐν φωτὶ τῶν ὠφελειῶν ὁ καρπός. **73.13** Ὑπὸ τοιούτου φρουρούμενος Ὀδυσσεὺς λογισμοῦ τὰ Κίρκης νενίκηκε φάρμακα.

74.1 Μεταβὰς δ' ἐκ τῶν[5] ὑπὲρ γῆς θεωρημάτων Ὅμηρος οὐδὲ τὴν ἀφανῆ καὶ νεκρὰν φύσιν εἴασεν ἀναλληγόρητον, ἀλλὰ καὶ τὰ ἐν Ἅιδου συμβολικῶς

---

1. Te; mss., Bu, read ὑπαναλύεται, "lentement se dégagent," but this word should mean "are gradually broken up," and this seems quite the wrong sense.

2. Text unsure. A has συρραφῆσαι αὐτῷ γινόμενος, D and the Homeric scholia have συρραφεὶς ἑαυτῷ. We follow this, but transpose ἑαυτῷ to precede συρραφείς, to avoid an illicit hiatus. Te emends to συρραφεύς, "stitcher"; Bu emends to συρραφής (reading αὐτῷ with A instead of ἑαυτῷ), a rare form meaning "sewn together."

3. Te inserts this (= "called") from D and the Homeric scholia; omitted by A, Bu.

4. Te inserts <εἰς> before μόνους, Bu after, unnecessarily: Heraclitus may be adopting the poetic usage of putting the preposition with only the second noun (Kühner and Gerth 1963, 2.1:550).

5. Te, following Mehler (δ' ἐκ) and D (τῶν); A, Bu read simply δέ.

73 This then is the counsellor who stands at Odysseus's side as he goes to see Circe. At first, carried away by anger and distress at what he has heard, Odysseus is in an uncontrolled state of excitement, but after a while, as these feelings fade, rational calculation of expediency slips in. So "Hermes Goldenwand" meets him:[1] "golden" stands for honorable and "wand" [*rhapis*] suggests *rhaptein*, "to stitch," a metaphor for putting things together and thinking them out. Homer says elsewhere:

We were busy stitching troubles for them.[2]

Similarly, he speaks of "woven words"[3] because words arising from one another and stitched together lead to the discovery of the right course of action. Thus speech is called "Goldenwand" [*khrysorrhapis*] because of its power to counsel well and stitch things together. So this reasoning power came to Odysseus's aid, took over from his outburst of anger, and reproached him for his foolish zeal:

Poor wretch, why walk the hills alone,
when you know nothing of the country?[4]

Odysseus says this to himself, curbing his former urge by having second thoughts. Homer plausibly called wisdom *moly*, because it comes only [*monous*] to humans, or because it comes to few and with difficulty [*molis*]. Its characteristic is a black root and "a milk-white flower,"[5] because all such important good things have steep and difficult beginnings, but if one submits bravely and faces up to the initial labor, sweet then in the light is the harvest of benefits. It is because he was protected by this sort of reasoning that Odysseus overcame Circe's drugs.

74 From these speculations concerning life above ground, Homer passes to the unseen world of the dead, not failing to allegorize this also, but giving a philosophical account in symbolic terms of Hades too. The

---

1. *Od.* 10.278.
2. *Od.* 3.118. For a different etymology, see Cornutus, *Theol.* ch. 16 = p. 21.15–18 Lang, with Ramelli (2003, 335 n. 90).
3. This seems to refer to *Od.* 13.295, where our texts of Homer read *klopiôn*, "thievish," but an ancient variant *plokiôn* is known (cf. Eustathius 1741.57).
4. *Od.* 10.281–282 (Hermes speaking).
5. *Od.* 10.304.

ἐφιλοσόφησε. **74.2** Κωκυτὸς γοῦν ὁ πρῶτος ὀνομάζεται ποταμὸς ἐπώνυμον[1] ἀνθρωπίνου πάθους κακόν, θρῆνοι γὰρ ἐπὶ τοῖς τεθνεῶσιν οἱ παρὰ τῶν ζώντων. **74.3** Πυριφλεγέθοντα δ᾽ ἐφεξῆς ὀνομάζει· μετὰ γὰρ τὰ δάκρυα ταφαὶ καὶ πῦρ ἀφανίζον ὅ ἐστι θνητῆς σαρκὸς ἐν ἡμῖν. **74.4** Ἀμφοτέρους δὲ τοὺς ποταμοὺς εἰς ἕνα τὸν Ἀχέροντα συρρέοντας οἶδεν, ἐπειδήπερ ἐκδέχεται μετὰ τοὺς πρώτους κωκυτοὺς καὶ τὴν ὀφειλομένην ταφὴν ἄχη τινὰ καὶ λῦπαι χρόνιοι πρὸς ὀλίγας ὑπομνήσεις ἐρεθίζουσαι τὰ πάθη. **74.5** Στυγὸς δ᾽ ἀπορρῶγες οἱ ποταμοὶ διὰ τὴν στυγνότητα καὶ τὴν ἐπὶ τῷ θανάτῳ κατήφειαν. **74.6** Ἀίδης μὲν οὖν ὁ ἀφανὴς τόπος ἐπωνύμως ὠνόμασται, Φερσεφόνη δ᾽ ἄλλως ἢ τὰ πάντα πεφυκυῖα διαφθείρειν· **74.7** ἐν ἧς[2] οὐκ

> ὄγχνη ἐπ᾽ ὄγχνη γηράσκει, μῆλον δ᾽ ἐπὶ μήλῳ,

τὰ δ᾽ ἐνερριζωμένα πρέμνα τοῖς ἄλσεσιν "αἴγειροι καὶ ἰτέαι ὠλεσίκαρποι." **74.8** Τὰς δὲ θυσίας συνῳκείωσε τῷ τόπῳ...

75.1 .... τῆς σελήνης[3] ἀμαυρούμενος ὁ τοῦ ἡλίου κύκλος ἀμβλύνεται καὶ πολλάκις ἄστρων διαφεγγεῖς μαρμαρυγὰς ὁρῶμεν. **75.2** Εὐλόγως οὖν τοῦτο Θεοκλύμενος εἶπεν, ὁ τὰ θεῖα κλύων (εὗρε γὰρ ἄξιον τῆς φυσικῆς θεωρίας καὶ τοὔνομα),

> νυκτὶ μὲν ὑμέων
> εἰλύαται κεφαλαί τε πρόσωπά τε νέρθε τε γοῦνα.

75.3 Καὶ μὴν ἐν ταῖς ἐκλείψεσιν αἵματι προσφερὴς χρόα τὸ βλεπόμενον,[4] ἐκφοινίσσεται γάρ· **75.4** διὰ τοῦτ᾽ ἐπήνεγκεν·

> αἵματι δ᾽ ἐρρέδαται τοῖχοι καλαί τε μεσόδμαι.

---

1. Russell, following D; Bu reads ἐπώνυμος, Τε ἐπωνύμως.
2. Τε; Bu, following mss., reads οἷς, "among which" (but translates "chez elle").
3. Sc., e.g., <ὑπελθούσης> (Russell); cf. Ps.-Plutarch, *Vit. poes. Hom.* 108, with Hillgruber's note (1994–1999, 2:241).
4. Mss., Bu; Te adopts Mehler's προσφερές and χρόαν, and inserts τὴν before χρόαν: "what is observed is red in color."

first river he names is Cocytus ("lamentation"),[1] an evil that takes its
name from human suffering, since the lamentations of the living are
dirges for the dead. Next he names Pyriphlegethon, for after the tears
comes the funeral and the fire that consumes what mortal flesh there is in
us. He knows that both these rivers flow into the single stream of
Acheron, because after the first lamentations and the due rituals of burial
come griefs [*akhê*] and sorrows that endure and rekindle the emotion at
the slightest recollection. These rivers are said to be outlets of the Styx,
because of the hatefulness [*stygnotês*] and gloom of death. Hades is so
named as the "the unseen place," and Persephone [Greek *Phersephonê*] is
she whose nature is to destroy [*dia-phtheirein*] all things: in her house is no

> pear maturing after pear,
> and apple after apple.[2]

The only trees that take root in her grove are "poplars and willows that
lose their fruit."[3] He has made the sacrifices to fit the place....[4]

75 <When> the moon <is in conjunction with it>, the sun's orb is
dimmed and we often see the bright twinkling of the stars. There is reason
therefore in the words of Theoclymenus—that man who hears [*kluôn*]
divine [*theia*] things (Homer has found a name for him suitable for his
scientific speculation):

> your heads, your faces, and your knees
> are shrouded all in night.[5]

Moreover, in eclipses, what is observed is a color like blood, for it is all
reddened: so Theoclymenus adds

> the walls and handsome pedestals
> all run with blood.[6]

---

1. Cf. Cornutus, *Theol.* ch. 35 = pp. 74–75 Lang for this and what follows, with Ramelli
(2003, 414 n. 301, 414 n. 302).
2. *Od.* 7.120. For a different derivation, cf. Cornutus, *Theol.* ch. 28 = p. 55.4–7 Lang,
with Ramelli (2003, 384 n. 222).
3. *Od.* 10.510. A good deal is lost here, though the mss. mark no lacuna. We resume
with *Od.* 20.
4. The sacrifices will be those described in *Od.* 11.23–37.
5. *Od.* 20.351–352.
6. *Od.* 20.354.

75.5 Προθεσμία δὲ τῆς ἐκλείψεως, ἣν ῞Ιππαρχος ἠκρίβωσε, κατὰ τὴν ὀνομα-ζομένην τριακάδα καὶ νουμηνίαν, ἣν ᾽Αττικῶν παῖδες ἔνην τε καὶ νέαν ὀνομάζουσιν· **75.6** οὐδ᾽ ἂν ἄλλην τις εὕροι τῆς ἐκλείψεως ἡμέραν. **75.7** ῞Οτε[1] οὖν Θεοκλύμενος ἱστορεῖ ταῦτα τίς ἦν ὁ χρόνος, ἔξεστι παρ᾽ αὐτοῦ μαθεῖν Ὁμήρου·

τοῦ μὲν φθίνοντος μηνός, τοῦ δ᾽ ἱσταμένοιο.

75.8 Τοσαύτη καὶ περὶ τῶν παρακολουθούντων καὶ τῆς προθεσμίας ἡ κατὰ τὴν ἔκλειψιν ἀκρίβεια.

75.9 Τί δεῖ τούτοις ἅπασι προστιθέναι τὴν ἐπὶ τέλει τῆς μνηστηρο-φονίας παρεστῶσαν ᾽Αθηνᾶν Ὀδυσσεῖ, τουτέστι τὴν φρόνησιν; **75.10** Εἰ μὲν γὰρ ἐκ τοῦ φανεροῦ καὶ βιαζόμενος ἠμύνατο τοὺς λελυπηκότας, ῎Αρης ἂν αὐτῷ[2] συνηγωνίζετο· **75.11** νῦν δὲ δόλῳ καὶ τέχνῃ περιελθών, ἵν᾽ ἀγνοούμενος ἕλῃ, διὰ συνέσεως κατώρθωσε. **75.12** Διὸ[3] δὴ πάντα καθ᾽ ἓν ἀθροίσαντες ἀλληγορίας πλήρη τὴν ὅλην ποίησιν εὑρίσκομεν.

76.1 ῏Αρ᾽ οὖν ἐπὶ τούτοις ὁ μέγας οὐρανοῦ καὶ θεῶν ἱεροφάντης ῞Ομηρος, ὁ τὰς ἀβάτους καὶ κεκλεισμένας ἀνθρωπίναις ψυχαῖς ἀτραποὺς ἐπ᾽ οὐρανὸν ἀνοίξας, ἐπιτήδειός ἐστι κατακριθῆναι δυσσεβεῖν, **76.2** ἵνα ταύτης τῆς ἀνοσίου καὶ μιαρᾶς ψήφου διενεχθείσης ἀναιρεθέντων τε τῶν ποιημάτων ἄφωνος ἀμαθία τοῦ κόσμου κατασκεδασθῇ, **76.3** καὶ μήτε νηπίων παίδων χορὸς ὠφελῆται τὰς σοφίας παρ᾽ Ὁμήρου πρῶτον, ὡς ἀπὸ τιθήνης ποτιζό-μενος[4] γάλα, **76.4** μήτ᾽ ἀντίπαιδες ἢ νεανίαι καὶ τὸ παρηβηκὸς ἤδη τῷ χρόνῳ γῆρας ἀπολαύῃ τινὸς ἡδονῆς, **76.5** πᾶς δ᾽ ὁ βίος ἀναιρεθεὶς τὴν γλῶτταν ἐν κωφότητι διάγῃ; **76.6** Φυγαδευέτω τοίνυν ἀπὸ τῆς ἰδίας πολιτείας Πλάτων ῞Ομηρον, ὡς αὐτὸν ἐξ ᾽Αθηνῶν ἐφυγάδευσεν εἰς Σικελίαν. **76.7** ῎Εδει δὲ ταύτης τῆς πολιτείας Κριτίαν ἀπωστὸν εἶναι, τύραννος γάρ, ἢ ᾽Αλκιβιάδην, τὸν ἐν παισὶ μὲν ἀπρεπῶς θῆλυν, ἐν δὲ μειρακίοις ἄνδρα, τὸν ἐν συμποσίοις Ἐλευσίνια παίζοντα καὶ Σικελίας μὲν ἀποστάτην, Δεκελείας δὲ κτίστην. **76.8** ᾽Αλλά τοι Πλάτων μὲν ῞Ομηρον ἐκβέβληκε τῆς ἰδίας πόλεως, ὁ δὲ σύμπας κόσμος Ὁμήρου μία φησὶν εἶναι πατρίς·

---

1. Reading ῞Οτε with Bu; Te reads ῞Ο τε and (following Mehler) inserts <δ᾽> after τίς.
2. Te, following D (which reads ὁ ῎Αρης); Bu, following A, reads ἄριστ᾽ ἂν ὁ πόλεμος, translating "la Guerre eût été toute indiquée pour l'assister."
3. Διό Russell (cf. 19.9, etc.); Διά A, Bu, translating "par tous ces exemples que nous avons rassemblés"; ῾Α Te, following D, Homeric scholia.
4. Te, following D, Homeric scholia; A, Bu omit the word (= "drink in").

The date when eclipses occur, which Hipparchus determined, is what is called the thirtieth day or the new moon: the Athenians call it "old and new." No other day can be found when an eclipse can happen. So we can discover from Homer himself what the date was when Theoclymenus tells this story:

one moon waning, and another waxing.[1]

Such is Homer's precision about the eclipse, covering both its concomitant circumstances and its timing.

Is it necessary to add to all this the presence of Athena (that is to say, wisdom) at Odysseus's side at the end of the Slaying of the Suitors?[2] If he had defended himself openly and by force against those who had harmed him, Ares would have been his ally; but as he has gone about it with craft and guile, so as to overcome them without being recognized, his success is brought about by wisdom. So, putting all these things together, we can see that the whole poem is full of allegory.

76 After all this, can Homer, the great hierophant of heaven and of the gods, who opened up for human souls the untrodden and closed paths to heaven, deserve to be condemned as impious? Were this vile and unholy verdict to be given and his poems destroyed, dumb ignorance would spread across the world; no help would come to the band of little children who drink in wisdom first from Homer, as they do their nurses' milk; nor would boys and younger men or the older generation that has passed its prime any longer have pleasure. Life's tongue would be ripped out, it would all dwell in dumb silence. So let Plato banish Homer from his private Republic as he banished himself from Athens to Sicily. It is Critias who ought to have been driven from that Republic as a tyrant, or Alcibiades, who was so disgustingly effeminate as a boy and so precocious an adult as a lad, the mocker of Eleusis at the dinner table, the deserter from Sicily, the founder of Decelea.[3]

Yet, while Plato banished Homer from his private city, the whole world claims to be Homer's only country: for

---

1. *Od.* 14.62.

2. *Od.* 22.205ff.

3. The highlights of Alcibiades' career are familiar in declamation (see Russell 1983, 123–28): this is a good instance of Heraclitus's rhetorical disposition. While Alcibiades was leading the Athenian naval expedition in Sicily, he was charged with the mutilation of the Herms back in Athens; he deserted to the Spartan side and advised the Spartans to occupy Decelea in Attica as a base from which to conduct year-round operations.

76.9 "Ποίας," γοῦν, "ἀστὸν Ὅμηρον ἀναγραψώμεθα πάτρης,
κεῖνον ἐφ' ᾧ πᾶσαι χεῖρ' ὀρέγουσι πόλεις,"

76.10 ἐξόχως δ' Ἀθῆναι, αἱ Σωκράτην μὲν ἀρνησάμεναι πολίτην μέχρι φαρ-
μάκου, μίαν δ' εὐχὴν ἔχουσαι δοκεῖν Ὁμήρου πατρὶς εἶναι; **76.11** Πῶς γε μὴν
αὐτὸς Ὅμηρος ἐμπολιτεύεσθαι τοῖς Πλάτωνος ἂν ἐκαρτέρησε νόμοις, οὕτως
ἐναντίᾳ καὶ μαχομένῃ στάσει διῳκισμένων αὐτῶν;[1] **76.12** ὃ μέν γε συμβουλεύει
κοινοὺς γάμους τε καὶ τέκνα, τῷ δ' ἄμφω τὰ σωμάτια γάμοις σώφροσι
καθωσίωται· **76.13** διὰ μὲν γὰρ Ἑλένην ἐστρατεύκασιν Ἕλληνες, διὰ
Πηνελόπην δ' Ὀδυσσεὺς πλανᾶται. **76.14** Καὶ θεσμοὶ μὲν δικαιότατοι παντὸς
ἀνθρωπίνου βίου δι' ἀμφοῖν τῶν Ὁμήρου σωματίων ἐμπολιτεύονται, **76.15** τοὺς
δὲ Πλάτωνος διαλόγους ἄνω καὶ κάτω παιδικοὶ καθυβρίζουσιν ἔρωτες, οὐδαμοῦ
δ' οὐχὶ τῆς ἄρσενος ἐπιθυμίας μεστός ἐστιν ἀνήρ. **76.16** Μούσας μὲν Ὅμηρος
ἐπικαλεῖται θεὰς παρθένους ἐπὶ τοῖς λαμπροτάτοις τῶν κατορθωμάτων,
ὅπου τι καὶ γεννικόν ἐστιν ἐπίταγμα καὶ τῆς Ὁμηρικῆς θειότητος ἄξιον, **76.17**
οὐκ ἔλαττον [ἤ][2] κατὰ πόλεις διαταττομένων ἤ[3] κἀπὶ[4] μεγάλων ἡρώων
ἀριστείαις[5].

77.1 Συνεχῶς οὖν καθάπερ εἰς χῶρον αὐτῷ συνήθη τὸν Ἑλικώνιον ἐφίσταται λέγων· **77.2**

Ἔσπετε νῦν μοι Μοῦσαι Ὀλύμπια δώματ' ἔχουσαι,
οἵτινες ἡγέμονες Δαναῶν καὶ κοίρανοι ἦσαν.

77.3 Ἢ πάλιν ἡνίκα τῆς Ἀγαμέμνονος ἀνδραγαθίας ἐνάρχεται τὸν τρισὶ
θεοῖς ἥρωα σύμμορφον ὑμνῶν· **77.4**

Ἔσπετε νῦν μοι Μοῦσαι Ὀλύμπια δώματ' ἔχουσαι,
ὅστις δὴ πρῶτος Ἀγαμέμνονος ἀντίος ἦλθεν.

77.5 Ἀλλ' ὅ γε θαυμαστὸς Πλάτων ἐν τῷ περικαλλεῖ **Φαίδρῳ** τῆς σώφρονος
ὑπὲρ ἐρώτων διακρίσεως ἀρχόμενος ἐτόλμησεν, ὡς ὁ Λοκρὸς Αἴας ἐν τῷ

---

1. Mss., Bu; Te emends to αὐτῷ, "when they [the laws] were divided from him [Homer],
etc.," but this involves an unlikely change of case (διῳκισμένων picking up νόμοις).
2. Deleted by Russell; retained by Te, Bu, following mss.; Te punctuates after ἔλαττον.
3. Polak, followed by Te; mss., Bu, read διατασσομένη.
4. Russell; καὶ <ἐν> Polak; καί mss., Te, Bu.
5. D, Te; A, Bu read ἀριστείαν.

of what land shall we count Homer citizen,
the man to whom all cities extend a hand[1]

—Athens above all, which denied Socrates as a citizen to the point of
giving him poison, and yet prays only to be thought Homer's native
land? But how could Homer himself have endured to live under Plato's
laws, when the two of them are divided by such contrary and conflicting positions? Plato recommends marriages and children in common,
Homer's two poems are both sanctified by chaste marriages: the
Greeks have gone to war because of Helen, Odysseus goes on his wanderings because of Penelope. Again, the most righteous principles of
human life are embedded in the society of both Homer's poems; Plato's
dialogues, in contrast, are disgraced through and through by ped-
erasty: there is not a passage which does not show the man bursting
with desire for a male partner. Homer invokes the Muses, virgin goddesses, for the most brilliant of his heroes' achievements, when there is
a really noble command to give them, worthy of Homer's divine quality,
no less for the exploits of armies drawn up city by city than for those of
mighty heroes.[2]

77 Thus he often, as it were, stands on his home ground of Helicon,
and says

Tell me now, Muses who dwell on Olympus,
who were the leaders and princes of the Danaans;[3]

or again, when he begins the heroic deeds of Agamemnon by praising the
hero who has a likeness to three gods:[4]

Tell me now, Muses who dwell on Olympus,
who was it first confronted Agamemnon?[5]

On the other hand, our wonderful Plato, in his beautiful *Phaedrus*, at
the start of that very moral distinction of the kinds of love, had the

---

1. *Planudean Anthology* 16.294, one of a large group (292–304) of epigrams on these
themes.
2. Invocations of the Muses occur both before the account of whole armies (*Il.* 2.484)
and before individual actions (*Il.* 11.218).
3. *Il.* 2.484, 487.
4. I.e., Zeus, Ares, and Poseidon: *Il.* 2.478.
5. *Il.* 11.218–219.

παρθενῶνι τῆς ἁγιωτάτης θεᾶς, ἄγος τι Μουσῶν κατασπείσας, τὰς σώφρονας ἔργων ἀσελγῶν καλέσαι βοηθούς· **77.6** " Ἄγετε δή, Μοῦσαι, εἴτε δι' ᾠδῆς εἶδος λίγειαι εἴτε διὰ γένος τι μουσικὸν ταύτην ἔσχετε τὴν ἐπωνυμίαν, σύμ μοι λάβεσθε τοῦδε τοῦ μύθου." **77.7** Περὶ τίνος, εἴποιμ' ἄν, ὦ θαυμασιώτατε Πλάτων; ὑπὲρ οὐρανοῦ καὶ τῆς τῶν ὅλων φύσεως ἢ περὶ γῆς καὶ θαλάττης; **77.8** ἀλλ' οὐδὲ περὶ ἡλίου καὶ σελήνης οὐδ' ὑπὲρ ἀπλανῶν τε καὶ πλανήτων κινήσεως. **77.9** Ἀλλὰ τί τῆς εὐχῆς πέρας ἐστίν, αἰσχύνομαι καὶ λέγειν· **77.10**

> Ἦν δὲ παῖς οὕτω καλός, μᾶλλον δὲ μειρακίσκος, οὗ πολλοὶ μὲν ἦσαν
> ἐρασταί, εἷς δέ τις αἱμύλος, ὃς ἐπεπείκει αὐτὸν ἐρῶν ὅτι οὐκ ἐρῴη
> καί ποτε αὐτὸν αἰτῶν ἔλεγεν ...

77.11 Ὧδε γυμνοῖς τοῖς ὀνόμασι[1] τὴν ἀσέλγειαν ὡς ἐπὶ τέγους ἀνέῳξεν, οὐδ' εὐπρεπεῖ σχήματι τὸ τοῦ πράγματος αἰσχρὸν ὑποκλέψας.

78.1 Τοιγαροῦν εἰκότως ὁ μὲν Ὁμήρου λόγος ἡρώων ἐστὶ βίος, οἱ δὲ Πλάτωνος διάλογοι μειρακίων ἔρωτες. **78.2** Καὶ πάντα τὰ παρ' Ὁμήρῳ γενικῆς ἀρετῆς γέμει· **78.3** φρόνιμος Ὀδυσσεύς, ἀνδρεῖος Αἴας, σώφρων Πηνελόπη, δίκαιος ἐν ἅπασι Νέστωρ, εὐσεβὴς εἰς πατέρα Τηλέμαχος, ἐν φιλίαις πιστότατος Ἀχιλλεύς· **78.4** ὧν <τί>[2] παρὰ Πλάτωνι τῷ φιλοσόφῳ; πλὴν εἰ μὴ νὴ Δία βιωφελῆ φήσομεν[3] εἶναι τὰ σεμνὰ τῶν ἰδεῶν τερετίσματα καὶ παρ' Ἀριστοτέλει τῷ μαθητῇ γελώμενα. **78.5** Διὰ τοῦτ' ἀξίας οἶμαι τῶν καθ' Ὁμήρου λόγων δίκας ὑπέσχεν, "ἀκόλαστον" ἔχων "γλῶσσαν, αἰσχίστην νόσον," ὡς Τάνταλος, ὡς Καπανεύς, ὡς οἱ διὰ γλωσσαλγίαν μυρίαις κεχρημένοι συμφοραῖς. **78.6** Πολλάκις ἐπὶ τὰς τυραννικὰς ἐφθείρετο θύρας, ἐν ἐλευθέρῳ δὲ σώματι δουλικὴν ἠνέσχετο τύχην καὶ μέχρι πράσεως· **78.7** οὐδὲ εἷς γὰρ ἀγνοεῖ τὸν Σπαρτιάτην Πόλλιν, [ῷ][4] οὐδ' ὡς Λιβυκοῦ χάριν

---

1. Muenzel, Τε, in place of ὄμμασι, i.e., "to naked eyes" (mss., Bu).
2. Te, followed by Bu.
3. Te, cf. βίου ὠφέλειαν φήσομεν (D); Bu reads τιμὴν <καὶ> ὠφέλ<ειαν φ>ήσομεν, i.e., "that there is honor and use in the twitterings" (cf. τιμὴν ... ὠφελήσομεν, A).
4. Bu, following a suggestion in Te apparatus criticus; Te retains ῷ and indicates a lacuna after it, e.g., "to whom <Dionysius handed him over>."

hardihood, just like Locrian Ajax in the maiden-chamber of the most holy goddess,[1] to pour a libation of filth over the Muses, and summon those chaste goddesses to aid his wicked works, saying "Come, ye Muses, whether it be for the nature of your song that you were called clear-voiced [*ligeiai*], or because of some musical nation, help me in this tale."[2] And what, I may ask, is the tale about, O most wonderful Plato? Heaven and the universe, or earth and sea? No, nor sun and moon and the motions of fixed stars and planets. What the goal of his prayer is, I am ashamed even to report:

> Once upon a time there was a beautiful boy, or rather young lad, who had many lovers, and one persuasive one who had convinced him that he did not love him, though in fact he did, and who said one day when asking for his favors....

In such naked language did he reveal his wickedness, from the rooftops as it were,[3] not even concealing the disgrace of the thing by a decent pretense.

78 It is only natural therefore that Homer's discourse should be the life of heroes, and Plato's conversation the loves of young men. In Homer, everything is full of noble virtue: Odysseus is wise, Ajax brave, Penelope chaste, Nestor invariably just, Telemachus dutiful to his father, Achilles totally loyal to his friendships. And what is there of this in philosopher Plato? Unless indeed we are to say that there is practical use in the solemn twitterings [*teretismata*][4] of the Ideas, which even his pupil Aristotle ridicules. He was rightly punished, I am sure, for his words against Homer. It is he who has "tongue unchastened, most shameful sickness,"[5] like Tantalus, like Capaneus, like all who have suffered innumerable disasters because of their loose tongue. Often did he journey wearily to tyrants' doors; born free, he endured the fate of slaves, even to the point of being sold. Who has not heard of Pollis the Spartan,[6] or

---

1. I.e., Athena: Ajax is said to have violated Cassandra in her temple. See Apollodorus, *Epitome* 5.22–23; Virgil, *Aen.* 2.403–408.

2. *Phaedr.* 237A. The "musical nation" are the Ligurians, whose name is supposed to come from *ligus*, "clear-voiced."

3. Perhaps with a suggestion of a brothel: see Gow and Page (1965) on *Palatine Anthology* 11.363 (= Dioscorides 37.4); cf. also Aristophanes, *Lys.* 389, 395 on sound traveling from a rooftop.

4. Cf. Aristotle, *An. post.* 83a32.

5. Euripides, *Orest.* 10. See above, 1.3.

6. Pollis is the man to whom Dionysius handed over Plato as a slave; cf. Diogenes Laertius 3.19.

ἐλέου σέσωσται, καὶ μνῶν εἴκοσι καθάπερ ἀνδράποδον εὐτελὲς ἐτιμήθη. **78.8** Καὶ ταῦτα τῶν εἰς Ὅμηρον ἀσεβημάτων ὀφειλομένην τιμωρίαν <ὑπέσχε>[1] τῆς ἀχαλίνου καὶ ἀπυλώτου γλώττης.

79.1 Πρὸς μὲν οὖν Πλάτωνα καὶ πλείω λέγειν δυνάμενος ἐῶ, τοὔνομα τῆς Σωκρατικῆς σοφίας αἰδούμενος. **79.2** Ὁ δὲ **Φαίαξ** φιλόσοφος Ἐπίκουρος, ὁ τῆς ἡδονῆς ἐν τοῖς ἰδίοις κήποις γεωργός, ὁ πᾶσαν ποιητικὴν ἄστροις σημηνάμενος οὐκ ἐξαιρέτως μόνον Ὅμηρον, ἆρ' οὐχὶ καὶ ταῦθ' ἃ μόνα τῷ βίῳ παρέδωκεν αἰσχρῶς ἀγνοήσας[2] παρ' Ὁμήρου κέκλοφεν; **79.3** ἃ γὰρ Ὀδυσσεὺς ὑποκρίσει παρ' Ἀλκίνῳ μὴ φρονῶν ἐψεύσατο, ταῦθ' ὡς ἀληθεύων ἀπεφήνατο τέλη βίου· **79.4**

> ἀλλ' ὅταν εὐφροσύνη μὲν ἔχῃ κατὰ δῆμον ἅπαντα,
> δαιτυμόνες δ' ἀνὰ δώματ' ἀκουάζωνται ἀοιδοῦ,
> τοῦτό τί μοι κάλλιστον ἐνὶ φρεσὶν εἴδεται εἶναι.

79.5 Λέγει δ' Ὀδυσσεὺς οὐχ ὁ παρὰ Τρωσὶν ἀριστεύων, οὐχ ὁ Θράκην κατασκάπτων οὐδ' ὁ τὰς παρὰ Λωτοφάγοις[3] ἡδονὰς παραπλέων οὐδ' ὁ τοῦ μεγίστου Κύκλωπος ἔτι μείζων, **79.6** ὃς ἐπέζευσε τὴν ἅπασαν γῆν, ὃς ἔπλευσε τὴν Ὠκεάνιον θάλατταν, ὃς ἔτι ζῶν εἶδεν Ἅιδην, **79.7** οὐχ οὗτος Ὀδυσσεύς ἐστιν ὁ ταῦτα λέγων, ἀλλὰ τὸ βραχὺ τῆς Ποσειδῶνος ὀργῆς λείψανον, ὃν οἱ βαρεῖς χειμῶνες ἐπὶ τὸν Φαιάκων ἔλεον ἐξεκύμηναν. **79.8** Ἃ δὴ παρὰ τοῖς ὑποδεξαμένοις ἐνομίζετο τίμια, τούτοις ἐξ ἀνάγκης συγκαταινεῖ, **79.9** μίαν γ'[4] εὐχὴν πεποιημένος, ἣν ἀτυχῶν[5] ἐπαρᾶται·

> Δός μ' ἐς Φαίηκας φίλον ἐλθεῖν ἠδ' ἐλεεινόν,

---

1. Russell (ὑποσχών Mehler); Te emends to ὀφειλομένη τιμωρία, "was his due punishment."
2. Mss., Bu; Te emends to ἀγνωμονήσας, "unjustly."
3. Te, following Mehler; τὰς περὶ Λωτοφάγους (D); Bu, following A, reads παρὰ τάς Λωτοφάγους (adjective with ἡδονάς), but παραπλέων at 70.3 takes a direct object.
4. Te in apparatus criticus, δ' mss., Bu; Te reads μίαν εὐχὴν.
5. D, Te; A, M, Bu read ἀτυχῶς.

how he was saved by the merciful act of a Libyan, and valued, as a poor-quality slave, at twenty minae? And this was the due punishment <he underwent> for the impieties against Homer of his unbridled and unfenced tongue.[1]

79 There is more I could say against Plato, but I let it pass, out of respect for the reputation of Socratic wisdom. But what about the Phaeacian philosopher Epicurus, the horticulturalist who grew pleasure in his private garden, who took a bearing on all poetry, not only Homer in particular, by relying on the stars?[2] Did he not steal ignorantly and shamefully from Homer the only doctrines which he has passed on to mankind? What Odysseus said falsely, unwisely, and hypocritically at the court of Alcinous, Epicurus proclaims as the goal of life, and claims to be speaking the truth:

> When joy possesses all the people,
> and in the house the feasters hear the singer,
> that seems to my heart to be best of all.[3]

Odysseus says this—not the Odysseus who fought heroically at Troy, not the man who destroyed cities in Thrace, not the man who sailed past the delights of the Lotus-Eaters, was greater than the mighty Cyclops, traveled the whole earth on foot and sailed the Ocean sea, and as a living man beheld Hades—that is not the Odysseus who said these things, but the poor leavings of Poseidon's anger, the man whom dreadful storms washed up to be pitied by the Phaeacians. He feels compelled accordingly to approve what was thought honorable by his hosts, for he has only one prayer, the one he makes in his misery:

> Grant that I come to the Phaeacians,
> a friend, and to be pitied.[4]

---

1. Apparently an allusion to Aristophanes, *Ran.* 838: *akhalinon akrates athurôton stoma*, with the variant *apulôton* favored by most of the secondary tradition (see Dover 1993, 297).

2. A proverb (Diogenianus 2.66) has it that travelers lost on a long journey can only (like sailors) plot their course by the stars; Epicurus is similarly lost as regards literature, for which he has only contempt. For the association between Epicurus's hedonism and the Phaeacians, cf. the scholia on *Od.* 9.28.

3. *Od.* 9.6–7, 11. Cf. Ps.-Plutarch, *Vit. poes. Hom.* 104.19.

4. *Od.* 6.327.

ἃ δὴ πραττόμενα φαύλως οὐκ ἐνῆν διδάσκοντα βελτίω ποιεῖν, τούτοις διὰ τὸ χρειῶδες ἠναγκάσθη μαρτυρεῖν. **79.10** Ἀλλ' ὅ γ' Ἐπίκουρος ἀμαθίᾳ τὴν Ὀδυσσέως πρόσκαιρον ἀνάγκην βίου κατεβάλετο δόξαν, ἃ παρὰ Φαίαξιν ἐκεῖνος ἀπεφήνατο κάλλιστα, ταῦτα τοῖς σεμνοῖς κήποις ἐμφυτεύσας. **79.11** Ἐπίκουρος μὲν οὖν οἰχέσθω, πλείονας οἶμαι περὶ τὴν ψυχὴν ἐσχηκὼς νόσους ἢ περὶ τὸ σῶμα. **79.12** Τὴν δ' Ὁμήρου σοφίαν ἐκτεθείακεν αἰὼν ὁ σύμπας, καὶ προϊόντι τῷ χρόνῳ νεάζουσιν αἱ ἐκείνου χάριτες, οὐδὲ εἷς δ' ἐστὶν ὃς οὐκ εὔφημον ὑπὲρ αὐτοῦ γλῶτταν ἀνέῳξεν. **79.13** Ἱερεῖς δὲ καὶ ζάκοροι τῶν δαιμονίων ἐπῶν αὐτοῦ πάντες ἐσμὲν ἐξ ἴσου·

Τούσδε δ' ἔα φθινύθειν, ἕνα καὶ δύο, τοί κεν Ἀχαιῶν
νόσφιν βουλεύωσ' — ἄνυσις δ' οὐκ ἔσσεται αὐτῶν.

He was therefore obliged for reasons of expediency to testify for bad practices that he could not remedy by teaching. Yet Epicurus, in his ignorance, made Odysseus's temporary necessity into a principle of living, and planted in his glorious garden the things that Odysseus told the Phaeacians were "best of all." But let us say goodbye to Epicurus: he doubtless suffered from more diseases of the mind than of the body.[1] Homer's wisdom, by contrast, the whole course of the ages has deified.[2] Time passes, but his charms stay young. No one opens his mouth to speak of him but in praise. We are all alike priests and ministers of his divine poetry:

> And let them waste away, those one or two,
> who counsel differently from all the Achaeans:
> in them there shall be no fulfillment.[3]

---

1. Epicurus's ill health was famous; see Usener (1887, 405).
2. Cf. Longinus, *Subl.* 36.2.
3. *Il.* 2.346–347.

SELECT BIBLIOGRAPHY

Abbenes, J. G. J., S. R. Slings, and I. Sluiter, eds. 1995. *Greek Literary Theory after Aristotle: A Collection of Papers in Honour of D. M. Schenkeveld*. Amsterdam: VU University Press.

Alesso, Marta. 2002. El Hades en Heráclito el alegorista. Pages 29–37 in *Los estudios clásicos ante el cambio de milenio: Vida, muerte, cultura*. Edited by Rodolfo P. Buzón, Pablo A. Cavallero, Alba Romano, and M. Eugenia Steinberg. Buenos Aires: Universidad de Buenos Aires.

Allan, D. J. 1952. *The Philosophy of Aristotle*. London: Oxford University Press.

Asmis, Elizabeth. 1995. Epicurean Poetics. Pages 15–34 in *Philodemus and Poetry: Poetic Theory and Practice in Lucretius, Philodemus, and Horace*. Edited by Dirk Obbink. New York: Oxford University Press.

Auden, W. H. 1951. *The Enchafèd Flood or the Romantic Iconography of the Sea*. London: Faber & Faber.

Babut, Daniel. 1969. *Plutarque et le stoïcisme*. Paris: Presses Universitaires de France.

Bernard, Wolfgang. 1990. *Spätantike Dichtungstheorien: Untersuchungen zu Proklos, Herakleitos und Plutarch*. Stuttgart: Teubner.

Blank, D. L. 1997. *Sextus Empiricus: Against the Grammarians (Adversus mathematicos I)*. Clarendon Later Ancient Philosophers. Oxford: Clarendon.

Blönnigen, Christoph. 1992. *Die griechische Ursprung der jüdisch-hellenistischen Allegorese und ihre Rezeption in der alexandrinischen Patristik*. Europäische Hochschulschriften, Reihe 15, Klassische Sprachen und Literaturen 59. Frankfurt am Main: Lang.

Boyancé, Pierre. 1936. *Études sur le Songe de Scipion*. Limoges: Bontemps.

Boys-Stones, G. R. 2001. *Post-Hellenic Philosophy: A Study of Its Development from the Stoics to Origen*. New York: Oxford University Press.

———. 2003a. The Stoics' Two Types of Allegory. Pages 189–216 in Boys-Stones 2003b.

————, ed. 2003b. *Metaphor, Allegory, and the Classical Tradition: Ancient Thought and Modern Revisions.* Oxford: Oxford University Press.

Buffière, Félix. 1956. *Les Mythes d'Homère et la pensée grecque.* Paris: Belles Lettres.

————, ed. 1962. *Héraclite: Allégories d'Homère.* Paris: Budé.

Coulter, James A. 1976. *The Literary Microcosm: Theories of Interpretation of the Later Neoplatonists.* Columbia Studies in the Classical Tradition 2. Leiden: Brill.

Dawson, David. 1992. *Allegorical Readers and Cultural Revision in Ancient Alexandria.* Berkeley and Los Angeles: University of California Press.

Demetrakos, D., and I. Spyridonos. 1949–1951. *Mega lexikon tês hellenikês glôssês.* 9 vols. Athens: Syntagmatos.

Denniston, J. D. 1954. *The Greek Particles.* 2nd ed. Oxford: Clarendon.

Deubner, Ludwig. 1932. *Attische Feste.* Berlin: Keller.

Dover, Kenneth, ed. 1993. *Aristophanes: Frogs.* Oxford: Clarendon.

Edelstein, Emma J., and Ludwig Edelstein. 1945. *Asclepius: A Collection and Interpretation of the Testimonies.* 2 vols. Baltimore: Johns Hopkins University Press.

Edelstein, Ludwig, and I. G. Kidd, eds. 1988–1999. *Posidonius.* 2nd ed. 3 vols. in 4. Cambridge: Cambridge University Press.

Ford, Andrew. 2002. *Origins of Criticism: Literary Culture and Poetic Theory in Classical Greece.* Princeton: Princeton University Press.

Frow, John. 1995. *Cultural Studies and Cultural Value.* Oxford: Clarendon.

Gale, Monica. 1994. *Myth and Poetry in Lucretius.* Cambridge: Cambridge University Press.

Gow, A. S. F., and D. L. Page, eds. 1965. *The Greek Anthology: Hellenistic Epigrams.* Cambridge: Cambridge University Press.

Griffiths, John Gwyn. 1970. *Plutarch's De Iside et Osiride.* Cardiff: University of Wales Press.

Grube, G. M. A. 1965. *The Greek and Roman Critics.* Toronto: Hackett.

Hardie, P. R. 1985. Imago mundi: Cosmological and Ideological Aspects of the Shield of Achilles. *JHS* 105:11–31.

————. 1986. *Virgil's Aeneid: Cosmos and Imperium.* Oxford: Clarendon.

Henry, Madeleine. 1986. The Derveni Commentator as Literary Critic. *TAPA* 116:149–64.

Hillgruber, Michael. 1994–1999. *Die pseudoplutarchische Schrift De Homero.* 2 vols. Beiträge zur Altertumskunde 57–58. Stuttgart: Teubner.

Jackson, Robin. 1995. Late Platonist Poetics: Olympiodorus and the Myth of Plato's Gorgias. Pages 275–99 in Abbenes, Slings, and Sluiter 1995.

Janko, Richard. 2001. The Derveni Papyrus (Diagoras of Melos, Apopyrgizontes Logoi?): A New Translation. *CP* 96:1–32.

————. 2002. The Derveni Papyrus: An Interim Text. *ZPE* 141:1–62.

Jones, W. H. S., trans. 1923–1931. *Hippocrates*. 4 vols. LCL. Cambridge: Harvard University Press.

Kennedy, George A., ed., 1989. *The Cambridge History of Literary Criticism*. Vol. 1: *Classical Criticism*. Cambridge: Cambridge University Press.

Kühner, Raphael, and Bernhard Gerth. 1963. *Ausführliche Grammatik der griechischen Sprache*. 3rd ed. 2 vols. Munich: Hueber.

Laks, André, and Glenn Most, eds. 1997. *Studies on the Derveni Papyrus*. New York: Oxford University Press.

Lamberton, Robert. 1986. *Homer the Theologian: Neoplatonist Allegorical Reading and the Growth of the Epic Tradition*. Berkeley and Los Angeles: University of California Press.

Lamberton, Robert, and J. J. Keaney, eds. 1992. *Homer's Ancient Readers: The Hermeneutics of Greek Epic's Earliest Exegetes*. Princeton: Princeton University Press.

Lausberg, Heinrich. 1998. *Handbook of Literary Rhetoric*. Edited by D. E. Orton and R. Dean Anderson. Leiden: Brill.

Long, Anthony A. 1992. Stoic Readings of Homer. Pages 41–66 in Lamberton and Keaney 1992.

Most, Glenn. 1989. Cornutus and Stoic Allegoresis. *ANRW* 2.36.3:2014–65.

Mynors, R. A. B., ed. 1990. *Virgil: Georgics*. Oxford: Clarendon.

Nisbet, R. G. M., and Margaret Hubbard. 1970. *A Commentary on Horace: Odes, Book 1*. Oxford: Clarendon.

Obbink, Dirk. 1995a. "How to Read Poetry about the Gods." Pages 189–209 in Obbink 1995b.

————. 2003. Allegory and Exegesis in the Derveni Papyrus. Pages 177–88 in Boys-Stones 2003b.

————, ed. 1995b. *Philodemus and Poetry: Poetic Theory and Practice in Lucretius, Philodemus, and Horace*. New York: Oxford University Press.

————, ed. 1996. *Philodemus: On Piety*. Part 1. Oxford: Clarendon.

Oelmann, Franciscus, et al., eds. 1910. *Heracliti quaestiones Homericae*. Stuttgart: Teubner.

Page, D. L. 1955. *Sappho and Alcaeus: An Introduction to the Study of Ancient Lesbian Poetry*. Oxford: Clarendon.

————, ed. 1962. *Poetae Melici Graeci*. Oxford: Clarendon.

Panchenko, Dmitri. 1994. The *Iliad* 14.201 and 14.246 Reconsidered. *Hyperboreus* 1:183–86.

Pease, A. S., ed. 1920–1923. *M. Tulli Ciceronis De divinatione*. 4 vols. Urbana: University of Illinois.

————, ed. 1955–1958. *Cicero: De natura deorum*. 2 vols. Cambridge: Harvard University Press.

Pépin, Jean. 1981. *Mythe et allégorie: Les origines grecques et les contestations judéo-chrétiennes*. 3rd ed. Paris: Études Augustiniennes.

Pingree, David. 1997. *From Astral Omens to Astrology: From Babylon to Bikaner*. Rome: Istituto Italiano per l'Africa et l'Oriente.

Ramelli, Ilaria. 2004. *Allegoria: I, L'età classica*. In collaboration with G. Lucchetta. Introduction by R. Radice. Milan: Vita e Pensiero.

——, ed. and trans. 2003. *Anneo Cornuto: Compendio di teologia greca*. Milan: Bompiani.

Russell, Donald A. 1981. *Criticism in Antiquity*. London: Duckworth.

——. 1983. *Greek Declamation*. Cambridge: Cambridge University Press.

——. 2003. The Rhetoric of the Homeric Problems. Pages 217–34 in Boys-Stones 2003b.

Russell, Donald A., and Michael Winterbottom, trans. 1972. *Ancient Literary Criticism: The Principal Texts in New Translations*. Oxford: Oxford University Press.

Spoerri, W. 1959. *Späthellenistische Berichte über Welt, Kultur und Götter*. Schweizerische Beiträge zur Altertumswissenschaft 9. Basel: Reinhardt.

Struck, Peter T. 1995. Allegory, Aenigma, and Anti-Mimesis: A Struggle against Aristotelian Rhetorical Literary Theory. Pages 215–33 in Abbenes, Slings, and Sluiter 1995.

——. 2004. *Birth of the Symbol: Ancient Readers at the Limits of Their Texts*. Princeton: Princeton University Press.

Thomas, Ivor, trans. 1951. *Selections Illustrating the History of Greek Mathematics*. Rev. ed. 2 vols. LCL. Cambridge: Harvard University Press.

Tompkins, Jane P. 1980. The Reader in History. Pages 201–32 in *Reader-Response Criticism from Formalism to Post-Structuralism*. Edited by Jane P. Tompkins. Baltimore: Johns Hopkins University Press.

Usener, Hermann, ed. 1887. *Epicurea*. Leipzig: Teubner.

Wehrli, Fritz. 1928. *Zur Geschichte der allegorischen Deutung Homers im Altertum*. Borna-Leipzig: Noske.

West, Martin L. 1965. Tryphon De Tropis. *CQ* 15:230–48.

——, ed. 1966. *Hesiod: Theogony*. Oxford: Clarendon.

——, ed. 1998. *Homeri Ilias*, vol. 1. Bibliotheca scriptorum Graecorum et Romanorum Teubneriana. Stuttgart: Teubner.

Wettstein, J. J., ed. 1751–1752. *Novum Testamentum Graecum*. Amsterdam: Ex officina Dommeriana.

Whitman, John. 1987. *Allegory: The Dynamics of an Ancient and Medieval Technique*. Cambridge: Harvard University Press.

INDEX NOMINUM ET RERUM

Index Locorum

Printed in the United Kingdom
by Lightning Source UK Ltd.
121008UK00003B/160